Diverse Methodologies in the Study of Music Teaching and Learning

A volume in
Advances in Music Education Research

Series Editors:
Linda K. Thompson, *Lee University*
Mark Robin Campbell, *SUNY at Potsdam*

Diverse Methodologies in the Study of Music Teaching and Learning

edited by

Linda K. Thompson
Lee University

and

Mark Robin Campbell
SUNY at Potsdam

Information Age Publishing, Inc.
Charlotte, North Carolina • www.infoagepub.com

Library of Congress Cataloging-in-Publication Data

Diverse methodologies in the study of music teaching and learning / edited by Linda K. Thompson and Mark Robin Campbell.
   p. cm. -- (Advances in music education research)
   Includes bibliographical references (p.).
   ISBN 978-1-59311-629-3 (pbk.) -- ISBN 978-1-59311-630-9 (hardcover) I. Music--Instruction and study. I. Thompson, Linda K. II. Campbell, Mark Robin.
   MT1.D58 2008
   780.71--dc22

                                       2008005376

ISBN 13: 978-1-59311-629-3 (pbk.)
          978-1-59311-630-9 (hardcover

Printed in the United States of America

CONTENTS

PART II: FOCUS ON SOCIAL AND
INSTITUTIONAL CONTEXTS AND ISSUES

EDITORIAL REVIEW BOARD

FOREWORD

Linda K. Thompson and Mark Robin Campbell

The publication of *Advances in Music Education Research* (AMER) is a landmark in the growth and development of the Music Education Special Interest Group of the American Educational Research Association (AERA). Designed as an ongoing book series for the group, AMER seeks to strengthen the research and educational base of music education. Titles in the series reflect the interests of AERA Music Education SIG members and include a broad range of disciplinary and interdisciplinary subjects and diverse methodologies. Content for each volume in the series is primarily drawn from selected conference papers presented at the annual AERA conference, but also may include invited manuscripts focused on a specific theme.

As the first volume in the series, it is apt to think about beginnings, and the idea of beginning. Beginnings conjure notions of commencements, openings, launches, inaugurations, and even laying foundations and creating establishments. Although connotatively different, each of these ideas has at root bringing something into existence and creating spaces and conditions for continuation. This is certainly the goal of the series, to advance music education research. Beginnings also suggest pathways and choices. The authors who have contributed to this collection of studies and essays provide numerous avenues for thinking about research and its implications. Their writings suggest a variety of possibilities, including actions, decisions, and options to pursue. Some write about new ways of thinking about the self and the various social contexts in which music education is understood, done, and interpreted. Others write about methods, processes, institutions and values, including the relationships individuals have with each other within and across diverse learning and research environments. All of these papers, however, are open for discussion and dialogue, and for interrogating our thinking about learners and learning, teachers and teaching, and the ways we go about studying and understanding each of these areas of interest.

Diverse Methodologies in the Study of Teaching and Learning is divided into two parts: Part I examines the topics of teaching and learning; Part II focuses on social and institutional contexts and issues. Part I includes the work of Peter Whiteman, Margaret Berg, Margaret Schmidt, Melissa Natale Abramo, Deborah Bradley, and Teryl Dobbs. Part II includes the work of James Austin, Warren Henry, Susan Conkling, and Linda Thornton. Liora Bresler's presentation at the Music Education Special Interest Group business meeting of the 2007 annual meeting of AERA in Chicago precedes these two sections.

In our invitation to Liora Bresler to speak at the Music Education Special Interest Group business meeting of the 2007 annual meeting of AERA in Chicago, we asked Bresler to speak on a topic of her own choosing, setting no restrictions. We knew Bresler's work and anticipated that her presentation would be thoughtful, engaging, reflective, and provocative. It was. Although different from the actual presentation at the meeting, the article included in this volume of the series communicates much of the power of the presentation, yet presents many more ideas. In "The Live/d Performance of Scholarship: Shared Structures and Ethos in Music and Research" Bresler explores the idea of "intensity of engagements" and draws analogies between the practices of musicians and qualitative researchers.

In thinking about "intensity of engagements," we are reminded of Dewey's work in experience and art. In *Art as Experience,* Dewey (1934/ 1980) expresses disappointment that the English language does not have a single word to capture the aesthetic/artistic dimensions of art. Yet this bifurcation serves a purpose. Only through the analysis of the relationships between both dimensions, however, do we come to see their intimate connection and essentially fused natures in art experiences. To have an art experience, according to Dewey, the aesthetic—the experience of perceiving—is integrally connected with the artistic—the experience of making. Thus in art experiences there is interaction, an undergoing and a doing. As most of Dewey's writing, there is concern for interaction, doing, reflection, the significance, and integrity of experience, agency, and interest in community. In other words, having "an art experience" is equivalent to having an "intense engagement."

In reading Bresler's examination of the sensibilities and processes of music (making)/research (researching), we are reminded that as musicians and researchers we share similar Deweyan concerns for interaction, doing, reflection, experience, and interest in community. Indeed, the sensibilities shared by both musician/researcher are those that are primarily of the felt kind—the embodiment of qualitative and particularized phenomenon that is acquired through our senses—perceptual focusing, scanning, patterning and organizing, and sensing textural intensities. The processes—the actions directed toward sharing our perceptions and understandings of primarily qualitative relationships—are technical, yet creative and responsive to the uniqueness of the particular, the situation at hand or "the thing" encountered. In other words, both musicians / researchers are engaged in a dynamic of action and reflection, and are by necessity informed by interests served—a praxis. The dynamism is one of intense engagement.

Bresler's article, like the writings of her informants (especially Dewey, Buber, Eisner, and others not named) asks us to think rather sophisticatedly about the significance of our work. It asks us to think about the aesthetic and artistic, the materiality and the symbolic, the analogous and the nonparallel. It also reminds us of Erich Fromm's (1976) idea of "being" of the world as opposed to "having" the world. That is, being concerned with shared experience and productive activity, and intensely committed to being engaged. To a group of music education teacher-researchers, her ideas fall on an appreciative audience.

Part I. Focus on Teacher and Learning

In his study of "Young Children's Constructions of the Musical Knowledgeable Other," Peter Whiteman looks at the social interactions that occur during preschoolers' spontaneous singing to determine the effects of these interactions on the acquisition of musical knowledge and skills. Basing his analysis on a 3-year longitudinal study of eight preschool children in a childcare center and their spontaneous singing, Whiteman describes the processes involved in how these children scaffold or assist the music learning of others. Seeking to understand how these children "make meaning," Whiteman draws upon the theoretical assertion that social interaction is fundamental in the development of cognition (Vygotsky, 1978; Wertsch, 1985). Furthermore, Whiteman, seeks to shed additional light on two key constructs in the social-cultural tradition of developmental cognition: "the more knowledgeable other" and the zone of proximal development.

At the theoretical level, Whiteman suggests that traditional notions such as age, experience, and role, that are associated with learning and development, as well as the manner in which the more knowledgeable other is defined, be reconsidered. Especially fruitful in thinking about the development of children's music making and the supports likely to facilitate their generativity and agency, he suggests, are the theoretical models posited by Bronfenbrenner (ecological systems theory, 1979), Corsaro (symbolic interactionist perspective or "Orb web model," 2005), and Thelen and Smith (dynamic systems approach, 1994). As the children in this study show, and as Whiteman's analysis and each of these theories suggest, music making and taking is centrally a multidimensional and interactive process that acknowledges the unique contributions that individuals make and take.

At the practical level, Whiteman offers persuasive arguments for reconsidering grouping practices in education and other settings where children are likely to be found, and for working within emergent curricular structures. And, finally, Whiteman provides suggestions for how researches might go about documenting children's musical learning processes. Most intriguing is the idea of having children document their own music making and taking; indeed becoming key agents in constructing what is potentially meaningful data.

Margaret Berg's study of beginning instrumentalists' music practice, "Getting the Minutes In," reminds us of the power of case studies in educational research. As Yin (1994) has observed, case studies clarify complicated processes and generate new knowledge about phenomenon. Case studies have the power to enrich and build our understanding of seemingly unrelated things. Metaphorically, case studies allow us to hear individual melodies within overall harmonic structures. This is the power of Berg's study. The study of musicians' practice is a phenomenon of perennial of interest to music educators, as is the exploration of young instrumentalists' music practices—their strategies, motivations, desires, goals, and thought processes. Of equal interest in studying music practices are environmental and contextual factors, such as resources, parental support, specific music pieces, and teacher-student relationships. Of additional interest is how music (in general) functions in the lives of individuals and how music is or becomes meaningful to them.

Berg's account of two adolescents' music practicing describes at various levels each of these factors and gives us a rich and multidimensional report of some of the things that "matter." That is, from each young instrumentalist we learn not only about their music practicing, but we also learn that, as a profession, we have much to learn about the construct of practice itself, especially its potential to be understand as an embedded and contextual phenomenon. In other words, Berg's central and underlying question of "What does it mean to practice?" has significant implications for music teaching and learning, curricular practice and continuing research.

The great strength of Berg's work is in helping us see into the lives of these two young students, and to question the efficacy of typical pedagogical approaches to motivating and assessing musical learning in instrumental music education. It helps us think more broadly, as Berg notes, about "the features of the music" itself, "student felt experience," and the "varied purposes served by learning to play an instrument."

Margaret Schmidt's study, "First-Year Teachers and Methods Classes: Is There a Connection?" looks at the relationship between three string music teachers' first year of teaching and their junior-year methods courses. More specifically, Schmidt explores the extent to which these teachers applied a specific teaching method (a rote-to-note method that was discussed and practiced with classmates and children in elementary and middle school during a year-long junior practicum course) to their current teaching. The connection between learning in preservice teacher preparation and inservice teaching is of substantive interest to music teacher educators and inservice mentors, and Schmidt's investigation suggests that there is carryover ... to some extent. That extent, however, is more accurately understood as *degrees of difference* dependent upon or constrained by site, context, depth of a teacher's pedagogical/theoretical understanding of a specific method, and a teacher's own temperaments and professional dispositions.

As a counterpoint in making sense out how novices teachers implement, modify or reject practices presented in the preservice education, Schmidt notes that neither level of musicianship nor quantity of preservice teaching experiences is likely to be a strong candidate for explaining the degree of connections made. What may be more important, she asserts, is a "readiness to learn" and "individual effort." From the perspective of some teacher educators, readiness and effort may seem like difficult qualities to quantify and assess. The relative extent to which both may be present in an individual's professional array of dispositions, however, is worth considering when it comes to both teacher candidate selection and qualifications.

Integrally linked to these dispositions are teacher beliefs. The growing and persuasive research base that preservice teachers' beliefs and dispositions may be one of the strongest determinants of future teacher thinking and actions is one that deserves considerable weight in thinking about professional preparation (see for example, Carter & Dolye, 1995, Raths, 2001; and Richardson, 2003 in general education; and Campbell & Thompson, 2001, Thompson & Campbell, 2003 in music education). A close reading of Schmidt's analysis suggests this, as she notes, "the complex relationships among existing beliefs, readiness to learn, effort, course work and initial teaching practices" deserve continued study in helping unravel both "the processes and time lines by which novices teachers implement, modify or reject practices" presented in preservice education. Rather than conceptualizing a teacher education curriculum as primarily a matter of content or method acquisition, our biggest challenge may be to conceptualize professional education and development as a continuum beginning with early childhood, with a primary goal of helping teachers uncover, explicate, affirm, modify and reject certain sets of beliefs (Raths, 2001).

In her study of "Music Educator as Social Agent: A Personal Narrative," Melissa Natale Abramo identifies and examines the factors involved in the work of a music educator working for change. Abramo seeks to describe what it means to be an agent of change—what it means to enact change and what it means to rupture structures and habits that define and circumscribe thoughts and actions about teaching and learning in order to create different ways of thinking and acting pedagogically. The process she uses to explore the experience of agency is reflection on her own teaching, her students' learning, and various professional contexts, including her school, her conversations with stakeholders and colleagues, and her own preparation as a music teacher.

Abramo's narrative raises important questions about the reproductive nature of music education pedagogy and music teacher education, especially in regard to hegemonic forces and processes that institutionalize and privilege certain forms of practice. Take for example, as Abramo discusses, the idea and use of exemplars and models in music education—a seemingly nonproblematic and commonsense idea. As a matter of fact, much music education practice is socially constructed around the "idea of the ideal"—for example, the ideal sound, the ideal performance, the ideal orchestration, the ideal conductor, the ideal singer, and so forth. The idea of the ideal (with its embedded values and assumptions) is an operating ideology. Submission to such an ideology, as Foucault (1977) has discussed, can be punishing and oppressive. Resistance to its reification and legitimization, and to what many music educators might see as "commonsense" (in the Gramscian [1971] sense), is indeed, a site of struggle. This is where Abramo provides an optimistic turn in her narrative. Abramo makes it clear that it is important to connect narrative inquiry to social action, thus underscoring the idea that teachers are not powerless; that through resisting dominant discourses and structures they can partake in acts of self-(re)creation. We can remake the given, so to speak, and create new pedagogical spaces of possibilities for our students and ourselves.

Deborah Bradley, in her study titled "Teaching in an Unforgiving Present for the Unknowable Future: Multicultural Human Subjectivity, Antiracism Pedagogy, and Music Education," continues the focus on social action and self-understanding in and through music. Her critical ethnography introduces readers to members of the Mississauga, Ontario youth choir, highlighting the singers experiences of being taught in an anti-racism pedagogy. A focus of the study is the idea of "multicultural human subjectivity." Bradley develops our understanding of this theoretical construct by connecting us to ideas of self-understanding (Brubaker & Cooper, 2000) influenced by multicultural globalization and cosmopolitanism. Contributing to the contextualization of this study is discussion of Canada's official multiculturalism policy, the idea of global song as opposed to multicultural music, Small's (1998) concept of "musicking," and the perspective of anti-racist pedagogy as distinctly different from definitions of multiculturalism found in educational policy.

Within this framework, Bradley recounts interviews with several members of the Mississauga Youth Choir, a group that reflects the transnationality and cultural hybridity of the community. As a result of a specific performance for an international audience, Bradley found that some of the choristers indicated a growing sense of multicultural human subjectivity, while for others the experience seemed to serve to reinforce static ideas of identity as well as cultural stereotypes.

Bradley concludes this study by posing challenges to consider as we think about the ways in which antiracism pedagogy and meaningful "musicking" can contribute to the development of multicultural human subjectivity. Although Bradley identifies barriers to developing this multicultural subjectivity that are pervasive in modern society (racialized stereotypes), she voices optimism that learning and performing global song in the context of antiracism pedagogy does open the door for the emergence of multicultural human subjectivity in the lives of the participants. In light of our increasingly diverse educational settings in North America this research provides an important new way of thinking about music education in relation to self, culture, and the development of understanding of self in culture—multicultural human subjectivity.

Teryl Dobbs focuses on the role of language in her study titled "Discourse in the Band Room: The Role of Talk in an Instrumental Music Classroom." Dobbs bases her study on the idea of discourse analysis grounded in speech act theory (Austin, 1962), wherein words function as performances within a specific social context. Implicit within discourse analysis is exploration of language as socially and culturally constructed, with each speaker's background and experiences recognized as part of the complex whole. From this theoretical point Dobbs seeks to investigate the ways that classroom discourse shapes teaching and learning, and also the impact of classroom discourse on young musicians' "induction" into a musical community.

Dobbs' study is situated in the middle school band room where she had been a music teacher. Data sources include video and audiotapes of the 113 participating middle-school students in both large ensembles and small-group lessons. Coding of video and field notes provided emergent themes, while audiotapes were coded according to an a priori structure based on speech act theory. Dobbs' analysis reveals two particular patterns of discourse that seem to impact the teaching and learning of music: musical uptake (discursive event in which students demonstrate knowledge of musical concepts through performance), and repetition framing (affirming a students' response by repeating part of the student's statement) (Tannen, 1989). Physical gestures (conducting, vocable performance, and instrumental music performance) also have embodied meaning and were coded as paralinguistic gestures. Dobbs concludes that these discursive patterns, paralinguistic gestures, and the concurrent performance of both shape the teaching and learning of music, and that both musical and social development occurs through classroom discourse, fostering an identify as musician.

This study provides a challenge for music educators and music teacher educators to examine the complexity of the use of language in a music-centered classroom. What is the role of verbal language in a nonverbal art form (instrumental music)? What is the nature of classroom discourse, and how does that impact a student's developing sense of identity? What community is created through the discourse in a music classroom? What is the quality as well as the quantity of the verbal discourse? How does this differ based on the background, age, and experiences of the students and/or the teacher in the classroom? On different music classrooms (general, choral, orchestral, theory, etc.)? Studying students' verbal descriptors of music is not new, but the impact of Dobbs' study lies in these new questions and ways of thinking about the power of language in classrooms, and in the continued exploration of the idea of discourse analysis in music education.

Part II. Focus on Social and Institutional Contexts and Issues

In their study, "Charter Schools: Embracing or Excluding the Arts?" James Austin and Joshua Reynolds provide an overview of the current status of arts in 122 public charter schools in 15 states. Specifically, this study is a beginning examination of music instruction in the often misunderstood or misinterpreted context of charter schools. The authors "demystify" these schools by providing important background information on the development and philosophy of charter schools, clarifying that these schools are publicly-funded schools of choice. They point out that although charter schools are responsible for student achievement and meeting standards, they do operate autonomously, free of local and state regulations.

Based on responses to the 27-item questionnaire sent to administrators, Austin and Reynolds report that music is included as part of the regular curriculum in 70% of charter schools, while other schools provide applied lessons and/or informal musical opportunities in after-school programs. The authors examine factors associated with the music instruction, including overall school enrollment, grade level configuration, and those responsible for designing and implementing that instruction. In their discussion, Austin and Reynolds also note that for charter schools offering music instruction, the curriculum is often somewhat informal, narrower in scope than in traditional public school settings, and fewer teachers are considered highly qualified.

Because, as the authors discuss, support for charter schools continues, with no expectation of decrease in the future, it is imperative for music educators and music teacher educators to be aware of the role of the arts, specifically music, in the overall philosophy and curriculum of public charter schools. Austin and Reynolds conclude that public charter schools seem to neither exclude nor embrace the arts.

It appears then, that similar to the general status of music education in traditional public schools, equitable access to arts instruction becomes a critical issue. The back-to-basics curricular emphasis, often evident in charter schools' philosophies (stated or implicit) can push the arts into the background, not unlike the impact of legislation such as No Child Left Behind in traditional public schools. So maybe the questions we are to ask are not fundamentally different from those we ask about music education in general. Who are the decision makers, and are the decisions related to music instruction reactions to experiences in traditional K-12 schools, or is there simply a lack of advocacy on the part of the organizers and stakeholders in charter schools? Who are the teachers and what has been their preparation? Are all students given the opportunity to engage in sequential, comprehensive, meaningful experiences in music? Austin and Reynolds have not only provided a valuable first broadscale look at the status of the arts in public charter schools, but have challenged us to continue to think deeply about the core values we hold related to music instruction for all students, regardless of a public, private, or charter context.

For many university teaching assistants (TAs) their work as a TA is their beginning experience in teaching. In "Doctoral Students in Music and Their Socialization Into Teaching: An Initial Inquiry," Susan Conkling and Warren Henry explore issues related to ways that doctoral students in music are socialized into the role of teacher, and how apprenticeship of observation (Lortie, 2002) impacts that socialization. Describing their work in two different universities with graduate students in a college teaching course, Conkling and Henry use ethnographic analysis techniques to identify aspects of the socialization process common to their students and to doctoral students described in the professional literature. They find that cultural concepts of teaching and learning impact the socialization process for international students, comprising 8 of the 18 students in the study (7 of the 8 students have a first language other than English). Learning theories, particularly those associated with adult learners, are new to the majority of the students in the study. Technology, a common thread between the two courses, is seen as an area of concern, with students expressing a feeling of being pressured to include technology in their teaching.

We are reminded in this study that socialization into the role of teacher —for graduates as well as undergraduates—is a complex and highly contextual process, intensified when considering the impact of various cultural perspectives of learning and teaching. Conkling and Henry suggest that doctoral education be intentionally recognized as a time of socialization into the role of faculty and a time to assist graduate students in "deconstructing" their experiences in teaching in higher education in order for them to further understand their role as teacher. While the authors assume apprenticeship of observation occurs, particularly with students' applied instructors, one must question the impact of that observation in light of the wide diversity of teaching models and cultural interpretations of observations.

Conkling and Henry conclude this initial exploration of doctoral students' socialization into the teaching role by posing questions for further consideration and investigation. At the time of application, is sufficient information gathered related to the applicant's teaching background and interests in and for teaching? How might students expand their understandings of adult learning theories? In what ways can integration of technology be encouraged in ways that are appropriate to the subject and context, enhancing the learner's engagement with the topic? Teaching assistants are the future professoriate. The beliefs they hold about teaching, as described in relation to Schmidt's study, will powerfully impact their work in university classrooms and studios in the future. Conkling and Henry have provided in their study a timely reminder of the need for awareness of, and mentoring in, this important time of socialization for future university faculty.

A beginning point for a majority of research in music education involves interaction with an institutional review board (IRB). Linda Thornton's study, "The Role of IRBs in Music Education Research," presents her perspectives as both an insider recounting her own experiences with multiple IRBs as well as her position as a researcher investigating issues related to the ethical responsibilities for protecting human subjects. Thornton's description of a specific research project in which she was a coinvestigator, and the impact of IRBs on that project, brings to light concerns related to the widely varying requirements she encountered when working with what was initially 26 IRBs at like institutions. While Thornton is careful to point out that she is not intending to criticize any specific institutions, the differences—in some cases extreme differences—in the processes of IRBs at these various institutions underscores the need for the social sciences to give pause to reconsider the appropriateness of the IRB's processes.

Through Thornton's experience and the related literature, she discusses the ways in which IRBs interpret the guidelines for protecting human subjects, questioning the appropriateness of these interpretations for current practice and scholarship in music education. Is informed consent possible in qualitative research? Does a guarantee of confidentiality diminish the credibility of historical research? Possibly an even larger question is related to the definition of research and the blurred boundaries between teaching and research for many educators, particularly as related to action research and as addressed in a recent *Educational Researcher* (Nolen & Vander Putten, 2007) in which the authors acknowledge the ethical issues related to teacher as researcher [see also Boser, 2007]. Are the guiding principles of respect for persons, justice, and beneficence "inherently contradictory," calling into question the probability of any research actually meeting the IRB criteria? Thornton concludes this study with suggestions for researching IRBs, possible changes in regulations, greater social science presence on the IRBs, and the involvement of professional organizations in setting guidelines and standards for the wide range of research methodologies evident in the social sciences.

It seems fitting to conclude this first volume with Thornton's "call to action" as it relates to IRBs. Truly "advancing" the research in music education requires that we have both the quantitative and qualitative data that informs our decisions about policy, teaching and mentoring, and life-long learning and participation in music. Although the localized interpretations of IRBs may create barriers or unnecessary delays for accessing our most important informants—students and teachers— Thornton's study emphasizes the need to take action in promoting an

IRB process that is realistic, appropriately ethical, and mindful of the many "ways of knowing" that exist in social science research.

In conclusion, we wish to thank the editorial board for their work with the preparation of this volume. We also wish to invite you, the reader, to consider being a part of future volumes. We encourage you to submit your comments and responses to studies presented in this volume. These responses may be published in a *Dialogue Column* in future volumes. If you are a member of the Music Education SIG of AERA you may also wish to submit a proposal for a themed volume in this book series, serving as editor for that volume. If you would like to contribute to future volumes as described above please send us your ideas. We look forward to your voice in future volumes of *Advances in Music Education Research*.

REFERENCES

Austin, J. (1962). *How to do things with words*. London: Oxford University Press.

Boser, S. (2007). Power, ethics, and the IRB. *Qualitative Inquiry, 13*(8), 1060-1074.

Bronfenbrenner, U. (1979). *The ecology of human development: Experiments by nature and design*. Cambridge, MA: Harvard University Press.

Brubaker, R., & Cooper, F. (2000). Beyond "identity." *Theory and Society, 29*(1), 1-47.

Carter, K., & Doyle, W (1995). Preconceptions in learning to teach. *The Educational Forum 59*, 186-195.

Campbell, M. R., & Thompson, L. K. (2001). Preservice music educators' images of teaching." In *Desert Skies Symposium on Research in Music Education* (pp. 24-38). Tucson, AZ: University of Arizona, School of Music and Dance.

Corsaro, W. A. (2005). *The sociology of childhood* (2nd ed.). Thousand Oaks, CA: Pine Forge Press.

Dewey, J. (1980). *Art as experience*. New York: Putnam. (Original work published 1954)

Fromm, E. (1976). *To have or to be*. New York: Harper & Row.

Foucault, M. (1977). *Discipline and punish: The birth of the prison*. (Translated from the French by Alan Sheridan). New York: Pantheon Books.

Gramsci. A. (1971). *Selections from the prison notebooks of Antonio Gramsci* (Q. Hoare & G. N. Smith, Eds. & Trans.). New York: International.

Lortie, D. C. (2002). *Schoolteacher: A sociological study (with new introduction)*. Chicago: University of Chicago Press.

Nolen, A. L., & Vander Putten, J. (2007). Action research in education: Addressing gaps in ethical principles and practices. *Educational Researcher, 36*(7), 401-407.

Raths, J. (2001). Teachers' beliefs and teaching beliefs. *Early Childhood Research & Practice, 3*(1). Retrieved November 12, 2007, from http://ecrp.uiuc.edu/v3n1/raths.html

Richardson, V. (2003). Preservice teachers' beliefs. In J. Raths & A. C. McAninch (Eds.), *Teacher beliefs and classroom performance: The impact of teacher education* (Vol. 6, pp. 1-22). Greenwich, CT: Information Age.

Small, C. (1998). *Musicking: The meanings of performing and listening.* Hanover: University Press of New England.

Tannen, D. (1989). *Talking voices: Repetition, dialogue, and imagery in conversational discourse.* New York: Cambridge University Press.

Thompson, L. K., & Campbell, M. R. (2003). Gods, guides, and gardeners: Preservice music education students' personal teaching metaphors, *Bulletin of the Council for Research in Music Education, 158,* 43-54.

Thelen, E., & Smith, L. (1994). *A dynamic systems approach to the development of cognition and action.* Cambridge, MA: MIT Press.

Vygotsky, L. S. (1978). *Mind in society: The development of higher psychological processes.* Cambridge, MA: Harvard University Press.

Wertsch, J. V. (1985). *Vygotsky and the social formation of mind.* Cambridge, MA: Harvard University Press.

Yin, R. K. (1994). *Case study research* (2nd ed). Beverly Hills, CA: SAGE.

CHAPTER 1

THE LIVE/D PERFORMANCE OF SCHOLARSHIP

Shared Structures and Ethos in Music and Research

Liora Bresler

My colleague and friend, philosopher of education Chris Higgins, has pointed out that all research is "me-search." Chris talks about a "torturing question" that motivates us in our life-long scholarship. If I may paraphrase to something less torturous, my own "lingering question" concerns the nature and power of intensified engagement: that is, shaping, and being shaped by personal, emotional and intellectual connections. Intensified engagement becomes most readily defined by its (alas, all too prevalent) absence: a lack of engagement manifested, for example, in the indifferent reading of a paper, or while attending a lecture that fails to engage us. Lack of connection is not exclusive to scholarship but can be present in all aspects of life, including music, for example, when hearing music that does not touch us, or, as I vividly recall from my earlier years, in the drudgery of music drills in preparation for the weekly lesson.

Diverse Methodologies in the Study of Music Teaching and Learning, pp. 1–21

1

Having identified intensified engagement (both as a subject *and* quality) as a key theme in my research, I found its presence in everything I wrote, (long before I articulated it as an issue), approached from various angles and perspectives: in my master's thesis in musicology, exploring the manifestation of personal and national identity grounded in powerful musical experiences; in my work in music and arts curriculum and the investigation of spaces that allow intensified engagement (as well as those that hinder it); and in methodological investigations of the ways in which empathic engagement facilitates knowing and understanding in conducting research. This chapter belongs to that last methodological strand, knowing and understanding as an emphatically engaged researcher.

In this paper, I suggest that the practices of musicians and qualitative researchers, in terms of structures and ethos, are analogous in their intensity of engagements.[1] On an elementary level, each is essentially a form of communication, and communicative actions have a basic triadic *structure* consisting of sender, addressee, and referent.[2] Beyond structures, musical processes, and experiences can illuminate significant aspects of qualitative research, including the overlapping processes of data collection, data analysis, and writing. Examining ways in which music provides rich and powerful models for perception, conceptualization, and engagement for both performers and audience members, I highlight the potential of these models to cultivate *sensibilities* that are directly relevant to the processes and products of qualitative research. These sensibilities and practices share a common spirit, an *ethos*, in that communication via music or qualitative research can intensify engagement with the phenomenon through the communication with an audience.

The first part of the paper examines the purposes of this *telos*[3] of engagement, its end and purposes. The ethos of researchers draws their intensity and power from the community of practice (Lave & Wenger, 1991) in which the researchers operate, a collective whose ethos is often intensified through the "live performances" of scholarship, much like musical performances. I suggest that the dialogical relationships between researcher and what is studied, similar to the relationship between performer and music, are intensified by the expectation of communication with an audience, creating an engaged tri-directional relationship. In the second part of the paper, I reflect on conferences as supporting the communities of practice of music educators, and specifically, on the site for the original talk on which this paper is based, the American Educational Research Association (AERA) annual meeting, as facilitating *strong and weak ties* (Putnam, 2000) among their members in ways that enhance scholarship in music education.

The sensibilities I address here are not exclusive to music—they are manifested in various forms in other arts, and probably in other disciplines. But as a musician turned educational researcher, I recognized the inherent musical qualities of qualitative research during my first educational research project, and my awareness of those questions was deepened through subsequent research experiences. These processes include two sets of seemingly oxymoronic states: (a) A "zoomed"/spacious state, characterized by an interplay between a focused analytic state of mind and an open, receptive one; and (b) an aesthetic space that combines intimacy with critical distance. As I became aware of the need to communicate my work (beyond my advisor and dissertation committee) in research papers and conference presentations, the triadic structure of the communication and its ethos of "reaching out," essential to musical experiences, became pronounced. This process of communication, in turn, sensitized me to the various ways that the scholarly world, including diverse communities of practice in distinct intellectual disciplines, affects my work.

SENSIBILITIES AND ETHOS IN MUSICIANSHIP AND RESEARCH

In this section I discuss the sensibilities and ethos of the three-pronged engagement and connection that operates in music and scholarship. References to engagement and connection can be found in various bodies of literature, including in the literatures on motivation, cognition, aesthetics and spirituality. Connection is implied in theories of the self,[4] for example in sociologist George Herbert Mead's (1934) discussion of the genesis of the self and of the peculiar character of human social activity. That character, Mead argues, is found in the process of communication, and more particularly in the triadic relation on which generation of meaning is based.[5] Intensified engagement and connection are implied in Dewey's notion of intensified experience, distinguishing it from the anesthetic. Intensified engagement is also acknowledged in Czikszentmihalyi's (1990) theory of flow. Both *flow* and *intensified experience* are specific, heightened forms of connection.

Although it was my encounter with Dewey that helped me identify and give a name to a forceful aspect of my experience, it was Buber's (1971) writing that deepened my understanding of the relationships inherent in intensified engagement. Buber contrasts two primary attitudes, two ways in which we approach existence, the "I-Thou," and the "I-It." The difference between these two relationships is not in the nature of the object to which one relates but rather in the relationship itself. I-Thou is the relationship of openness, directness, mutuality, and presence

(Friedman, 1947). "I-It is the more typical subject-object relationship in which one knows and uses other persons or things without allowing them to exist for oneself in their uniqueness" (Friedman, 1947, p. xii). Buber (1947/2002) refers to "real listening," becoming personally aware of the "signs of address" that "address one not only in the words of but in the very meeting with the other." It is the attainment of the sphere of the "between" that Buber holds to be the "really real." The relationship of I-Thou teaches us to meet others and at the same time, "to hold our ground when we meet them" (p. xiv).

Indeed, the notion of empathy is now gaining interest in various intellectual disciplines. We note it in the phenomenologically-based realm of *verstehen* (e.g., van Manen, 1990 who talks about the tact of teaching,) or in the related ideas of empathic teaching, for example in Arnold's (2005) writing. The concept of empathy is also present in literature on theater education (see, for example, Klein (2005), and Schonmann's (2006) discussion of catharsis and children's emotional responses to drama).

Just as it is the *quality* of relationship rather than the nature of the object to which one relates that distinguishes "I-I" from "It-It," it is the quality of engaged activity that is of essence. (Clearly teachers, like researchers, have an important role in arousing that quality and thus generating the nature of the educational encounter.) Activity itself does not fully determine how it will be experienced, though certainly some activities are more conducive to engagement than others. Potentially rich activities like listening to music, having a conversation, conducting research, or attending conferences can provide a continuum of connections even for the same individual. Even seemingly routine activities can be experienced as providing spaces for engagement, as Studs Terkel's (1974)[6] study of people's relationships with their work manifests vividly, It is this quality that arises from being able to engage in music, in ideas, in the world, that characterizes, in my opinion, great musicians, and great researchers. The great, too, have their preferred arenas. Dewey is reported to have connected poorly to students within formal classroom settings (Jackson, 1998) (and often, as my students complain, in a first reading of his work). Still, his ideas engage us vibrantly 80 years after he articulated them.

As a "lingering question," the issue of engagement is not an abstract concern but one that shapes powerfully my everyday life, in my choices of friends, advisees, research topics and book projects. As a learner and a teacher, I am aware that intensified engagements and connections, although they cannot be forced, can be cultivated. While an initial spark can be useful, connection involves investment and a sustained relationship with the material learned. In my teaching of research methodology and aesthetics, my most important goal is the cultivation of engagement with material (readings, research project, or artwork, depending on what the focus of the class is) and connections with this material by providing an intellectual space for interaction and some tools for engaging, with both research and artwork.[7]

The commonalities between engagement in research and in music, and the awareness of their shared features, hit[8] me in my very first research project as a doctoral student in what was a completely new area for me (or so I thought)—education. While the bodies of knowledge in education were indeed unfamiliar and the discursive language style novel, the commonalities of engagement between my "musical identity" (a mix of the performer, the musicologist, and always the listener) and the educational researcher were striking. I often felt that it was these "musical identities" that shaped my research in more fundamental ways than the conceptual frameworks and theories I learned in school. Certainly it was the quality of engagement that fulfilled me in my new (and later, not so new) researcher role. This intensity of connection experience was a complete surprise: my (implicit) expectations of research were of a highly textual, formal, and disembodied activity, a "cooler" rather than "warmer" relationship (Thagard, 2006). The vibrancy and emotional intensity (up and down) of my fieldwork and writing were unexpected. Equally unexpected were the highly engaged embodied aspects of presenting. It took me several presentations to experience the positive intensity of the live performance of research.

The topic of intensity of engagement is addressed in the field of aesthetics, going back to Aristotle's classic concept of *catharsis* in drama, through Tolstoy's (1898/1969) communicative concept of art and Dewey's (1934) and Rosenblatt's (1978) notion of transaction, to contemporary Richard Shusterman's (2000, 2004) pragmatism and John Armstrong's (2000) discussion of perception of art work. Contemporary thinking recognizes the intricate ways that cognition and affect work together.[9] Armstrong for example, offers these five aspects of the process of perceptual contemplation of an artwork: (a) noticing detail, (b) seeing relations between parts, (c) seizing the whole as the whole, (d) the lingering caress, and (e) mutual absorption.

Armstrong's (2000) first aspect, becoming aware of detail which our habitual and rapid seeing and hearing tend to gloss over, requires a conscious effort to attend to different parts of the composition. The second aspect, that of noting relations, involves apprehending how every element performs with respect to the whole. The third aspect has to do with completeness and coherence, the grasping of unity in the face of diverse elements. These aspects, fundamental of course to musical analysis, are presented as cognitive but have an important role in facilitating an emotional relationship with the work.

The fourth and fifth aspects of experiencing visual art, what Armstrong (2000) terms the "lingering caress" and "mutual absorption," involve a new set of relationships between viewer and artwork. Lingering caress is characterized by the lack of instrumental purpose—a form of engagement that is traditionally associated with the concept of aesthetics. When we linger, Armstrong points out, "Nothing gets achieved, nothing gets finished—on the contrary, satisfaction is taken in spinning out our engagement with the object" (p. 98). The process of a deepening relationship allows for artistic and aesthetic discoveries. The fifth aspect, mutual absorption, refers to the possible transformative character of connection. Armstrong writes, "When we keep our attention fixed upon an object which attracts us, two things tend to happen: we get absorbed in the object and the object gets absorbed into us" (p. 99). I find musical experiences epitomize this absorption on bodily, cognitive and affective levels, which weave together so that "I become the music."

The intimate, reciprocal relationship between viewer and viewed is a recent theme, part of a postmodern consciousness. In discussing Velasquez' painting *Las Meninas,* philosopher Michel Foucault (1973) evokes the reciprocity and dialectic of looking: We can look at the painting, and the painting looks back at us. This notion of reciprocity seems to emerge independently in different domains. From her perspective as a science educator, Margery Osborne (2006) makes a similar claim: The act of looking at another can enable a heightened awareness of self, a self-reflexivity. I have made a similar observation in relation to the dialogical relationship of music and research, sensibilities and interactions that are the basis of aesthetic encounters (Bresler, 2006).

Of particular relevance to the triadic structure and ethos that I describe here is what I suggest as a sixth aspect, centrally present not only in the performing arts but also in academic research: communication with audience through lived performance. Drawing on music's ability to create a community, live performances unify performers and listeners in what can be an intensely shared experience.

These six aspects of engagement—interactive and cyclical rather than hierarchical and linear (hence Armstrong's use of the term *aspects* rather than stages)—are at the core of qualitative research. Shaping perception and interpretation, these features of engagement are inherent to qualitative research during observing interviewing, analyzing, and writing. The first three aspects are analytic and task-oriented as we focus on detail, note relations and patterns, and grapple to see a coherent whole. Just as they function in art and music, these aspects of perception and engagement in a research context involve an interplay between part and whole, tightening one's focus and widening it, alternating among description, incubation, and interpretation.

The activities of noting and perceiving create engagement and connection, and in turn are shaped by engagement and connection. The open, receptive space of the lingering caress and mutual absorption, facilitated by prolonged engagement and immersion in both fieldwork and data analysis, allows the researchers, in the words of Armstrong's book title, to "move closer" in order to connect—to establish intellectual and emotional intimacy.

Taking the theme of connection to a seemingly different arena, love, Armstrong (2002) writes in his second book *Conditions of Love: The Philosophy of Intimacy:*

> Love is an achievement, it is something we create, individually, not something which we just find, if only we are lucky enough. But although it is a creation and a achievement it is not something which can be forced simply by effort … this is unsurprising if we reflect that love is dependent upon many other achievements: kindness of interpretation, sympathy, understanding, a sense of our own needs and vulnerability. And these kinds of capacity and awareness do not spring suddenly into being. Each requires patient cultivation: we have to take whatever fragile presence each has in our lives and build upon that. (p. 158)

Here, too, there is an emphasis on the cultivation of relationship, an openness, a giving of oneself. The experience of both fieldwork and analysis requires a connection, the cultivation of (in Armstrong's words, "kind") perspectives, the acknowledgement of vulnerabilities.[10] This awareness of the role of the self, a sense of "our own needs and vulnerability" in interpretation and understanding and in connecting to what we study is relatively new to educational research. Traditionally, social science emphasized detachment from the "subjects," for fear of what is regarded as its opposite, *attachment*, and emotional entanglement. While an understandable taboo in the field of laboratory psychology, given the expectation of uncontaminated "data," and the structures of the laboratory settings, the concern about attachment has also operated in disciplines that, in fact, relied on connection to enable understanding and generate a meaningful study. As a result, sociological and anthropological studies used to present narratives that provided little information about researchers' engagement and interactive experiences of fieldwork and how these engagements facilitated their understandings and interpretations.

The spread of the postmodern paradigm and the expansion of qualitative research methods in the past 40 years has changed the assumptions and expectations of relationship in research. The increasing expectation of *verstehen*, empathic understanding, is a key goal of research in the social sciences, and it acknowledges that qualitative research depends upon authentic, meaningful connections with participants and their worldviews. Such research entails getting inside these worldviews and letting them get inside us, simultaneously internalizing as well as analyzing them, thus combining empathy with distance.

While relatively new in research methodology, these reciprocal relationships have been long present in experiences of music performances. The openness to connect to the music one rehearses and plays (which also involves an analytic, cognitive relationship) propels a dialogic connection with oneself, drawing on one's emotions and sensibilities. The triadic element enters due to the ethos of communication. The dialogical connections in both music and research are enhanced by communication (actual or anticipated) with the audience within a public aesthetic space. Because of this inherent similarity in both structure and ethos between music and qualitative research, I regard musical processes as rich resources for the understanding and conceptualization of engagement and connection during research.

Anticipation of communication deserves a comment. Communication has a much deeper and more sustained character than the moment of actual encounter. Mead (1934) pointed out that the importance of what we term "communication" lies in the fact that it provides a form of behavior through which a person may become an object to himself. Thus, the communication is directed not only to others but also to the individual himself (p. 139). Mead suggested that it is when one responds to that which one addresses to another, and when that response of one's own becomes a part of one's conduct, when one not only hears oneself but respond to oneself, talks and replies to oneself as truly as the other person replies to the communication, that we have behavior in which individuals become objects to themselves.

Anticipated communication, the awareness of a future audience when conducting research, is present at various stages from the very start. The processes of research, like musical performances, involve the discovery and shaping of meanings for oneself as well as for others. Already in the early stages of fieldwork, observations attend to what is observed but are shaped by the responsibility of the observer's intent to communicate to others.[11] Researchers are motivated by their intellectual-emotional curiosity, intensified by the commitment to an outside audience. Losing that sense of audience is akin to losing their motivation as ethnographers, the danger of "going native." The awareness of a potential audience is, I believe, essential to both music performance and research. It is the act of communication that defines them as such, heightening perception and focus, rendering what could be a private act into a social one, an act undertaken within a community of practice.

Nonverbal Aspects of Engagement

Richard Shusterman (2000), in his book *Performing Live*, speaks of the exclusivity of the verbal in arguing against hermeneutic universalism, the claim that all understanding is linguistically mediated. The only form of experience, writes Shusterman, that disembodied philosophers (and academics in general) recognize and legitimate is linguistic, thinking in words, talking, writing.

> But neither we nor the language that admittedly helps shape us, could survive without the unarticulated background of pre-reflective, nonlinguistic experience and understanding. Hermeneutic universalism thus fails in its argument that interpretation is 'the only game in town' because language is the only game in town. (p. 135)

This argument applies to the role of language in the interpretive process of qualitative research. Engagement and connection can be facilitated and supported by narrative and language, but they are not exclusively linguistic. Traditionally qualitative researchers have regarded interpretation as aimed at linguistic formulation.[12] Qualitative research is typically identified with writing and narrative. However, it goes way beyond written discourse (obviously, fieldwork including relationship with participants, requires much more than language.)

The idea that many, perhaps most experiences are not linguistic and that interpretation does not require language is of course a given for musicians. Musicians create musical interpretations that are not verbal but that attend to important qualities of temporal experience. They have also developed an elaborate, sophisticated nonverbal vocabulary for the elements and qualities of musical experience. In an earlier paper, I discussed musical qualities that are at the basis of analysis and interpretation, including form, rhythm, dynamics, and texture (Bresler, 2005). These terms may be new to nonmusicians, but the experiences which they represent are clearly not.[13] Naming them is important in sensitizing us to their presence. An adequate vocabulary is important because the concepts we use to make sense direct both our perceptions and our actions. We pay attention to what we expect to see, we hear what we can place in our understanding. This is why the sensibilities of musicians can contribute greatly to researchers studying personal and communal lived experience.

The scholar who first framed the arts explicitly as models for knowledge as well as for the *process* of inquiry is Elliot Eisner (1991). In his conceptualization of connoisseurship and educational criticism, Eisner, drawing on the visual arts, expanded the modes of inquiry from the verbal and numerical to the senses, and in particular, to vision. By choosing the art critic as his model, Eisner identified a figure that could translate the visual world to a linguistic medium (a role that Eisner himself filled with eloquence and elegance, as I have personally witnessed on several occasions). His notion of the *enlightened eye* invited me to explore the possibilities and implications of an enlightened *ear*, in research settings and beyond, in perceiving the world. However, my own metaphor, rather than that of a music critic, is that of a musician, solo or ensemble player. Art critics and musicians employ two different levels of embedded interpretation: The musician participates as an active creator of the music, interpreting and performing, taking into account contextual knowledge of current conventions and performance practices, while the critic plays the part of engaged but somewhat removed outsider,[14] interpreting the performance and providing a commentary. Both combine intimacy and distance but the starting point of each is different.

The communication of research, in writing and in live presentation, is crucial for its dissemination and usefulness. The topic of writing research has been explored extensively (e.g., Becker, 1986; Richardson, 1994; Wolcott, 2002). In contrast, actual, lived presentations seem to be fairly unexplored. The fear of demagogy that will numb if not destroy the listener's "objectivity" and critical skills have shaped a typical abstract, analytical format for scholarly presentation. However, making something dull does not guarantee its objectivity. Additionally, we should hope that scholarly audiences are not easily swayed by a superficial performance. The next section examines more closely live performances of scholarship in their natural habitat, conferences.

THE PERFORMANCE OF SCHOLARSHIP:
WEAK AND STRONG TIES IN COMMUNITIES OF PRACTICE

Communication is inevitably addressed to individuals or members of a group with some shared understandings and assumptions. Others outside this group are outsiders to the communication. In this section I discuss *strong and weak ties* (Putnam, 2000) as they operate in *communities of practice* (Lave & Wenger, 1991; Wenger, 1998) as useful concepts for understanding and furthering academic scholarship in general and research in music education in particular.

People become members of a community of practice through mutual endeavor, for example, shared practices and common activities (Lave & Wenger, 1991). The process of social learning occurs when people who have a shared interest in some subject or problem collaborate over an extended period and exchange ideas, find solutions, and build innovations. Such activities bind members of a community of practice together as a social entity. Anthropologist Jean Lave and social learning theorist Etienne Wenger coined the term community of practice in relation to situated learning as part of an attempt to rethink scholarly conceptualizations of learning. More recently, communities of practice have become associated with knowledge management with an emphasis in the scholarship on communities of practice on ways of nurturing new knowledge, stimulating innovation, and sharing existing tacit knowledge within an organization. The AERA provides a space that allows intellectually for both what I will define as strong ties (for example, the music special interest group (SIG) for music educators), and what I will define as weak ties among numerous AERA divisions and dozens of AERA SIGs with their distinct scholarly traditions and bodies of knowledge.

From another perspective, the sociologist Robert Putman (2000), in his book *Bowling Alone* writes about strong ties that link us to friends whose sociological niche is very like our own. Weak ties link us to distant acquaintances who move in different circles from ours (p. 23). Communities of practice, I suggest, are spaces where strong ties operate centrifugally toward a shared core, whereas weak ties operate centripetally, away from that core to outside sources of knowledge.

In the milieu of scholarship and academe, two major media that bind the community together and essentially function as the "oxygen of scholarship" are (a) the written texts of books and journals, and (b) the textural, multisensory spaces of conferences. While the latter are as essential to contemporary scholarship as the written media, they are rarely addressed explicitly beyond referring to their existence as having hosted the earlier oral version of a published paper. In addition to the interesting, complex relationship between the temporal lived presentation and the "fixed" written manuscript (Bresler, 2005), live performances create different dynamics within a community. A live community has more affinity with the ancient (and still very much alive!) functions of music in society, as compared, for example, with the more recent invention of print. The power of live performances is dealt with extensively in the fields of anthropology and sociology (see, for example, Bet-El & Ben-Amos, 1994; Gennep, 1960; Kapferer, 1986; Moore & Myerhoff, 1977; Schechner, 1988; Turner, 1969, 1982; Turner & Bruner, 1986).

In the contemporary worlds of scholarship, books parallel the texts of music compositions, whereas conferences parallel textured live performances with their shared temporal presence. These two modes are often intimately related, as this paper clearly manifests. The written paper you read was initially presented in a conference, an encounter that heightened my attention to the specific role of intensified engagement in performance of scholarship, akin to the role of a live audience in a musical performance. Here, the medium certainly shapes the style. The textual/textural provide an interplay between the fixed/fluid. Thought and the activity of thinking are motivated (at least in the contemporary world of scholarship, if not in those of Socrates and Jesus) by the quest for a product. The fixed product—a research paper, a musical composition— typically serves as a fixed target in the act of creation, parallel to the emphasis of text in classical music.[15] However, thinking—like breathing, talking, lecturing, advising, and writing this paper—is fluid, constantly moving. Our engagement as musicians with the fluidity of sound and music, I argue, can sensitize us to the fluidity of personal and cultural experience, the heart of qualitative research.[16] The relationship between presentation and paper, as those readers who attended the conference can tell, is far from identical. In contrast to scripted written manuscripts my live performances tend to be improvisational in response to audience's presence and my perceptions of their interests and background.

Big conferences like AERA can facilitate the establishment of weak ties by the conference's embodied social/intellectual presence. Wenger points out that learning occurs in the context of our lived experience of participation in the world (Wenger, 1998, p. 3). His concept of legitimate peripheral participation, whether in classrooms or in conferences, describes an important type of learning experiences. The community of practice of the music education SIG is affected by the broader AERA conference, for example, in the formats of sessions and the critical role of discussants, and in the structures of paper presentations and symposia, which often share in the same session research issues across different disciplines. This can, of course, be a process of mutual shaping and reciprocal relationship. We as musicians and music educators can expand AERA beyond its traditions, heightening attention to musical qualities that are an inherent part of scholarship (and life). The function of weak ties and how they operate in communities of practice relates to aesthetician Claire Detels' (1999) notion of "softening of boundaries." The softening of the boundaries of what used to be well-defined musical and artistic genres and intellectual disciplines is an important characteristic of the twenty-first century.

In an earlier writing (Bresler, 2003) discussing the cross-fertilization of school disciplines, I noted how the softening of boundaries results in increasing "border crossing" (Giroux, 1992). In music, performers like Nigel Kennedy, Daniel Barenboim, and Yo Yo Ma cross genres to perform music of various cultures and subcultures, including rock and popular music. Performance centers, traditionally dedicated to classical music, now host what used to be "music untouchables" (Nettl, 1995) performers of music traditionally played only in nightclubs.

Crossing genres often results in the generation of new entities, genres, and styles. In music, the boundaries between classical and folk, in Bruno Nettl's (1995) words, "the high caste of music," as evidenced in the works of the great masters, from Bach and Haydn through Beethoven, Liszt, and Tchaikovsky to Bartok and Ives, has never been bounded. However, traffic across this boundary was on a limited scale, typically consisting of an adoption of a folk theme within a classical form. There was a clear distinction between borrower and borrowed, and the borrowing involved no blurring of the "dominant style." This is markedly different from contemporary musical compositions, for example, Osvaldo Golijov's *La Pasión Según San Marco*, which mixes together Jewish and Argentinean folk music within a Christian passion genre, or Simunye's music which blends English Madrigal with South African musical styles.[17] The number of musical works that juxtapose traditionally incompatible styles to create new, hybrid creations is increasing. Their success and popularity among sophisticated musicians are a strong testimony to the changing norms, expectations, and tastes in communities of practice of musicians.

The same pattern is evident in scholarship. The crossing of boundaries is most noticeable at the emergence of new disciplines, from biochemistry, astrophysics, and computational neuroscience to cultural anthropology and psychological economics. Interdisciplinary work can, of course, cause its own difficulties and disappointments (Sperber, 2005), often revolving around the difficulty of creating criteria that can be shared by the different intellectual traditions (Boix-Manilla & Gardner, 2005). However, crossing borders seems to be rewarding enough that it is here to stay. Often emerging from the ground up by individual researchers, it is also facilitated by institutional structures and funding agencies, in both the sciences and the humanities.

Putnam (2000) regards weak ties as particularly valuable for social capital (Bourdieu, 1984). I argue that weak ties and the cross-fertilization they engender are increasingly vital to our conceptualization of knowledge[18] and its organization into new, hybrid disciplines. Just like the concept of art (Weitz, 1956), a discipline, too, can be constructed as an open-ended entity. Yet, in order to exist, it needs boundaries. At the same time, to maintain its vibrancy and respond to changing realities, an art medium, or a discipline, needs to be able to extend these boundaries to venture into new territories.

Intellectually, the juxtaposition of strong and weak ties has made for an extraordinarily stimulating environment for qualitative education researchers. One of its products is the development of new methodological genres, such as "mixed methods" and the more recent "arts-based research" (e.g., Barone 2001a, 2001b; Bresler, 2008a, in press b, in music; Cahnmann & Siegesmund, 2008, in the literary arts; Irwin & DeCosson, 2004; and Sullivan, 2005 in the visual arts).

Neither AERA nor weak ties are, of course, new phenomena. However, it seems that now, more than ever, scholars thrive on the coexistence of weak/strong ties and their interactions. Academics have more to gain, and less to lose, institutionally (and personally) from venturing into hybrid forms of research.

THE LIFE CYCLE AND POWER OF SCHOLARSHIP

Papers, at least my own papers, go through many cycles and metamorphoses. Each stage leaves its mark, adds a layer. The final version (in the sense of being printed and circulated, rather than the sense of a "final thought"), the one you are reading now, feels, at least in contrast to the preceding cocoons, like a butterfly in its mobility, the movement out of (my) private space into public space, the possibility of entering others' private spaces and interacting with them. All papers have multiple origins and many shoulders upon which they stand.[19] Writing, as Wenger (1998, p. xiv) has acknowledged, is always the product of a community. Mine can be easily traced to the gigantic shoulders of Martin Buber and John Dewey. Structurally it was enabled by Linda Thompson's and Mark Campbell's kind invitation to talk to AERA's music SIG. Its written version is indebted to the related inauguration of Advances in Music Education Research, a new book series generated out of the Music SIG, a cause for celebration for the music education community.[20]

The moment of intellectual encounter, the act of communication, is typically seen as the "end" of scholarship, the culmination of effort to articulate ideas within an aesthetic form. However, good encounters are also beginnings, beginnings of relationships where others enter the conversation, at best, in a dialogue (in a Buberian language—the meeting of I and Thou; in Gadamerian language, the *fusing of horizons*). Spaces like AERA can be used to create a communal space that generates personal intellectual encounters and sometimes the beginnings of "live" companionships and friendships. This communication, propelled by an interaction between the textural live performance and encounter and textual manuscripts (and e-mails) is often the step to the next project. Most fundamentally, they allow us to grow, and risk our current opinions by being open to others' perspectives.

Clearly, there are important differences between musical performances and scholarly presentations. In the case of AERA, one difference has to do with the format of a conference that allocates public time for questions, allowing audience members to share thoughts, to contribute to the content, texture, and dynamics of the encounter. This dynamic, typically unacknowledged, is, as I suggest below, an integral part of mutual endeavor within the community of practice. To explicate how this dynamic operates, I will revert to a "vignette mode," common to qualitative research, grounding the theoretical theme of live performance and engagement within the concrete situation of the past conference presentation.[21]

In the defined temporal boundaries, beginning and ending of this particular "business meeting" session, activities and experiences were sequenced, much like notes in a musical performance, yet allowing space for individual constructions in this "public/private" setting for cocreation of understanding. Unlike the reading of a text, the experience of the session, as all concrete experiences do, provided a "whole environment"—where the text is embodied, multisensory, and communal. Even at 8 P.M., the fresh energy of the first day of the annual meeting of the *American Education Research Association*, which can easily feel like a big, sweeping wave, had the distinct ambiance of a beginning. The audience, fifty or so bright, alert SIG members accommodated in a cozy room in Chicago's Hyatt's fourth floor, had just arrived from their various destinations—Ireland, China, New Zealand, and different parts of the United States. In their leadership roles Mark Campbell and Linda Thompson provided clear yet open, inclusive, and flexible structures of support. The audience, a cross-section of researchers in music education and AERA members, a diverse yet cohesive group, consisted of mostly faculty and doctoral students. In response to my question, all the people in the room raised their hands to indicate that they were qualitative researchers.

A concrete moment of encounter, in this case, 6-8 P.M. on a Monday in early April, exists uniquely in space and time. In contrast, the conceptualizations and interpretations of this moment are multiple. This productive tension between the concrete and the abstract is the stuff that qualitative research is made of: making sense of communal and personal lived experience, theorizing, interpreting, drawing on conceptual frameworks, and in the process, giving these frameworks new meaning. The concrete seems (deceptively) self-evident; interpreting is, many would say, what makes us human: sophisticated, incisive, grounded interpretations distinguish excellent scholars and researchers from more mediocre ones. Scholarship aims at creating increasingly sophisticated conceptualizations. My own choice of conceptualizations in this paper exemplifies the process of engagement with research, in this case research in preparation for speaking as a musician to a group of musicians and music educators. These conceptualizations evoke similarities to musical engagements—communal as well as individual, pulling together strong and weak intellectual ties.

While Buber and Dewey have an explicit presence in the conceptual framework of this paper, there are other important contributors that do not have such a well-defined place in the written text.[22] The marks of lively interactions with philosopher of education Chris Higgins, psychologist Yakov Epstein, art educator Terry Barrett, early childhood educator Su-Jeong Wee, and education and literacy scholar Alyson Whyte, all outside the field of music education, and music and art educator Regina Murphy, have left important marks on this paper. Other interactions can be traced to the questions raised by the music education audience present at the AERA talk, indicating diverse and at the same time deeply shared concerns and questions that followed me for these past few months.

Seated at the back of the room, a doctoral student commented that she never thought about research as performance but was rather intimidated by the power structure of the dissertation committee. This comment deepened my commitment to reflect on the role and usefulness of musical sensibilities and ways of being in the world of scholarship. My own change of view from being "under examination" to "having a stage to present something dear to my heart" has proven helpful to me: I hoped it may be of use to others. From the front row, to my right, Ryan asked about intentionality (I learned later that this theme emerged in his dissertation defense), a topic that prompted a discussion of the different genres of research—from the more applied evaluation and action research to the "basic" genres of anthropology and ethnomusicology with their respective goals and intentions. Still, across these different genres, an engaged *verstehen*, expanding our knowledge about the human condition, was a shared intension, motivating the use of qualitative methods. From the middle of the room, Glenda's question about teaching qualitative research stayed with me through another paper I wrote in the spring, focusing on the teaching and learning of research. Close by, Margaret Schmidt's query on how to juggle it all—in-depth research, solid, communicative teaching, committed service—is acutely shared by all academics I know, especially since connection and intensified engagement imply the investment of energy.[23] This issue of multiple demanding tasks defined by the meso, institutional context of academe, operates as powerfully on the macro, scholarly level on the micro personal level as we improvise our lives, engaging meaningfully with the world and ourselves.

The communities of practice that come together for the performance of scholarship at a conference as sites of performance (as well as those private dialogues with colleagues through the earlier cycles) engender in a stretta like fashion new and expanded themes, creating the multilayered fugues of scholarship (and life).

ACKNOWLEDGMENTS

Many thanks to Terry Barrett, Yakov Epstein, Chris Higgins, Regina Murphy, Su-Jeong Wee, and Alyson Whyte for their reading of this work and their insightful comments.

NOTES

1. These structures and ethos are also present in teaching, a theme that I have explored in Bresler (in press a).
2. I am grateful to Yakov Epstein for indicating that the triadic nature of communication has been explored by various scholars in sociology and psychology, for example by George Herbert Mead (1934) and by Hovland, Janis, and Kelley (1953).
3. The term *telos* (from the Greek word for "end") used by Aristotle in his theory of biology as well as by other Greek philosophers, is the root of the term "teleology," the study of aims and intentions. I am indebted to Chris Higgins for pointing out Jonathan Lear's translation: "that for the sake of which" which is superior to aim or end since we often tend to see think of aims in a literal way as target or terminus. Here, the *telos* of archery is not the target but the cultivation of accuracy, strength, patience, self-control, and so forth. (see Higgins 2003, p. 280; Lear, 1988, p. 35).
4. A complex and contested concept.
5. Mead, a symbolic interactionist, was one of the classical "Chicago school of sociology" that included the sociologist Charles Horton Cooley and philosopher, psychologist and educator John Dewey. It is interesting to note how each of these three major figures developed this concept as part of their broader scholarship.
6. Sadly, Terkel's study points at more incidences of alienation rather than connection.
7. I elaborate on these tools in Bresler (in press a).
8. A visceral, as well as intellectual and emotional realization.

9.   For compelling examples of the interaction of social, affective, and cognitive aspects in math, see for example, Dai and Sternberg (2004), Hannula (2002), and Epstein et al. (2007).

10. The literature on love is relatively new, boosted by humanist psychology, particularly Abraham Maslow (1962) and his theory of needs. Zick Rubin (1970) in his social-psychological construct of romantic love identifies attachment, caring, and intimacy as three elements of love. Educationist Leo Buscaglia (1972) in his widely read books gained enthusiastic audiences when addressing these qualities in a popular domain.

11. That awareness can be very much at the background rather than the foreground, coexisting with the experience that the more a person gets engaged by his/her observations (or with the music), the less s/he is likely to think about *how* they will communicate to others.

12. This view is now eroding with the increasing popularity of arts-based research, which employs different modes of representation that include but are not restricted to discursive verbal modes of representation.

13. My colleague Alyson Whyte commented that creative writing specialists will readily see parallels of each of the four musical qualities named.

14. The traditional view of the critic as distanced is critiqued by postmodernists (for a compelling discussion of these various perspectives (see Barrett, 2007).

15. If not necessarily in the explicitly improvisational cultures of the middle East, Indian and African cultures, see for example, Nettl (in press).

16. This sensitization is not automatic: Musicians are as creatures of habits like the rest of us, and the transfer from one domain, music, to another, that of research, takes active, conscious cultivation.

17. The existence of hybrid genres consisting of "world musics" in pop musics, combining indigenous folk and popular cultures, has been a regular feature of the process of intensifying globalization (for example, in the music of Sting, Frank Zappa, Jaques Loussier, and Winton Marsalis).

18. It is that interplay between strong and weak ties, which allows a cross fertilization of disciplines that motivated me to embark on the *International Handbook of Research in Arts Education* (Bresler, 2007) with its mission of promoting discourse among the various arts education disciplines.

19. To paraphrase Isaac Newton's comment in his letter to his fellow scientist, Robert Hooke.

20. As a note intended for insiders to the music education community I would like to acknowledge the supporting shoulders of the AERA audience— colleagues like Frank Abrahams, Janet Barrett, Margaret Barrett, Eve Harwood, Koji Matsunobu, Marie McCarthy, Regina Murphy, Sandy Stauffer, and other, familiar and not-yet-familiar faces.

21. I realize that some readers of this paper were not present at the conference. Still, like much of qualitative research, I aim to provide some (admittedly limited) vicarious experience that heightens attention to the two main centers of scholarship and their differences, conferences and written publications.

22. Often relegated to footnotes.

23.   Admittedly, connections are also recharging and provide energy.

REFERENCES

Armstrong, J. (2000). *Move closer: An intimate philosophy of art.* New York: Farrar, Straus, & Giroux.

Armstrong, J. (2002). *Conditions of love: The philosophy of intimacy.* New York: Norton.

Arnold, R. (2005) *Empathic intelligence: Teaching, learning, relating.* Sydney, Australia: University of New South Wales Press.

Barone, T. (2001a). Science, art, and the predispositions of educational researchers. *Educational Researcher, 30*(7), 24-28.

Barone, T. (2001b). Pragmatizing the imaginary: On the fictionalization of case studies of teaching. *Harvard Educational Review, 7*(4), 735-742.

Barrett, T. (2007). Teaching toward appreciation in the visual arts. In L. Bresler (Ed.), *International handbook of research in arts education* (pp. 639-654). Dordrecht, the Netherlands: Springer.

Becker, H. D. (1986). *Writing for social scientists: How to start and finish your thesis, book, or article.* Chicago: University of Chicago Press.

Bet-El, I., & Ben-Amos, A. B. (1994). Rituals of democracy. In N. Sammlung (Ed.), *Fierteljahres-seitshcrift Fur Erziehung Und Gesellschaft* (pp. 51-58). Germany: Sonderdruck.

Boix-Manilla, V., & Gardner, H. (2005). *Assessing interdisciplinary work at the frontier. An empirical exploration of "symptoms of quality."* Retrieved September 20, 2007, from www.interdisciplines.org/interdisciplinarity/papers/6/paper

Bourdieu, P. (1984). *Distinction: A social critique of the judgement of taste* (R. Nice, Trans). London: Routledge & Kegan Paul.

Bresler, L. (2003). Out of the trenches: The joys (and risks) of cross-disciplinary collaborations. *Bulletin of the Council of Research in Music Education, 152,* 17-39.

Bresler, L. (2005). What musicianship can teach educational research. *Music Education Research, 7*(2), 169-183.

Bresler, L. (2006). Toward connectedness: Aesthetically based research. *Studies in Art Education, 48*(1), 52-69.

Bresler, L. (Ed.). (2007). *International handbook of research in arts education.* Dordrecht, the Netherlands: Springer.

Bresler, L. (2008). The music lesson. In J. G. Knowles & A. Cole (Eds.), *Handbook of the arts in qualitative inquiry: Perspectives, methodologies, examples, and issues* (pp. 226-237). Thousand Oaks, CA: SAGE.

Bresler, L. (in press a). Research as music: New ways of conceptualizing research education. *Bulletin of the Council of Research in Music Education.*

Bresler, L. (in press b). Music and qualitative research. In L. M. Given (Ed.), *The SAGE encyclopedia of qualitative research methods.* Thousand Oaks, CA: SAGE.

Buber, M. (1971). *I and Thou.* New York: Simon & Schuster.

Buber, M. (2002). *Between man and man.* New York: Routledge. (Original work published in 1947)

Buscaglia, L. (1972). *Love.* New York: Fawcett Crest.

Cahnmann, M., & Siegesmund, R. (2008). *Arts-based inquiry in education: Foundations for practice.* Mahwah, NJ: Erlbaum.

Czikszentmihalyi, M. (1990). *Flow: The psychology of optimal experience.* New York: Harper & Row.

Dai, D. Y., & Sternberg, R. J. (Eds.). (2004). *Motivation, emotion, and cognition: Integrative perspectives on intellectual functioning and development.* Mahwah, NJ: Erlbaum.

Detels, C. (1999). *Soft boundaries: Re-visioning the arts and aesthetics in American education.* Westport, CT: Bergin & Garvey.

Dewey, J. (1934). *Art as exprerience.* New York: Perigee Books.

Eisner, E. (1991). *The enlightened eye: Qualitative inquiry and the enhancement of educational practice.* New York: Macmillan.

Epstein, Y., Schorr, R., Goldin G., Warner L., Arias, C., Sanchez L., Dunn M., et al. (2007). Studying the affective/social dimension of an inner-city mathematics class. *Proceedings of the Twenty-ninth annual meeting of the North American Chapter of the International Group for the Psychology of Mathematics Education, Lake Tahoe, NV,* 649-656.

Foucault, M. (1973). *The order of things: An archeology of the human sciences.* New York: Vintage Books.

Friedman, M. (1947). Introduction. In M. Buber (Ed.), *Between man and man* (pp. ix-xx). New York: Routledge.

Gennep, A. (1960). *The rites of passage.* London: Routledge & Kegan Paul.

Giroux, H. (1992). *Border crossings.* New York: Perigee Books.

Hannula, M. S. (2002). Attitude towards mathematics: Emotions, expectations and values. *Educational Studies in Mathematics, 49*(1), 25-46.

Higgins, C. (2003). MacIntyre's moral theory and the possibility of an aretaic ethics of teaching. *Journal of Philosophy of Education, 37*(2), 279-292.

Hovland, C., Janis, I., & Kelley, H. (1953). *Communication and persuasion.* New Haven, CT: Yale University Press.

Irwin, R., & de Cosson, A. (2004). *A/r/tography: Rendering self through arts-based living inquiry.* Vancouver, Canada: Pacific Educational Press.

Jackson, P. W. (1998). *John Dewey and the lessons of art.* New Haven, CT: Yale University Press.

Kapferer, B. (1986). Performance and the structuring of meaning and experience. In V. Turner & E. Bruner (Eds.), *The anthropology of experience* (pp. 188-203). Urbana, IL: University of Illinois Press.

Klein, J. (2005). From children's perspectives: A model of aesthetic processing in theatre. *The Journal of Aesthetic Education, 39*(4), 40-57.

Lave, J., & Wenger, E. (1991). *Situated learning: Legitimate peripheral participation.* New York: Cambridge University Press.

Lear, J. (1988). *Aristotle: The desire to understand.* Cambridge, England: Cambridge University Press.

Maslow, A. (1962). *Toward a psychology of being.* Princeton, NJ: D. Van Nostrand.

Mead, G. H. (1934). Development of self. In C. W. Morris (Ed.), *Mind, self, and society* (pp. 135-226). Chicago: University of Chicago Press.

Moore S., & Myerhoff, B. (1977). Introduction. In S. Moore & B. Myerhoff (Eds.), *Secular rituals* (pp. 3-24). Amsterdam: Van Gorcum.

Nettl, B. (1995). *Heartland excursions.* Urbana, IL: University of Illinois Press.

Nettl, B. (in press). Preface. In G. Solis & B. Nettl (Eds.), *Improvisation in music—Society, education, art.* Urbana, IL: University of Illinois Press.

Putnam, R. (2000). *Bowling alone.* New York: Simon & Schuster.

Osborne, M. D. (2006). A rose in a mirror. In K. Tobin & W-M. Roth (Eds.), *Auto/biography and auto/ethnography: Praxis of research method* (pp. 205-225). London: SENSE.

Richardson, L. (1994). On writing. In N. Denzin & Y. Lincoln (Eds.), *The handbook of qualitative research* (pp. 133-155). Thousand Oaks, CA: SAGE.

Rosenblatt, L. (1978). *The reader, the text, the poem: The transactional theory of the literary work.* Carbondale, IL: Southern Illinois University Press.

Rubin, Z. (1970). Measurements of romantic Love. *Journal of Personality and Social Psychology, 16*(2), 265-273.5

Schechner, R. (1988). *Performance theory.* New York: Routledge.

Schonmann, S. (2006). *Theatre as a medium for children and young people: Images and observations.* Dordrecht, the Netherlands: Springer.

Shusterman, R. (2000). *Performing live: Aesthetic alternatives for the end of art.* Ithaca, NY: Cornell University Press.

Shusterman, R. (2004). SomaAesthetics and education: Exploring the terrain. In L. Bresler (Ed.), *Thinking minds, moving bodies: Towards an embodied teaching and learning* (pp. 51-60). Dordrecht, the Netherlands: Kluwer.

Sperber, D. (2005). *Why rethink interdisciplinarity?* Retrieved November 1, 2007, from www. interdisciplines.org/interdisciplinarity/papers/1/printable/paper

Sullivan, G. (2005). *Art practice as research: Inquiry in the visual arts.* Thousand Oaks, CA: SAGE.

Terkel, S. (1974). *Working: People talk about what they do all day and how they feel about what they do.* New York: Pantheon Books.

Thagard, P. (2006). *Hot thought mechanisms and applications of emotional cognition.* Cambridge, MA: MIT Press.

Tolstoy, L. (1969). *What is art?* London: Oxford University Press. (Original work published 1898)

Turner, V. (1969). *The ritual process: Structure and anti-structure.* Chicago: Aldine.

Turner, V. (1982). *From ritual to theater.* New York: Performing Arts Journal Press.

Turner, V., & Bruner, E. (1986.) *The anthropology of experience.* Urbana, IL: University of Illinois Press.

van Manen, M. (1990). *Researching lived experience: Human science for an action sensitive pedagogy.* Albany, NY: The State University of New York.

Wenger, E. (1998). *Communities of practice: Leaning, meaning, and identity.* Cambridge, England: Cambridge University Press.

Weitz, M. (1956). The role of theory in aesthetics. *The Journal of Aesthetics and Art Criticism, 15*(1), 27-35.

Wolcott, H. (2002). *Writing up qualitative research.* Thousand Oaks, CA: SAGE.

PART I

FOCUS ON TEACHER AND LEARNING

CHAPTER 2

YOUNG CHILDREN'S CONSTRUCTIONS OF THE MUSICAL KNOWLEDGEABLE OTHER

Peter Whiteman

ABSTRACT

Contemporary views of children and childhood position children as valued coconstructors of their cultures, supporting the notion that learning and development are bound to a social context. Through this lens, scaffolding can be seen broadly as a collection of techniques employed by a knowledgeable other to assist a novice to internalize cultural signs. This paper reports images of the knowledgeable other constructed by a group of preschool-aged children engaged in spontaneous singing. Video-recordings of eight children singing during free-play over a period of 3 years were transcribed, and the songs and accompanying play episodes were analyzed using QSR NUD•IST software. Results revealed the children constructed a range of images of the knowledgeable other, employing a variety of techniques to define this role. Cultural experience did not seem to rely

Diverse Methodologies in the Study of Music Teaching and Learning, pp. 25–43

strongly on chronological age, with younger children often viewed in the role of the knowledgeable other.

INTRODUCTION

Contemporary reconstructions of children and childhoods acknowledge children as valued and valuable coconstructors of their cultures (Broström, 2006; Corsaro, 2005; Dahlberg & Moss, 2005; James & Prout, 1997; Kjørholt, 2002). This position, in turn, lends strong support to the sociocultural notion that learning, development, and cultural construction entail complex, socially located, collective activity, where more experienced members of a culture (hereinafter referred to as knowledgeable others) scaffold novices in the internalization and interpretive reproduction of cultural signs. From this sociocultural perspective, it is possible to gain insight into how young children construct the knowledgeable other, and the ways in which musical signs and behaviors are transformed and transferred during everyday music making in the early years. Accordingly, Small's (1977, 1998) designation of music as an act ("musicking") rather than a thing is adopted herein. This stance places explicit value on who is musicking and the context in which he or she is doing so.

SCAFFOLDING IN EARLY CHILDHOOD

We have come to know scaffolding as good pedagogy when working with young children. As a child attempts to piece together and refine new knowledge, a high-quality learning environment is characterized, among other things, by a teacher responding sensitively, using a range of strategies to model, question, challenge, and support the child's endeavors. Although in general, this notion is not new, its evolution has been shaped over time by cultural and political contexts. Vygotsky (1986) offered procedures for utilization by a knowledgeable other while guiding a novice on his/her journey from the inter- to the intrapsychological plane. Wood, Bruner, and Ross (1976) identified the fundamental features of scaffolding employed by experts in their support of novices as:

1. recruitment (engaging the interest of the novice);
2. reduction of degrees of freedom (simplifying the components of the task so that the novice recognizes the requirements);
3. marking critical features (underscoring relevant responses and their constituent parts);

4. direction maintenance (maintaining the novice's interest in the task at hand), and

5. demonstration (modeling task solutions).

In recent times, scaffolding has become a more fluid concept, generally referring to temporary strategies that are employed in the support of novices or learners making meanings. Teachers are no longer seen as the only people who scaffold. Parents, peers, and other members of children's cultures are now also regarded as taking on this role.

Scaffolding has been an integral part of a variety of recent studies of and with young children in a range of domains. In the field of literacies, researchers have investigated such things as how teachers scaffold beginning readers, the impact of maternal scaffolding on later literacy skills, and kindergartners' collaborative endeavors in a technology-rich learning environment. Cole (2006) identified a range of strategies employed by teachers working with novice readers. Teachers were found to use a range of remarks and gestures related to four cueing systems. The study showed that these strategies evolved as the readers became more fluent. In a case study of two teachers classified as "effective," Rodgers (2005) provided rich descriptions of the depth, breadth, and quality of support provided on a one-to-one basis to first grade students presenting with severe reading difficulty. She highlighted the multifaceted nature of scaffolding in light of on-the-fly decisions made by insightful teachers. Using structural equation modeling to investigate predictors of children's later reading in elementary school, Dieterich, Assel, Swank, Smith, and Landry (2006) found that maternal verbal scaffolding indirectly affected comprehension and decoding, and 4 year-old language directly affected comprehension at 10 years. This study provides direct evidence that an early language-rich social environment facilitates language and later reading skills. Discourse analysis of 5-6 year-old children's talk while using computers in a mapping project revealed the children's perceptions of computer-based learning (Hyun & Davis, 2005). The children's collaborative endeavors were found to scaffold development and their purposeful talk had a noticeable effect on emergent technoliteracy. Peer collaboration was also the focus of another study that paired third grade children with preschoolers to undertake craft activities (Fair, Vandermaas-Peeler, Beaudry, & Dew, 2005). Interviews with the older children and analyses of their reflective journals indicated that appropriate scaffolding was provided to the preschool-aged children. Moreover, the older children's metacognitive abilities were characterized by understanding of the scaffolding practices in which they engaged and the advantages these provided for themselves and the younger children.

Scaffolding has also been of interest in the province of music. Adults (parents and teachers) have been found to assume various roles and employ a range of techniques when scaffolding young children's musical endeavors. After surveying early childhood music teacher educators and early childhood music supervisors, Persellin (2003) concluded that respondents held strong beliefs about the best way to scaffold young children in their acquisition of new songs. However, no consensus was reached on what scaffolding techniques were best, beyond rejecting the use of recordings. For a period of 12 months, De Vries (2005) studied his son's vocal improvisation and song acquisition from 2 years of age. An examination of the child's movement through the zone of proximal development outlined a range of explicit scaffolding techniques for parents and teachers to utilize in fostering musical development. In a study of young children's musical socialization, Adachi (1994) identified three significant roles assumed by close adults: transmitter of musical signs, practice partner, and finally, that of coplayer. She found that musical signs such as sung pitches and self correction of pitch were transmitted from adult to child during social interaction and later surfaced in the child's independent musicking. Adults became practice partners when children had progressed beyond the initial acquisition of a musical sign and wanted to practice its use. When the child became involved in the same musical play situation with a different person, they tended to substitute their role with that of the adult, as the child perceived it, in the initial interaction. Finally, as a coplayer, the adult would participate equally with the child in making music.

Studies of collective musicking and peer collaboration have given rise to rich understandings of the dynamics surrounding such enterprises. Wiggins (2005) reported on peers sharing ideas with each other and the process of producing work that, according to members of the learning community, meets the requirements of the task. She highlights the "mutual effort" in which students engage so that eventual public performance of their compositions sees positive outcomes for all. Examining the collective musicking of a group of young children (4.3-5.9 years old), St. John's (2006) descriptive narratives illustrate the roles of others as children share ideas and make decisions moment by moment. The power of social influence, participants' transforming behaviors, and space to explore musical content were identified by St. John as three central themes materializing from the study.

Research in this area has not been limited to scaffolding as employed by people. A study of children using computer software to compose music (Reynolds, 2005) designated a computer as the knowledgeable other.

Results showed that the children scrutinized their compositions from visual, musical and aural perspectives.

The current paper examines a range of constructions of the musical knowledgeable other by a group of eight preschool-aged children. Data are drawn from a 3-year longitudinal study of the children's spontaneous singing during play. The purpose of this study was to ascertain the social interactions that occur during preschoolers' spontaneous singing and to determine the effects of these interactions on the acquisition of musical knowledge and skills.

METHOD

The study was undertaken over three years in a child care center in a large city. The center opens for 48 weeks each year. Participants were eight of the youngest children (four boys and four girls) who attended the center. At the beginning of the first year, the children's ages ranged from 2 years 6 months to 3 years 6 months. These children were chosen because of the potential length of time they would spend at the centre prior to attending school. All eight children remained part of the study until the end of the second year. At the beginning of the third year of the study, three left the center to attend school.

The children's spontaneous singing was systematically observed and recorded on videotape over the 3 years, during morning free-play times. Throughout these observation periods, the children were mainly involved in free play, but observations sometimes included routines such as packing away the indoor play area, and morning tea. Each child was observed monthly for 1 hour. Minor changes were made to the observation schedule as needed, to allow for unforeseen absences (e.g., due to illnesses). For example, if a child was absent, the focus child for the following observation day was brought forward, and the absent child was observed on the next available observation day.

During each observation period, all the activities undertaken by the focus child were recorded on videotape, yielding a total 140 hours of recordings over the project. These camera tapes were then reviewed, and all footage pertaining to the spontaneous singing of the focus children was extracted for analysis. The songs were manually transcribed using traditional Western notation with the addition of diacritics (Abraham & von Hornbostel, 1994; Gerson-Kiwi, 1953) such as "+" or "−" above a note to indicate a microtonal increase or decrease in pitch of less than a semitone and "↑" or "↓" to mark glissandi which often occurred when the children were using a vocal technique that sits between singing and speaking (e.g., sprechstimme). The resultant dataset consisted of 443 spontaneous songs and their associated play episodes. Over the life of the project, the four girls initiated the singing of 66, 60, 52, and 31 songs respectively (in rank order of frequency) while 69, 67, 52, and 46 were initiated by the four boys.

After transcription, each song was analyzed and coded for the following musical aspects: song type (standard, standard-variation, improvised); temporal organization (ranging from freeform, through motivic to metrical); melodic contour, based on Davidson's (1985) melodic contour schemes; and form, based on Dowling's (1984) phrase-contour type/token ratio. Coding continued with social aspects of the play episode according to: social category of play, based on the work of Parten (1932), Saracho (1984), and Wyver and Spence (1995); and song function, according to Bjørkvold's (1990) functions of song. Coding of social aspects was augmented with narrative records of observations made during repeated viewings of the video footage about the roles that the children assumed, focusing particularly on that of the knowledgeable other, and the onset and offset behaviors that defined each play episode. This conglomeration of fixed and open-ended data was stored in a relational database developed using Microsoft Access.

After base data such as children's names, and date of observation were added to each record, data were imported from the database into a NUD•IST project (Richards & Richards, 1994), using a mixture of automated procedures for fixed response data such as demographic information, temporal organization and melodic contour and manual procedures for the narrative records. Analysis was undertaken in a recursive manner. Automated coding of fixed-response data was followed by coding the open-ended data for themes, which were in turn, organized into patterns drawn from the data themselves rather than from an a priori perception.

The issue of validity was addressed through the notion of "trustworthiness" and realized by way of four specific strategies (Lincoln & Guba, 1985). One strategy was that of "prolonged engagement." Data were collected regularly over 3 years, allowing the researcher to understand daily occurrences in the way that the children do. Another strategy, "persistent observation," facilitated such engagement by observing and interpreting in combination with evolving analysis. A further strategy, "referential adequacy," involved ensuring the provision of information to contextualize the data collection. This was achieved by extended periods of observation including free play, routines, meals and the like. Also, the strategy of "peer debriefing" was utilized. This involved discussing observations and evolving analysis with professionals experienced in the field, but removed from the immediate environment of the study.

RESULTS

From the corpus of songs collected during the study, three images of the knowledgeable other emerged. Typically, children corrected each other, modeled songs and invited their peers to sing. Illustrated with examples, an outline of these follows.

The Overt Corrector

Transmitter behaviors have previously been broadly defined as facilitating musical signs being conveyed from a more experienced member of a culture (the knowledgeable other) to a less experienced member of that culture. A common transmitter construct in this study was that of the overt corrector. Here, a more experienced child corrected another child with a blatant verbal declaration that the song they were singing was incorrect; a model of the "correct" song often followed the announcement. In some instances, the resulting song was more of a coconstructed endeavor involving the original singer and the knowledgeable other who augmented the "correct" song.

Early in the study, Jacqui (2 years 10½ months) was involved in a play episode with a slightly older child, Ben, and sang the song in Figure 2.1.

In this play episode, Ben sang a song with some text that matched a standard song known to Jacqui. She responded with "No, not like that!" and then modeled a version of the first phrase of the standard song with an approximate contour that followed the requisite direction, but with unstable tonality towards the end of the phrase. At this point in the study,

Jacqui (Spoken) No, not like that

Figure 2.1.   Ben and Jacqui.

Figure 2.2.   Jacqui correcting.

Jacqui was not yet 3 years old, but apparently felt socially (and cognitively) capable of making overt corrections to a song produced by an older child of 3 years and 3¼ months.

Approximately 2 months later, aged 3 years and 1¼ months, Jacqui demonstrated similar behavior, attempting to correct a child aged 3 years and 5½ months (Figure 2.2 above).

In this case, Jacqui appeared to know more of the standard song, which was then taken up by her playfellow, and the two children ended up partners in coconstructing the finished song which had elements of two standard songs along with a small amount of improvised material. The initial correction that Jacqui attempted to make seemed to result in her providing a much less accurate model than in the previous example. In fact, in this case, her comment of "No, no, like this" and the model that immediately followed resulted in the other child extending the song, rather than repeating Jacqui's model. This indicates that Jacqui was probably not aware that her playfellow already knew the material, but once this fact was (implicitly) established she was able to take the cue to extend the song, equalizing the partnership and resulting in a coconstructed outcome.

Other instances of overt correction were played out in similar fashions. Predictably, in these cases, small variations in the language used in these announcements were observable, but the underlying meaning remained the same.

The Modeler

Modeling, in various guises was also observed in a range of play episodes and songs. In some cases, a knowledgeable other began singing and other (less experienced) children used that material as musical models for their own contribution to the song. The original singer often made no overt attempts to correct or encourage others to sing, but in some instances, provided a form of support in continuing to contribute to a jointly constructed song.

Children's singing was rarely an exact copy of the model, although this was occasionally evident. More common was the use of musical and/or textual material as a starting point for interpretive reproduction or innovation by the second singer. Sometimes this would result in the production of a solo, but quite common, were jointly constructed songs with ongoing involvement of the knowledgeable other and one or more other singers.

Generally, in the case of the modeler, the role of the knowledgeable other was conferred by the second singer and his or her actions, rather than the knowledgeable others themselves.

Consider the song in Figure 2.3. In this case, Lucy began singing and other (less experienced) children used her material as musical models for their own contribution to the song. Lucy made no overt attempts to correct or encourage children to sing, but in some instances, provided some form of support, by continuing to contribute sections to a jointly constructed song based on her initial singing. Lucy's singing in response to Jacqui in this case, may well have acted as a signal of corroboration that what Jacqui was doing was in fact a desirable phenomenon.

Another song that Lucy jointly constructed provides a similar picture. This episode saw her engrossed in parallel play, beside another child of approximately the same age, and Martha, who was 1 year younger. Lucy began the song with two motifs (Figure 2.4) that were to form the basis for later segments of the songs. While these two motifs appear somewhat rhythmically dissimilar, there is a reasonably close relationship between their melodic contours. Removing the rhythm imposed on the first motif by Lucy's choice of text, the outline of its melodic contour becomes (with diacritics removed) that in Figure 2.5.

Figure 2.3.   Musical model.

Figure 2.4.   Opening motifs—Lucy.

Figure 2.5.   Melodic contour of motif one.

Figure 2.6.   Motif two.

Figure 2.7.   Response to Lucy's opening motifs.

Comparing this to the second motif (Figure 2.6) reveals that the two share identical melodic frameworks (albeit at different pitches), focusing on a descending minor third.

The child closest in age to Lucy contributed the next part of the song shown in Figure 2.7 above.

This child's singing was not an exact copy, but did display some characteristics reminiscent of Lucy's material. Combined, these two motifs outlined the pitches that Lucy sang. The rhythm patterns employed by the second child mirrored those that Lucy used with a slight variation. Lucy's singing (Figure 2.8) became that shown in Figure 2.9 when her playmate was singing. The reason for this similarity is unclear. Melodically, the second child's singing did not display the emphasized descending minor third, and the text was not modeled on Lucy's original motifs. The unrelated melody was particularly clear in the second bar of the second child's singing.

Despite her rhythm being clearly reflected in her playmate's singing, there was no discernible response from Lucy, and beyond the actual singing, nothing from her playmate. In this observation, the second child made a sophisticated innovation on Lucy's model, unknowingly or otherwise, without needing to be prompted to do so.

Martha (a year younger than Lucy) also used Lucy's initial singing as a model for her contribution to this song, but her innovation was less

Figure 2.8.   Fragment of opening.

Figure 2.9.   Variation on opening.

[inaudible   ]   draw - ing

Figure 2.10.   Repetition of opening.

intricate. Taking over from the other child, Martha repeated part of Lucy's melodic material (Figure 2.10 above) and extended it by repeating the final two notes, shown in Figure 2.11. Martha utilized a direct rhythmic and melodic copy of Lucy's material, but incorporated her own text, possibly indicating that the message or information that she was singing was more important than the music itself.

This small transaction between the three children demonstrates some reasonably clear roles and results of participating in the singing of the song. Lucy was the oldest and (anecdotally) the more culturally experienced child, and often showed evidence of feeling secure in play and singing. The child closest to her age (and presumably more knowledgeable about their culture since she also played more frequently with Lucy than Martha did) presented a somewhat sophisticated innovation on Lucy's model. Martha, on the other hand (younger and presumably less culturally knowledgeable), extended the model, producing material consisting of far less intricate transformations.

The joint construction of the above song was realized without any explicit instruction on Lucy's part; her playmates apparently taking the lead from her initial singing and extending this model to form the song. A similar situation arose between Alex (5 years and 3 months) and a playmate approximately 1 year his junior.

Figure 2.11.   Repetition to finish song.

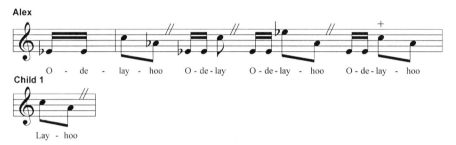

Figure 2.12.   Short echo.

While they were playing, the younger child (who seemed substantially less secure in social situations) eventually echoed a very small component of Alex's singing as shown in Figure 2.12 above. Alex responded with more animated singing of the original motif (Figure 2.13), which was then taken up and reproduced by an even younger child.

Alex finished the song by singing an extended variation of the original motif (Figure 2.14).

Alex and his playmates responded to opportunities to reproduce certain musical elements and also participate in using song in a question/ answer dialogue. However, the difference in this case appears to be the amount and detail of musical material that Alex's playmate utilized in his echo of Alex's initial singing. While Lucy and her playmate ultimately produced a relatively sophisticated joint construction, Alex's song consisted mainly of his material, with a small contribution from his playmate, in the form of an echoed interval.

The (Implied) Inviter

In contrast to the modeler described above was the (implied) inviter. This knowledgeable other was the initiator of another child singing, especially in the form of laying down a challenge. For example, the knowledgeable other issued an implied challenge to a playfellow in the

Figure 2.13.   Variation of original motif.

Figure 2.14.   Extended variation of original motif.

form of a song with a taunting melody and text, which in turn, was taken up and returned in the form of a musical retort by the other child.

Some time into the study, Alex and Jackson sang the song in Figure 2.15. The motivation for Alex to begin this song appeared to be linked to Jackson attempting to kick him by swinging past on a rope. Although Jackson did not make contact, Alex responded immediately by singing. The taunting text and tune, especially Alex's final three notes seemed to function as a challenge or some kind of implied invitation for Jackson to respond. Jackson's rejoinder incorporated rhythmic and textual aspects of Alex's singing, but these were not the only signs to which Jackson was exposed. By laying down the challenge and implying the need for some retort, Alex was (possibly without knowing) demonstrating that musical speech acts (that may well involve call and response or some other conversational devices) are valid and valued functions of songs in the culture of which he and Jackson are a part. That is, Alex was not only transmitting purely musical signs, but functional ones as well.

IMPLICATIONS

The findings of this study contribute to the growing body of knowledge about children's agency in their own learning and development. The data address two key tensions surrounding the more traditional notions of scaffolding and the knowledgeable other:

1. the relationship among age, experience and role, and
2. the manner in which the knowledgeable other is defined.

O - de - lay - hoo   o - lay - hoo

Figure 2.15.   Challenge.

The children demonstrated that within their cultures, it is not always an adult who acts as the knowledgeable other nor is it always the oldest child in the group who assumes or is assigned this role. Cultural maturity or experience with cultural signs, it seems, is not necessarily dependent on chronological age. Throughout the study, a range of children of varying ages both scaffolded and were scaffolded as they musicked within their zones of proximal development. Knowledgeable others tended to be children who were apparently familiar and secure with particular musical signs, rather than necessarily the oldest or older children in the group, while teachers or other adults were rarely seen in this role (it is important to note here that data were collected during free play and not during the more planned teaching and learning experiences throughout the day). In more traditional models of scaffolding (e.g., Wood, Bruner, & Ross, 1976) the expert or knowledgeable other has taken a relatively analytical approach to instructional design, involving such actions as nominating a desired outcome, and putting specific strategies into service. In the current case, the children realized a more fluid, contemporary form of scaffolding actively constructing sophisticated musical cultures as part of everyday life. The origins of these knowledgeable other behaviors have not been the focus of this study. Further research is needed to investigate their derivation and the possible relationships between them, particularly in light of Slobin's (1993) notion of an intersection of "supercultures," "subcultures" and "intercultures."

With chronological age not necessarily indicating status of knowledgeable other, practitioners would be well positioned to group children in multiage clusters where this is deemed appropriate. There are few situations across the lifespan where people are forced to limit their interactions with others to those who are within 12 months of their age. However, many education settings seem committed to such grouping. The benefits of multiage grouping have been demonstrated in a range of settings (Gerard, 2005; Kappler & Roellke, 2002; Katz, Evangelou, & Allison, 1990; Lennon & Middlemas, 2005), but in an age characterized by standardized testing and normalization, such practices are sometimes met with skepticism. Multiage grouping would provide the ideal opportunity to capitalize on naturally occurring peer scaffolding and support the children's meta-awareness of the process in the context of their own musical development.

In the more traditional, teleological models of human development, it is reasonable to assume that the decision about taking on the role of the knowledgeable other will, in fact, be made by that knowledgeable other. After all, in these types of models, decisions about teaching, learning and construction of the culture will be made by those who have made substantial progress through an often predetermined and unilateral pathway towards the end-state. That is, older members of the culture determine what it is that the younger members of the culture need to do in order that they move towards the end-state in a timely and efficient manner.

Interestingly, the children and their songs in this study provided little evidence to support end-state models, but instead, presented a deal of evidence to support more generative/adaptive models such as the orb web (Corsaro, 2005), bioecological systems (Bronfenbrenner, 1979) or dynamic systems (Thelen & Smith, 1994). The children's musicking and the roles that they assumed clearly demonstrated their agency in the construction of their musical cultures. The role of the knowledgeable other was not always determined by the knowledgeable other him/herself, but instead by other children. This was particularly obvious on a number of occasions where an apparently less knowledgeable child used the singing of another child as a model, thus conferring the role of knowledgeable other onto the original singer. Sometimes such actions resulted in more active involvement by the knowledgeable other (for example, the overt corrector), at other times little or no further action was evident on the part of the knowledgeable other, with the novice using the model as a kind of sounding board or testing ground. Still other transactions occurred where joint constructions initiated by the less knowledgeable child, but based on the singing of the knowledgeable other, resulted in some subtle feedback from the knowledgeable other and application of new musical signs by the novice child. It seems then, that for this group of children, the knowledgeable other can be functionally defined from several perspectives in both the inter- and intrapsychological planes.

This gives rise to some appealing possibilities for pedagogical documentation and the business of making learning visible. For instance, making use of video as a scaffold to revisit learning (see for example, Forman, 1999; Hong & Broderick, 2003; Makin & Whiteman, 2006) may allow children to provide insight into how and why the knowledgeable other can be defined in musical circumstances. Furthermore, the active involvement of the children in this process depicts a rich environment to which an emergent curriculum model (Edwards, 2002; Jones & Nimmo,

1994) is well suited. Realizing such a curriculum empowers the children and acknowledges them as key agents in their own learning and development.

Young children make music as a natural part of being. They construct complex and rich musical cultures resplendent with dynamic and clearly assigned roles. It is of the utmost importance that we capitalize on these naturally occurring phenomena with the provision of musicking opportunities that value children as coconstructors of their musical cultures. We must come to see music education in the early years from a true sociocultural perspective where musical learning and development is not merely affected by social context but firmly embedded in it.

REFERENCES

Abraham, O., & von Hornbostel, E. M. (1994). Suggested methods for the transcription of exotic music. *Ethnomusicology, 38*(3), 425-456.

Adachi, M. (1994). The role of the adult in the child's early music socialization: A Vygotskian perspective. *The Quarterly Journal of Music Teaching and Learning, 5*(3), 26-35.

Bjørkvold, J. R. (1990). Canto-ergo sum: Musical child cultures in the United States, the Soviet Union and Norway. In F. R. Wilson & F. L. Roehmann (Eds.), *Music and child development: Proceedings of the 1987 biology of music making conference* (pp. 117-135). St. Louis, MO: MMB Music.

Bronfenbrenner, U. (1979). *The ecology of human development: Experiments by nature and design.* Cambridge, MA: Harvard University Press.

Broström, S. (2006). Children's perspectives on their childhood experiences. In J. Einarsdottir & J. T. Wagner (Eds.), *Nordic childhoods and early education* (pp. 223-255). Greenwich, CT: Information Age.

Cole, A. D. (2006). Scaffolding beginning readers: Micro and macro cues teachers use during student oral reading. *Reading Teacher, 59*(5), 450-459.

Corsaro, W. A. (2005). *The sociology of childhood* (2nd ed.). Thousand Oaks, CA: Pine Forge Press.

Dahlberg, G., & Moss, P. (2005). *Ethics and politics in early childhood education.* Milton Park, Oxfordshire: Routledge.

Davidson, L. (1985). Tonal structures of children's early songs. *Music Perception, 2*(3), 361-374.

de Vries, P. (2005). Lessons from home: Scaffolding vocal improvisation and song acquisition with a 2-year-old. *Early Childhood Education Journal, 32*(5), 307-312.

Dieterich, S. E., Assel, M. A., Swank, P., Smith, K. E., & Landry, S. H. (2006). The impact of early maternal verbal scaffolding and child language abilities on later decoding and reading comprehension skills. *Journal of School Psychology, 43*(6), 481-494.

Dowling, W. J. (1984). Development of musical schemata in children's spontaneous singing. In W. R. Crozier & A. J. Chapman (Eds.), *Cognitive processes in the perception of art* (pp. 145-163). Amsterdam: Elsevier Science.

Edwards, C. P. (2002). Three approaches from Europe: Waldorf, Montessori, and Reggio Emilia [Electronic Version]. *Early Childhood Research & Practice, 4(1).* Retrieved January 15, 2007, from http://ecrp.uiuc.edu/v4n1/edwards.html

Fair, C., Vandermaas-Peeler, M., Beaudry, R., & Dew, J. (2005). "I learned how little kids thin": Third-graders' scaffolding of craft activities with preschoolers. *Early Child Development and Care, 175(3),* 229-241.

Forman, G. E. (1999). Instant video revisiting: The video camera as a "tool of the mind" for young children [Electronic version]. *Early Childhood Research and Practice, 1.* Retrieved September 1, 2004, from http://ecrp.uiuc.edu/v1n2/forman.html

Gerard, M. (2005). Bridging the gap: Towards and understanding of young children's thinking in multiage groups. *Journal of Research in Childhood Education, 19(3),* 243-250.

Gerson-Kiwi, E. (1953). Towards an exact transcription of tone-relations. *Acta Musicologica, 25(1),* 80-87.

Hong, S. B., & Broderick, J. T. (2003). Instant video revisiting for reflection: Extending the learning of children and teachers [Electronic version]. *Early Childhood Research and Practice, 5.* Retrieved September 1, 2004, from http://ecrp.uiuc.edu/v5n1/hong.html

Hyun, E., & Davis, G. (2005). Kindergarteners' conversations in a computer-based technology classroom. *Communication Education, 54(2),* 118-135.

James, A., & Prout, A. (Eds.). (1997). *Constructing and reconstructing childhood: Contemporary issues in the sociological study of childhood* (2nd ed.). New York: Falmer Press.

Jones, E., & Nimmo, J. (1994). *Emergent Curriculum.* Washington, DC: NAEYC. (ERIC Document Reproduction Service No. ED382343)

Kappler, E., & Roellke, C. (2002). The promise of multiage grouping. *Kappa Delta Pi Record, 38(4),* 165-170.

Katz, L. G., Evangelou, D., & Allison, J. (1990). *The case for mixed-age grouping in early education.* Washington, DC: National Association for the Education of Young Children.

Kjørholt, A. T. (2002). Small is powerful: Discourses on "children and participation" in Norway. *Childhood, 9(1),* 63-82.

Lennon, P. A., & Middlemas, D. (2005). The cultural maelstrom of school change. *School Administrator, 62(3),* 32-35.

Lincoln, Y. S., & Guba, E. G. (1985). *Naturalistic inquiry.* Beverly Hills, CA: SAGE.

Makin, L., & Whiteman, P. (2006). Young children as active participants in the investigation of early literacy. *European Early Childhood Education Research Journal, 14(1),* 33-42.

Parten, M. (1932). Social participation among pre-school children. *Journal of Abnormal and Social Psychology, 27,* 143-263.

Persellin, D. (2003). Teaching songs to young children: What do music-teacher educators say? *General Music Today, 17(1),* 18-27.

Reynolds, R. (2005). The computer as scaffold, tool and data collector: Children composing with computers. *Education and Information Technologies, 10*(3), 239-248.

Richards, T., & Richards, L. (1994). Using computers in qualitative data analysis. In N. Denzin & Y. Lincoln (Eds.), *Handbook of qualitative research* (pp. 445-432). Thousand Oaks, CA: SAGE.

Rodgers, E. M. (2005). Interactions that scaffold reading performance. *Journal of Literacy Research, 36*(4), 501-532.

Saracho, O. N. (1984). Construction and validation of the play rating scale. *Early Child Development and Care, 17*, 199-230.

Slobin, M. (1993). *Subcultural sounds: Micromusics of the west.* Hanover, NH: University Press of New England.

Small, C. (1977). *Music, society, education: A radical examination of the prophetic function of music in Western, Eastern and African cultures with its impact on society and its use in education.* London: Calder.

Small, C. (1998). *Musicking: The meanings of performing and listening.* Hanover, NH: University Press of New England.

St. John, P. A. (2006). Finding and making meaning: Young children as musical collaborators *Psychology of Music, 34*(2), 238-261.

Thelen, E., & Smith, L. B. (1994). *A dynamic systems approach to the development of cognition and action.* Cambridge, MA: MIT Press.

Vygotsky, L. S. (1986). *Thought and language* (A. Kozulin, Trans.). Cambridge, MA: MIT Press.

Wiggins, J. (2005). Fostering revision and extension in student composing. *Music Educators Journal, 91*(3), 35.

Wood, D., Bruner, J., & Ross, G. (1976). The role of tutoring in problem solving. *Journal of Child Psychology and Psychiatry, 17*, 89-100.

Wyver, S. R., & Spence, S. H. (1995). Cognitive and social play of Australian preschoolers. *Australian Journal of Early Childhood, 20*(2), 42-46.

CHAPTER 3

"GETTING THE MINUTES IN"

A Case Study of
Beginning Instrumentalists' Music Practice

Margaret H. Berg

ABSTRACT

The purpose of this study was to (1) describe two beginning instrumentalists' practice regulation and motivation and (2) identify the functions of music practice for the study participants. Data were collected during videotaped practice sessions and audiotaped interviews with the participants, parents and school orchestra teacher. Videotapes were coded using a graphic display of practice segments (Chaffin & Imreh, 2001) and practice strategy matrices (Miles & Huberman, 1994) while interviews were coded using low-level descriptors (LeCompte & Schensual, 1999) of practice session routines, practice strategies, practice environment, affect during practice, and use of effort. Although both participants were motivated by a practice time requirement, the use of different practice routines, strategies, environments and behaviors as well as motivational catalysts contributed to varied practice effectiveness. Findings suggest music practice served multiple and varied functions for these two adolescent-aged instrumentalists.

Diverse Methodologies in the Study of Music Teaching and Learning, pp. 45–65

INTRODUCTION

Although practice is necessary for the development of musical skill and knowledge, many beginning instrumentalists' practice may be characterized as inefficient (Barry, 1990; Gruson, 1988; McPherson & Renwick, 2001) and unenjoyable. Recent research on beginning instrumentalists' music practice has used self-regulation theory to identify effective, goal-oriented practice as well as some individual and environmental factors that influence practice. Self-regulated practice includes planning, organizing, monitoring, and evaluating a practice session (Austin & Berg, 2006; McPherson & Renwick, 2001; Nielsen, 2001); using a minimally distracting practice environment and appropriate resources (Barry & McArthur, 1994) and seeking help from others (Austin & Berg, 2006; Davidson, Howe, Sloboda, 1997; Hallam, 2000; Zdzinski, 1996). In addition, self-regulated learners use more effective practice strategies including mental rehearsal, mapping (playing through a piece to identify problem spots), marking the music, repetitive drill of sections in a piece of music, varying the tempo, recording practice, listening to recordings of and researching a piece, and engaging in an appropriate balance of required and motivational activities (Barry & Hallam, 2002; Gruson, 1988; McPherson & McCormick, 1999; McPherson & Zimmerman, 2002; Sloboda & Davidson, 1996; Zimmerman, 2000). Conversely, most beginning instrumentalists tend to play through entire pieces, rarely stopping to correct mistakes or practice sections of a piece longer than one measure; get distracted and express frustration (Austin & Berg, 2006; Gruson, 1988; Hallam, 1997; McPherson & Renwick, 2001; Pitts, Davidson, & McPherson, 2000a). [For a more extensive description of self-regulation theory and research, see McPherson & Zimmerman, 2002; Zimmerman, 2000].

The degree to which students engage in self-regulation while practicing may be affected by their motivation (Dweck, 1986). During practice, motivation is often manifested through effort, persistence when faced with a challenge and affect. In addition, a students' approach to practice and specific practice behaviors are influenced by future importance and value of an activity for the student (Pintrich & Schunk, 1996), as evident in student response to extrinsic or intrinsic factors and perceived cost of practicing (Eccles, Wigfield, & Schiefele, 1998); the balance between technical and musical challenge in the repertoire and student skill level resulting in flow, boredom, or frustration (Csikszentmihalyi, 1991); the perceived causes of success and failure including ability, effort, luck, and task characteristics (Austin & Vispoel, 1998; Stipek, 1998); whether students attribute their ability to practice effectively to factors within or outside their control (Weiner, 1986); and how confident the learner feels as manifested in persistence or such maladaptive/helpless behaviors as avoiding challenges, using less effective strategies, and experiencing negative emotions (Dweck, 1986; O'Neill, 1997) [see O'Neill & McPherson, 2002; Maehr, Pintrich, & Linnenbrink, 2002 for an extensive review of motivation theory and research].

While self-regulation and motivation theories provide a framework for describing practice, these theories do not adequately take into account the impact of a variety of contextual factors that influence student behavior, the malleability of student commitment or the multiple functions of practice beyond increasing musical skills and knowledge. As a result, the "meta" construct "engagement," which utilizes some concepts from self-regulation and motivation research, is increasingly being used to provide a more holistic and nuanced view of student learning. Engagement is defined as the amalgamation of cognition, behavior, and emotion. These three facets of engagement are dynamically related and impacted by school-level factors, the classroom context and an individual's need for relatedness, autonomy, and competence. [For a more detailed explanation of engagement concepts and research see Fredricks, Blumenfeld, & Paris, 2004.] Although some research on beginning instrumentalists' music practice has accounted for more than one facet of engagement and/or influential contextual factors (Austin & Berg, 2006; O'Neill, 1997; Pitts, Davidson, & McPherson, 2000a, 2000b), most research on music practice has focused on cognitive engagement with cursory consideration of the long-term impact of students' affective experience while practicing.

Recent writings suggest a "natural intellectual progression" (Sloboda, 2005, p. viii) within the research community from the investigation of individual cognitive processes, to motivational structures, to functions of music, an area that is most strongly influenced by culture. By utilizing concepts from anthropological research on the impact of context on learning and the multiple functions of music (Campbell, 1998; Kaplan, 1990; Merriam, 1964; Sloboda & O'Neill, 2001; Vygotsky & Kozulin, 1986), our awareness of the complexity of music practice can increase. For instance, Merriam (1964) delineated 10 functions of music in society, 5 of which (emotional expression, aesthetic enjoyment, entertainment, communication, integration of society) are most closely aligned with music practice. Campbell (1998) aggregated Merriam's functions into three "sides of music": the personal, social-familial, and functional. It may be the case that, for adolescent-aged beginning instrumentalists, music practice serves multiple functions not accounted for in research that utilizes only regulation and/or motivation theories as a conceptual framework.

Furthermore, there is limited research focused on beginning string instrumentalists' practice (Austin & Berg, 2006; Hallam, 1997; Hamann

& Frost, 2000; Pacey, 1993). These studies have used self-report (Austin & Berg, 2006; Hamann & Frost, 2000), semistructured interviews with students (Hallam, 1997) and audio recording of practice sessions (Hallam, 1997) to collect data. Research is needed that uses multiple data sources including videotaped practice sessions as well as structured and informal interviews with students, parents, and teachers to allow for methodological triangulation (Stake, 1995). This study will add to the existing research on beginning string instrumentalists' music practice through the use of observation as well as interviews with students, the teacher and parents.

The purpose of this study was to (1) describe two beginning instrumentalists' practice regulation and motivation and (2) identify the functions of music practice for study participants.

METHOD

Participants

Study participants were two seventh-grade, age 12, female string instrumentalists in their third year of instruction who were subjects in a previous study (Austin & Berg, 2006). Due to student transfer to other school districts, student attrition and teaching schedules, one middle school was selected for this second in a series of studies on beginning instrumentalists' music practice. Two of the four students from this school —Katy and Hannah—(pseudonyms are used to protect the identity of the participants) were selected to participate in the study.

Table 3.1 data were collected during the initial (Austin & Berg, 2006) study using a researcher-developed questionnaire (The Music Practice Inventory or MPI). The MPI, also utilized in a previous investigation (Austin, 1997), is organized into three sections. Section 1 includes 36 statements that address various aspects of practice motivation and practice regulation. In section 2, study participants are asked to provide two brief narratives based on given practice scenario prompts. Section 3 includes 12 items that address various background factors, including student and parent instrument experience, private lesson experience, average number of days and hours of practice per week, typical practice time, and home practice environment.

Median splits were calculated for practice regulation and motivation subscale scores to determine individual practice regulation and motivation profiles (e.g., low, medium, or high regulation and motivation). Frequency distributions were determined for dichotomous variables (whether students: play other instruments, take private string instrument lessons, have a parent who plays a musical instrument, and practice in a quiet environment) as well as for the time of day the student typically practices (early morning, during school, late afternoon, early evening, or late evening). Participant practice regulation, motivation and background characteristics for this study are located in Table 3.1.

Stratified purposeful case sampling procedures (Kuzel, 1992; Patton, 2001) were used since this sampling procedure facilitates portrayal of and comparisons between subgroups. As evident in Table 3.1, the participants share some characteristics including not taking private string instrument lessons, practicing in a quiet environment and taking piano lessons. In addition, both students were enrolled in honors—level language arts and social studies classes and from middle-income level families. However, these students are representative of varied motivation, strategy use, practice time, and parent musical background profiles, thus enabling comparisons between the two participants on these factors.

Procedures

Data were collected Spring 2005 over a period of 14 weeks (the equivalent of one trimester grading period) during bi-weekly, 20-minute videotaped practice sessions for a total of 56 recorded practice sessions (28 sessions of each participant's practice). Two formal interviews and several informal interviews were conducted with each participant. One formal interview was conducted with a parent and the school orchestra teacher as well as several informal interviews with the school orchestra teacher. A cassette recording was made during each formal interview and transcribed within 1 week. Similar to other

Table 3.1. Participant Characteristics

Name (Instr)	Motivations	Regulation	Other Instr	Private Lessons	Parent Bkgrd	Time Practice	Quiet Environment
Katy Jordan (Violin)	H	M	yes	no	yes	LA	yes
Hannah Hand (Viola)	M	L	yes	no	no	EE	yes

Note: H = high; M = medium; L = low; LA = late afternoon; EE = early evening; Instr = instrument; Bkgd = music background.

research (Hallam, 1997), participants were asked during one interview to look at a piece of unfamiliar music while explaining how they would approach practice, thus enabling a comparison between projected and actual practice of a new piece. In addition, participants watched a practice session videotape and were instructed to stop the video or comment anytime they noticed something they did well or would change in their practicing. Retrospective verbal reporting procedures (Ericsson & Simon, 1999) were also used whereby the researcher periodically stopped the videotape to ask questions about the participant's thinking and observed behaviors.

Practice sessions took place during orchestra rehearsals in the music technology room. Participants were asked to practice as they would at home for approximately the same length of time. Over the course of the trimester, participants practiced orchestra music at various stages of preparation as well as scales and pieces from the class method book *Spotlight on Strings, Book 2* (Gazda & Stoutmire, 1997). Although other studies of novice instrumentalists' practice have collected videotaped data during home practice sessions (Pitts, Davidson, & McPherson, 2000a, 2000b), due to the more limited scope of this study, budgetary constraints, and student schedules, practice sessions were videotaped at the school. In order to verify participants' description of the home practice environment and behaviors, the researcher observed a portion of one home practice session and asked parents to describe typical practice behaviors.

Practice session videotapes were transcribed using a graphic display of practice segments (Chaffin & Imreh, 2001). Practice segments were determined by noting the measure in the music where practice started and stopped. A practice segment was considered to be any combination of continuous playing and/or practicing of the music. Segments were considered to have ended when the student began to practice a different measure of music or paused for more than one second. This chapter contains a graphic display of two transcribed practice sessions that were selected as best examples of each participant's typical approach to practice. Also, a practice strategy matrix (Miles & Huberman, 1994) was created for each practice session. The matrix included a checklist of possible practice strategies and measure number(s) during which the strategy was used. Interviews were coded using low-level descriptors (LeCompte & Schensul, 1999) of practice session routines, practice strategies, practice environment, affect experienced while practicing and use of effort. Reliability and validity of the findings were increased through the use of low-level descriptor codes, checking for representativeness and negative case analysis (Lincoln & Guba, 1985; Miles & Huberman, 1994).

FINDINGS

Katy Jordan, Violin, Age 13

Katy was one of eight children, many of whom play or played an instrument. Katy began playing violin because she could apply her knowledge from 2 years of piano lessons and it "kinda looked cool … and I liked how it sounded." Although Katy's Mom played piano, she suggested Katy's abilities originated from her father's side of the family since Katy's great-grandfather played violin in a semiprofessional orchestra. After playing violin for nearly 3 years, Katy was intrinsically motivated to continue to play in orchestra since "I like how it sounds together in the whole orchestra."

At home, Katy practiced in the living room, sitting at the baby grand piano. Since she played competitive soccer and was in honors classes, she usually practiced 4 days a week, often practicing for a greater length of time on Sundays. While her Mom would remind her to practice during her first year of study, beginning her second year she determined the days of the week and amount of time she practiced each session. Katy hinted that getting started was sometimes a challenge, but "once I start I'm fine, I just have to get myself there."

A typical practice session at school would begin with Katy placing her music in order on the music stand, then warming-up on scales from the *Spotlight on Strings* method book. She then played current orchestra music, beginning with the pieces she liked the least "to get them out of the way." Sometimes, she played these pieces twice and would often end practice by playing from a new book of Disney tunes or previously performed orchestra music.

When practicing a new piece of music Katy used a systematic approach:

> First I play through to see how bad I am in some spots, and then (I) go back. If it seems there are a lot of timing things, I count it out or write in the beats with my pencil. Then I play it through slower just because it's easier to focus on notes. I go through and find the hard parts, like places where it falls apart in orchestra. Then I work on bowings if they're hard … if there are slurs or two up-bows. Then I look at dynamics.

Katy's approach to practicing a new piece was evident in her practice of the piece *Sonata Vivant* by Elliott DelBorgo (see Figure 3.1). The measure number in the score is placed on the horizontal axis and the practice segment number is located on the vertical axis. Figure 3.1 is read from left to right, beginning at the bottom of the graph. Each line represents a practice segment and the next practice segment begins on the line above the previous segment.

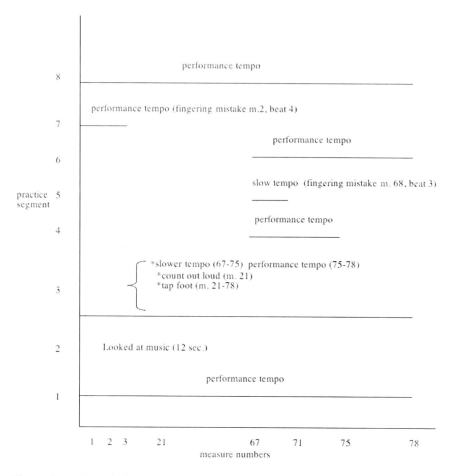

Figure 3.1.   Cumulative practice record for the first practice session of *Sonata Vivant* for Katy Jordon.

Note the use of specific strategies in this session mentioned in the description above (counting the beats, playing at a slower tempo, practicing smaller sections) as well as others including looking over the music, simultaneously playing while counting and foot tapping, repeating a section and altering the performance tempo. As evident in practice segments 5 and 7 in Figure 3.1, Katy would make a mistake, followed by playing from the same starting point (see segments 6 and 8). However, it was unclear whether she understood the cause of the error since segments 5 and 7 were followed by a performance tempo play-through of a large section rather than focused practice of the measure in which the mistake occurred. Overall, Katy used a "whole-part-whole" approach where she would play through a piece, work on a difficult section using one or more of the strategies illustrated in Figure 3.1, then play the entire piece again.

Although Katy seemed to follow an established practice routine, the amount of time she practiced each session was influenced by her teacher's 100 minutes per week requirement. Katy explained that "I practice to try to get my minutes in. If Mrs. _____ didn't have the 100 minute requirement, I'd practice less." At the same time, Katy expressed an interest in learning more difficult music since "(i)f I had more challenging music, I'd practice more." However, there were moments when Katy could have provided challenges for herself by using additional strategies to practice difficult sections in the music. Katy admitted this when watching a practice videotape since "that was off … I should have done that again. I was being lazy."

In summary, Katy's approach to practice might be characterized as moderately effective since she had an established practice routine that included the use of varied practice strategies. However, there was evidence that her practice could have been more effective by using her varied repertoire of strategies more frequently as well as additional strategies. Also, the practice time requirement established by her orchestra teacher as well as the lack of challenge provided by the repertoire seemed to mitigate growth in *intrinsic* motivation to practice, although Katy was *extrinsically* motivated to practice by the practice time requirement.

Hannah Hand, Viola, Age 13

In contrast to Katy's reasons for playing a string instrument, Hannah Hand's decision to play viola was more serendipitous.

> I was originally thinking about playing the clarinet or flute, but the band teacher told me that once I got my braces tightened, it would take about three weeks to get used to playing it again. When I went over to the viola I thought it was a violin, but it turned out that I really liked it.

Hannah noted the unique aspects of playing viola she enjoyed since

> I felt special since there were only three violas (in first year orchestra). I like the viola because it has a deeper sound. With the violin and cello, you get the same music as the piano. But with the viola there's this whole different clef and so I had to learn something completely new. That was really fun for me.

An only child of parents with limited musical backgrounds, Hannah practiced in her bedroom. Hannah would prop the music up in an open dresser drawer since she had misplaced her music stand. Sometimes she would play the radio between songs to "take a little break." Occasionally, she used the metronome she purchased for piano practice, an instrument she had been studying for 4 years. Hannah typically practiced after her homework was finished for 25 minutes on school (Monday through Thursday) evenings. Like Katy, she found getting started a challenge and realized the distinctions between piano and viola practice since "with the viola you have to set it up, tighten the bow, rosin it, and then tune it. So it makes it a little harder instead of just taking it out and playing it."

Hannah's practice sessions at school typically began with a warm-up that consisted of beginning at the start of *Spotlight on Strings*, playing familiar pieces for 10 to 15 minutes. These pieces were played "attaca" at a quick tempo and no scales or exercises related to the pieces were practiced. She would then play orchestra pieces for the remainder of the session, beginning with the pieces she liked the best. She explained that "I still practice the ones I don't like, but not as much." During a typical practice session, Hannah used such effective practice strategies as playing a difficult section in a piece at a slower tempo as well as less effective strategies including returning to the beginning of a piece when a mistake was made and discontinuing practice of a challenging song. Overall, Hannah seemed less focused on practicing to improve performance, as indicative in the comment at the end of one practice session that "I just started playing some stuff over, but I'm done now because I don't have anymore music left."

Hannah's explanation of her approach to practicing a new piece of music differed from observed practice. Rather than "playing at a medium speed, checking the rhythms, and working on dynamics," Hannah's observed practice consisted of playing through the entire piece, playing three short sections, and finally playing the entire piece again, all at performance tempo (see Figure 3.2).

Like Katy, Hannah was motivated to practice 100 minutes each week in order to earn a good grade in orchestra since "practicing gets you the grade, pretty much. It's 25% of our grade," a fact confirmed during an interview with the orchestra teacher. Her parents also motivated Hannah by occasionally reminding her to practice. However, since her parents had limited music experience—her Mom played violin and flute in school for one year and her Dad had no instrumental music experience—they assumed a supportive role where "they still just listen to me ... and I like it when they listen to me."

Practice challenges often resulted in an affective response from Hannah. For instance, she might get frustrated by a difficult rhythm that

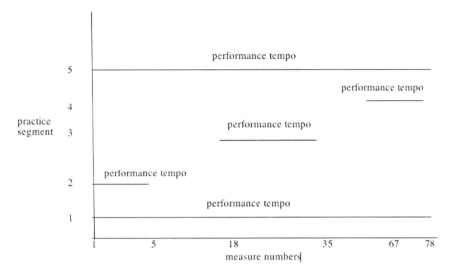

Figure 3.2.   Cumulative practice record for the first practice session of *Sonata Vivant* for Hannah Hand.

"I would practice wrong and I'd be mad and have to learn it all over again." Other times she reacted to a challenging, slow piece with boredom since "it's harder to count and we all thought it was boring cause it's slow." Hannah's response to challenge seemed to relate to whether she enjoyed the piece, as well as her mood.

> Some pieces I just didn't enjoy playing a whole lot and there were some that I would practice over and over to get it. There were some nights where I'm willing to practice and practice until I've got it down. And then there are other nights where I say "no, I don't want to try it anymore." I'd just do the songs I knew how to do. I think it just depends on my mood because some days I'm not in the very best mood. But other days I'm happy and willing to take a challenge.

Hannah was able to name such pieces as *Orpheus and the Underworld* and the *Can-Can* song as "pieces I know a lot" and were "really fun for me." In fact, her description of "fun pieces" revealed the mood altering function of viola practice since "I liked practicing the really fun songs because it would put me in a better mood." Like Katy, Hannah characterized her lack of persistence as laziness since

> some (pieces) you just have to think about them, and most of the time I was just too lazy to think. If I liked them they would probably be kind of easy. I enjoy a challenge but sometimes, easier is better for me.

While Hannah initially gained some satisfaction from practicing viola and participating in orchestra, when faced with choosing electives for the next school year, the perceived cost of continuing to participate in orchestra was too great, given increased homework and her competitive volleyball schedule. Hannah's mother supported the decision to stop playing viola since "we just want her to be well-rounded, not a concert violist or pianist. It just seems a half-hour of practice was too much, on top of piano."

Interestingly, both Hannah and her mother characterized the year as "getting off to a bad start." In addition to having rented a viola that was difficult to tune, Hannah was discouraged by the teacher from auditioning for the seventh-grade honors orchestra since "Mrs. _____ said the music was too hard and she didn't let me see it." As a result, it seemed that even though Hannah continued to practice viola, her interest decreased and her skills increased very little, as indicative in her mother's assessment that "her piano has improved, but viola less this year."

In summary, Hannah's reasons for orchestra participation and practice emerged from such extrinsic factors as the opportunity for recognition provided by playing viola and the mood altering function of playing. In general, Hannah's practice could be characterized as unstrategic based on the use of a limited number of practice strategies and the tendency to get frustrated by and avoid practicing more challenging pieces. However, Hannah sometimes practiced more challenging pieces, which suggests the features and style of a piece can have an impact on student motivation to practice. In the end, the positive experience of learning some challenging pieces and the ability to play familiar folk songs was not enough to ensure Hannah's continued participation in orchestra.

DISCUSSION

Through the use of observations and interviews to collect data, this case study of two beginning instrumentalists' practice helps us to better understand differences, beyond those previously identified through self-report data collection techniques (Austin & Berg, 2006), between more and less regulatory and motivated students, as well as the relative impact of the home environment, practice resources, teacher and parent support. For instance, Katy's practice, which included the use of both more and less efficient practice strategies, provides a more nuanced understanding of moderate strategy use. Also, this research seems to suggest motivation is multidimensional, a feature not represented in the high or medium motivation labels assigned to Katy and Hannah (Austin & Berg, 2006).

Although participants were similarly motivated by the teacher-initiated practice time requirement, the use of different practice routines, strategies, environments, resources and behaviors as well as motivational catalysts contributed to varied practice effectiveness. Overall, Katy's practice was more strategic and oriented toward improvement through the use of a clear practice routine that included preparation and warm-up activities as well as a greater variety of practice strategies. The practice strategies used and verbally identified by Katy, including playing at a slow tempo, repetition, simplifying a challenging passage, and using a "whole-part-whole" approach have been identified in previous research as effective practice strategies (Barry & Hallam, 2002; McPherson & McCormick, 1999). Katy used some strategies not identified in previous research on effective practice including simultaneously playing while counting, and/or tapping her foot and altering performance tempo during play through of a piece. Interestingly, Katy did not mention these strategies when describing violin practice, which might suggest a lack of awareness or the existence of a production deficit where transfer has not occurred between practice activity and discussion of the activity (Hallam, 1997). Katy seemed motivated by the sound of the ensemble, ensemble experience, and favorite pieces that were used as a reward by being played at the end of practice sessions.

Conversely, Hannah's decision to play and practice viola had less to do with the music and more to do with such external factors as getting attention from playing a unique instrument and the mood altering function of playing. Rather than playing a favorite piece as a reward near the end of practice, Hannah chose to begin practice with favorite pieces, using them for both their mood alteration potential and to help her either avoid practicing or prepare to practice more challenging pieces. Her practice might be characterized as less strategic since practice consisted primarily of playing through pieces and returning to the beginning of the piece if she made a mistake, although she did periodically use a moderately effective strategy of playing short sections of music at a slower tempo. These less effective strategies have been used by beginning instrumentalists in other research (Austin & Berg, 2006; Gruson, 1988; Pitts, Davidson, & McPherson, 2000a). Like Katy, Hannah also demonstrated a production deficit since a discrepancy existed between her description of and researcher observations of practice strategies typically used during practice.

At times, her affective reaction to challenge provided by the music, her equipment, or teacher seemed to negate the motivational potential of a piece of music or effective practice. Hannah's description of the impact of mood on effort expenditure ("(there are) days I'm happy and willing to take a challenge") adds to our understanding of causal attributes given by students to explain success or failure (O'Neill & McPherson, 2002; Weiner, 1986). Hannah's statement suggests an entity belief (Dweck, 2000) that mood, like ability, is beyond her control.

The practice routines and strategies used by the participants, the impact of the environment—including instrument quality and available practicing resources—and influence of the extrinsic practice time requirement, teacher, and parents on practice motivation correspond to the findings from other research on beginning instrumentalists' music practice (Austin & Berg, 2006; Gruson, 1988; Hallam, 1997; McPherson & Renwick, 2001; Morehouse, 1987; O'Neill, 1997; Pitts, Davidson, & McPherson, 2000a, 2000b). In order to glean more from practicing, both students needed a better balance among the challenges provided by the music, strategies used, and skill level (Csikszentmihalyi, 1991). Furthermore, Hannah's use of "surface level" practice strategies, effort avoidance, and need to be judged a competent violist by the teacher is aligned with concepts from engagement (Fredricks et al., 2004), self-regulation and motivation theories (Dweck, 1986, 2000; O'Neill, 1997; Weinstein & Mayer, 1986). For Hannah, the perceived cost (Pintrich & Schunk, 1996) of orchestra participation and viola practice was too great, thus contributing to her decision to not enroll the following year.

An argument could be made for the influence of piano study on the practice strategies used by the participants. Some previous research (Barry & McArthur, 1994; Hamann & Frost, 2000) suggests many students learn how to practice from their private instructor rather than the ensemble director. However, the previous study on which this research is based found no clear relationship between private lesson experience and practice regulation (Austin & Berg, 2006). The skill level of the participants in this study, the fact that students might not implicitly transfer strategies learned from one instrument context to another, and the resultant need for the ensemble teacher to explicitly teach for transfer by engaging students in metacognition when learning a new piece (Shuell, 1988) helps to explain the findings in this study. We might have expected the participants to use a greater variety of practice strategies given their years of piano study. However, this was not the case since Hannah had studied piano for twice as many years as Katy and yet her practice could be characterized as less strategic. Certainly, further study is needed to better understand the impact of private lesson study, whether it be private study of the ensemble or an additional instrument like piano, on students' practice regulation.

Although Katy and Hannah's practice can be characterized using dichotomous labels (e.g., strategic vs. unstrategic, adaptive vs. maladaptive), this framework masks the multiple functions of music practice for beginning instrumentalists (Campbell, 1998; Merriam, 1964).

For instance, music primarily served functional and social purposes for Katy as evident in meeting the practice time requirement; use of reasonably effective practice routines and strategies; her family's musical background and her motivation to participate being based primarily on the *ensemble* sound and experience. However, while playing viola also served the functional purpose of earning a good grade in orchestra for Hannah, the mood altering potential of practicing "fun" songs as well as her primary reasons for choosing to play viola and positive response to parental support indicate viola playing and practice served a broader spectrum of functions including personal, entertainment, and social functions.

While playing and practicing an instrument served a social function for both participants, it is interesting to note the varying degree of emphasis given to this function since Hannah commented more frequently on the positive recognition she received from peers and family for playing viola. While Katy might be considered a stronger musician based on practice effectiveness and orchestra program retention, the connection Hannah made between the emotional potential of the music, her emotional state, and the social environment as well as her interest in the timbre of the instrument indicated a stronger affinity for "aesthetic enjoyment" (Merriam, 1964) of music. Her comments also indicate a personal function for playing viola since:

> music offers children powerful aural images by which they come to under-stand themselves symbolically and emotionally. Music is a repository for their varied moods, a means by which they can relate to who they are (or are in the process of becoming) at particular times and places. (Campbell, 1998, p. 175)

IMPLICATIONS FOR FUTURE RESEARCH

Since both participants in this study recognized moments during practice when they were "lazy" and did not always use the most efficient practice strategies, it would be useful to better understand the catalysts for student use of appropriate practice strategies. Research on the impact of various approaches to practice for students with different strategy and motivational profiles could help teachers provide more targeted practice suggestions. Although some research suggests teachers should use different methods of communication with parents based on their socioeconomic status (Crozier, 1999), additional research is needed on how instrumental music teachers might more effectively collaborate with the parents of students from varied backgrounds to monitor home practice and encourage musical growth.

While the findings from this study imply the 100-minute weekly practice time requirement had a predominantly negative influence on the *intrinsic* motivation of the participants, further research is needed on the positive influence of a time requirement, the impact of teachers' using a variable time requirement, and the results—both positive and negative—of coupling a practice time requirement and course grade. The aforementioned additional research could help us begin to better articulate the motivational underpinnings of student behavior as related to the malleability of student commitment to practice.

Although the findings from this study seem to suggest an individual's need for personal relatedness with the music impacts the level of cognitive engagement while practicing, we need to know more about the relationship between students' need for relatedness, autonomy and competence and their engagement while practicing and rehearsing, particularly with older students and students of diverse backgrounds (Fredrick et al., 2004). In addition, longitudinal research is needed to better understand how engagement changes and how context influences engagement over time, particularly as students transition from elementary to middle and middle to high school.

In addition, further research is needed to delineate the varied social functions of music in children's lives including social-familial, social-peer, social-teacher, and social-community. An analysis of the relationships that form as a result of playing an instrument can help us to better understand how fostering and utilizing the various types of social functions might result in more efficient practice as well as instrumental music program retention.

At the same time, research is needed to explore connections between concepts from motivation and sociological theories. For instance, both participants in this study mentioned instrument timbre and ensemble sound as intrinsically motivating aspects of playing their instruments. These references might also be characterized based on the aesthetic enjoyment function of music. Kaplan's discussion of Huizinga's analysis of the term "play" suggests a connection between these two theoretical strands:

> We speak of "playing" music, of "playing" an instrument, of attending a "play." Is there something more here than a figure of speech? Play goes beyond the confines of a purely biological activity. It is a *significant* function … there is something 'at play' which transcends the immediate needs of life and imparts meaning to the action. (Kaplan, 1990, p. 33)

By probing the connection between musical motivation and function for beginning instrumentalists, we might be able to better understand and offer appropriate practice and ensemble experiences for these students.

Finally, although similar practice behaviors were observed during bi-weekly school practice sessions and one home practice session, thus adding credence to the results, environmental differences between school and home as well the impact of practicing at a different time of the day can be viewed as limitations of this study. More longitudinal research is needed where data is gathered during home practice in order to better understand not only practice regulation and motivation, but also how practice changes over time as a result of various factors including increased skill, parent and teacher influence, and the changing role of music in the lives of students.

IMPLICATIONS FOR MUSIC TEACHING

While the implications of this study are limited based on the small number of participants, the findings from this study seem to suggest that teachers need to design differentiated approaches to practice so that students with varied backgrounds, approaches to practice and motivations for playing and practicing an instrument will realize improved skill while maintaining or increasing motivation. Differentiated approaches might include assigning more challenging repertoire coupled with instruction on and monitoring of additional practice strategies for some students and positive reinforcement of student use of a more varied practice routine, coupled with assignment of additional 'fun' pieces for other students.

At the beginning of the school year or grading period, teachers could administer a brief survey that would help them to assess student knowledge and application of various practice strategies as well as the various ways music functions in their students' lives. This information could guide repertoire selection and daily discussions with students as well as practice suggestions. Recently published resources exist to help relate features of the music to growth in personal knowledge, ensemble community and intrinsic motivation (Buchanan & Mehaffey, 2005; Gruselle, 2006; Littrell, 2003; Miles, 2004; Miles & Dvorak, 2000; O'Toole, 2003).

Also, rather than having students complete weekly practice charts which merely track practice quantity, teachers could create or utilize commercially available practice resources (Wachsman, 2001; Winner, 1992) that have students document practice routines, practice strategies used, problem areas in a piece and/or specific steps used to improve performance of a problem area. While ensemble teachers are more limited in the amount of assistance they can provide to individual students, by assessing practice behaviors rather than just amount of practice, they can help to foster more efficient student practice.

The findings from this study seem to suggest that although both participants were motivated by a practice time requirement, the use of different practice routines, strategies, environments, and behaviors as well as motivational catalysts contributed to varied practice effectiveness. Music practice seemed to serve multiple and varied functions for the two adolescent-aged instrumentalists in this study. By teaching about the connections between features of the music, student felt experience when practicing and the varied purposes served by learning to play an instrument, more students might choose to learn to play an instrument and seek out opportunities for lifelong musical involvement (Reimer, 2002). Indeed, students could conceptualize practice, not just as "getting the *minutes* in," but rather more broadly as getting the self, the community and, most importantly, getting the *music* in.

REFERENCES

Austin, J. R. (1997, April). *Does perfect practice make perfect? An examination of strategic effort among middle school band students.* Paper presented at the annual meeting of the American Educational Research Association, Chicago.

Austin, J. R., & Berg, M. H. (2006). Exploring music practice among 6th-grade band and orchestra students. *Psychology of Music, 34*(4), 535-558.

Austin, J. R., & Vispoel, W. P. (1998). How American adolescents interpret success and failure in classroom music: Relationships among attribution beliefs, self-concept and achievement. *Psychology of Music, 26*(1), 26-45.

Barry, N. (1990). The effects of different practice techniques upon technical accuracy and musicality in student instrumental performance. *Research Perspectives in Music Education, 1*, 4-8.

Barry, N., & Hallam, S. (2002). Practicing. In R. Parncutt & G. E. McPherson (Eds.), *The science and psychology of music performance: Creative strategies for teaching and learning* (pp. 151-166). New York: Oxford University Press.

Barry, N., & McArthur, V. (1994). Teaching practice strategies in the music studio: A survey of applied music teachers. *Psychology of Music, 22*, 44-55.

Buchanan, H. J., & Mehaffey, M. (Eds.). (2005). *Teaching music through performance in choir* (Vol. 1). Chicago: GIA.

Campbell, P. S. (1998). *Songs in their heads: Music and its meaning in children's lives.* New York: Oxford University Press.

Chaffin, T., & Imreh, G. (2001). A comparison of practice and self-report as sources of information about the goals of expert practice. *Psychology of Music, 29*, 39-69.

Crozier, G. (1999). Is it a case of "We know when we're not wanted?" The parents' perspective on parent-teacher roles and relationships. *Educational Research, 4*(3), 315-328.

Csikszentmihalyi, M. (1991). *Flow: The theory of optimal experience.* New York: Harper & Row.

Davidson, J. W., Howe, M. J. A., & Sloboda, J. A. (1997). Environmental factors in the development of musical performance skill over the life span. In D. J. Hargreaves & A. C. North (Eds.), *The social psychology of music* (pp. 188-206). Oxford, England: Oxford University Press.

Dweck, C. S. (1986). Motivational processes affecting learning. *American Psychologist, 41*, 1040-1048.

Dweck, C. S. (2000). *Self-theories: Their role in motivation, personality and development.* Philadelphia: Psychology Press.

Eccles, J. S., Wigfield, A., & Schiefele, U. (1998). Motivation to succeed. In W. Damon & N. Eisenberg (Eds.), *Handbook of child psychology: Social, emotional and personality development* (5th ed., Vol. 3, pp. 1017-1095). New York: Wiley.

Ericsson, K. A., & Simon, H. A. (1999). *Protocol analysis: Verbal reports as data* (3rd ed.). Cambridge, MA: MIT Press.

Fredricks, J. A., Blumenfeld, P. C., & Paris, A. H. (2004). School engagement: Potential of the concept, state of the evidence. *Review of Educational Research, 74*(1), 59-109.

Gazda, D., & Stoutmire, A. (1997). *Spotlight on strings: Technique and program music for string orchestra and individual instructions (level 2).* San Diego, CA: Kjos.

Gruselle, C. L. (2006, July). *Comprehensive musicianship through performance.* Clinic presentation at annual summer CASTA (Colorado American String Teachers Association) Conference, Cherry Creek, CO.

Gruson, L. M. (1988). Rehearsal skill and musical competence: Does practice make perfect? In J. A. Sloboda (Ed.), *Generative processes in music* (pp. 91-112). Oxford, England: Clarendon Press.

Hallam, S. (1997). Approaches to instrumental music practice of experts and novices: Implications for education. In H. Jørgensen and A. C. Lehmann (Eds.), *Does practice make perfect? Current theory and research on instrumental music practice* (pp. 89-108). Oslo, Norway: Norges Musikkhøgskole.

Hallam, S. (2000). The development of performance planning strategies in musicians. In C. Woods, G. B. Luck, R. Brochard, S. A. O'Neill, & J. A. Sloboda (Eds.), *Proceedings of the sixth international conference on music perception & cognition.* Keele, Staffordshire, England: Keele University Department of Psychology (CD-ROM).

Hamann, D. L., & Frost, R. S. (2000). The effect of private lesson study on the practice habits and attitudes towards practicing of middle school and high school string students. *Contributions to Music Education, 27*(2), 71-93.

Kaplan, M. (1990). *The arts: A social perspective.* Cranbury, NJ: Associated University Presses.

Kuzel, A. J. (1992). Sampling in qualitative inquiry. In B. F. Crabtree & W. L. Miller (Eds.), *Doing qualitative research: Research methods for primary care series,* (Vol. 3, pp. 31-44). Newbury Park: SAGE.

LeCompte, M. D., & Schensul, J. J. (1999). *Analyzing and interpreting ethnographic data* (Ethnographer's toolkit, Vol. 5). New York: Altamira.

Lincoln, Y. S., & Guba, E. G. (1985). *Naturalistic inquiry*. Beverly Hills, CA: SAGE.

Littrell, D. (Ed.). (2003). *Teaching music through performance in orchestra* (Vol. 2). Chicago: GIA.

Maehr, M. L., Pintrich, P. R., & Linnenbrink, E. A. (2002). Motivation and achievement. In R. Colwell & C. Richardson (Eds.), *The new handbook of research on music teaching and learning* (pp. 348-372). New York: Oxford Oxford University Press.

McPherson, G., & McCormick, J. (1999). Motivational and self-regulated components of musical practice. *Bulletin of the Council for Research in Music Education, 141*, 98-102.

McPherson, G., & Renwick, J. (2001). Longitudinal study of self-regulation in children's musical practice. *Music Education Research, 3(1)*, 169-186.

McPherson, G. E., & Zimmerman, B. J. (2002). Self-regulation of musical learning. In R. Colwell & C. Richardson (Eds.), *The new handbook of research on music teaching and learning* (pp. 348-372). New York: Oxford University Press.

Merriam, A. (1964). *The anthropology of music*. Evanston, IL: Northwestern University Press.

Miles, M. B., & Huberman, A. M. (1994). *Qualitative data analysis: An expanded sourcebook*. Thousand Oaks, CA: SAGE.

Miles, R. (2004). *Teaching music through performance in band* (Vol. 5). Chicago: GIA.

Miles, R., & Dvorak, T. (2000). *Teaching music through performance in beginning band*. Chicago: GIA.

Morehouse, T. L. (1987). The relationship of selected attitudinal factors to dropout and retention in beginning string students (Doctoral dissertation). *Dissertation Abstracts International, 49*, 0757A, University of Houston, TX.

Nielsen, S. (2001). Self-regulating learning strategies in instrumental music practice. *Music Education Research, 3(2)*, 155-167.

O'Neill, S. A. (1997). The role of practice in childrens early performance achievement. In H. Jørgensen & A. C. Lehmann (Eds.), *Does practice make perfect? Current theory and research on instrumental music practice* (pp. 53-70). Oslo, Norway: Norges Musikkhøgskole.

O'Neill, S. A., & McPherson, G. E. (2002). Motivation. In R. Parncutt & G. E. McPherson (Eds.), *The science and psychology of music performance* (pp. 31-46). New York: Oxford University Press.

O'Toole, P. (2003). *Shaping sound musicians: An innovative approach to teaching comprehensive musicianship through performance*. Chicago: GIA.

Pacey, F. (1993). Schema theory and the effect of variable practice in string teaching. *British Journal of Music Education, 10*, 91-102.

Patton, M. Q. (2001). *Qualitative research and evaluation methods* (3rd ed.). Thousand Oaks, CA: SAGE.

Pintrich, P. R., & Schunk, D. H. (1996). *Motivation in education: Theory, research and applications*. Englewood Cliffs, NJ: Prentice–Hall.

Pitts, S., Davidson, J., & McPherson, G. (2000a). Models of success and failure in instrumental learning: Case studies of young players in the first 20 months of learning. *Bulletin of the Council for Research in Music Education, 146*, 51-69.

Pitts, S., Davidson, J., & McPherson, G. (2000b). Developing effective practice strategies: Case studies of three young instrumentalists. *Music Education Research, 2*(1), 45-56.

Reimer, B. (2002). *A philosophy of music education: Advancing the vision* (3rd ed.) New York: Prentice Hall.

Shuell, T. J. (1988). The role of transfer in learning and teaching music: A cognitive perspective. In C. Fowler (Ed.), *The Crane symposium: Toward an understanding of the teaching and learning of music performance* (pp. 143-167). Potsdam, NY: Potsdam College of the State University of New York.

Sloboda, J. A. (2005). *Exploring the musical mind: Cognition, emotion, ability, function*. New York: Oxford University Press.

Sloboda, J. A., & Davidson, J. W. (1996). The young performing musician. In I. Deliege & J. A. Sloboda (Eds.), *Musical beginnings: Origins and development of musical competence* (pp. 171-190). New York: Oxford University Press.

Sloboda, J. A., & O'Neill, S. A. (2001). Emotions in everyday listening to music. In P. N. Juslin & J. A. Sloboda (Eds.), *Music and emotion: Theory and research* (pp. 415-430). New York: Oxford University Press.

Stake, R. E. (1995). *The art of case study research*. Thousand Oaks, CA: SAGE.

Stipek, D. J. (1998). *Motivation to learn: From theory to practice* (3rd ed.). Boston: Allyn & Bacon.

Vygotsky, L. S., & Kozulin, A. (1986). *Thought and language* (Rev. ed.). Cambridge, MA: MIT Press.

Wachsman, D. (2001). *How to get to Carnegie Hall: Weekly music practice organizer.* New York: MMB Music.

Weiner, B. (1986). *An attributional theory of motivation and emotion.* New York: Springer.

Weinstein, C., & Mayer, R. (1986). The teaching of learning strategies. In M. C. Wittrock (Ed.), *Handbook of research on teaching and learning* (3rd ed., pp. 315-327). New York: Macmillan.

Winner, E. (Ed.). (1992). *Arts PROPEL: A handbook for music*. Princeton, NJ: ETS.

Zdzinski, S. F. (1996). Parental involvement, selected student attributes, and learning outcomes in instrumental music. *Journal of Research in Music Education, 44*, 34-48.

Zimmerman, B. J. (2000). Attaining self-regulation: A social cognitive perspective. In M. Boekaerts, P. Pintrich, & M. Zeidner (Eds.), *Handbook of self-regulation* (pp. 13-39). San Diego, CA: Academic Press.

CHAPTER 4

FIRST-YEAR TEACHERS AND METHODS CLASSES

Is There a Connection?

Margaret Schmidt

ABSTRACT

This qualitative study explored the ways that three first-year string teachers applied a song-teaching method emphasized in their junior-year instrumental methods course. The teachers all led students from preparatory aural activities to music reading, suggesting that the course did influence their teaching strategies. However, they demonstrated different degrees of theoretical understanding in their application of those strategies, related to whether they conceptualized the method as a series of activities or as an entire process of teaching music literacy. Readiness to learn and effort as a university student, as well as mentoring received as a first-year teacher, partially accounted for, but did not completely explain, those differences. Additional longitudinal studies of beginning teachers are recommended to help teacher educators assess the effectiveness of their own teaching and to better understand the processes by which preservice teachers accept, modify, or reject ideas presented in methods courses.

Diverse Methodologies in the Study of Music Teaching and Learning, pp. 67–90

INTRODUCTION

Teacher educators have long studied and debated the most effective and efficient ways to design methods courses. Early research focused on training preservice teachers in specific observable behaviors (Clift & Brady, 2005). Practice with skills such as nonverbal instruction (Lawes, 1987), teacher intensity (Madsen, Standley, & Cassidy, 1989), the use of sequential patterns of instruction (Price, 1992), or approving and disapproving feedback (Madsen & Duke, 1985) has been effective in modifying teaching behaviors. Later researchers conducted studies of preservice teachers' cognition, finding that preservice teachers do not automatically adopt ideas presented in methods courses, but individually construct their beliefs and choose their practices guided by perceptions of their own current and prior experiences as a guide (Ferguson, 2003; Leglar & Collay, 2004; Schmidt, 1998). These studies identified a variety of influences on preservice teachers' practices, in turn leading to studies of the interactions among individual preservice teachers and the institutional contexts of their teacher education programs (Clift & Brady, 2005). Such factors are often hidden and may interrelate in complex ways, making it difficult to determine direct relationships between experiences in a teacher preparation program and the practices novices adopt and refine in their early years of teaching.

To increase the likelihood that preservice teachers will adopt ideas presented in the university program, teacher educators have included a variety of activities in courses and field experiences designed to assist preservice teachers in uncovering the influence of their own experiences and beliefs. Assignments such as examining metaphors of teaching (Harwood & Wiggins, 2001; Thompson & Campbell, 2003), journaling (Robbins, 1993; Fredrickson & Pembrook, 2002; Pembrook & Fredrickson, 1999), research projects (Campbell, 1999; Miranda, Robbins, & Stauffer, 2006), or reflection on teaching activities (Gore, 1990; Robbins, 1999) have been shown to effect changes in preservice teachers' thinking, with the hope of influencing their long-term teaching behaviors. Consistent field experiences throughout a program or concurrent with methods classes also seem to increase the effectiveness of methods courses (Clift & Brady, 2005; Grossman & Richert, 1988).

Most of these studies have examined changes in preservice teachers' thinking and practices within the confines of particular methods courses, field experiences, or student teaching; few longitudinal studies have documented whether those changes are sustained into the early years of teaching (Clift & Brady, 2005; Nierman, Zeichner, & Hobbel, 2004). In fact, Bauer and Berg (2001) found that inservice teachers rated music education methods courses among the least important influences on their current teaching practices. In this study, I explore how three elementary string teachers applied learning from a junior-year methods class in their first year of teaching. An earlier study (Schmidt, 2006) found that six prior-year graduates at the university identified Gordon's (1993) music learning sequence as the most important learning from the methods class, so I chose it as a focus for this study. Specifically, this study focuses on how—or whether—the three teachers used elements of this aural approach in teaching method book songs to elementary string classes.

METHOD

Participants and the Practicum Course

Karen, Jing-Wei, and Jennifer (pseudonyms) graduated in 2006 and were hired to teach in area school districts, giving me the opportunity to study their longitudinal development into their first year of teaching. I selected them to participate in this study because they had taken the Practicum course together, and represented the range of teaching ability demonstrated by the nine string education majors in that cohort (Stake, 2005). More detailed information about each participant is given below with a teaching vignette; here, I provide some general background information about the Practicum course.

Instrumental Practicum is a two-semester junior-year course for preservice band and orchestra teachers, team-taught by the university's instrumental (band) specialist and myself. It meets twice a week for 3 hours each time on campus, with concurrent required field experience in local schools for a total of 72 contact hours per semester. It is taken in the year before student teaching, and covers many instructional and administrative aspects of band and orchestra teaching in elementary through high school.

To provide context for my analysis of the participants' teaching, I describe the approach that my colleague and I hoped the Practicum students would adopt in their future instruction, basically a rote-to-note approach to teaching music reading emphasizing the development of aural skills. Throughout the year, we referred to Gordon's (1993) music learning theory and Froseth's (2002) "feels like-sounds like-looks like" approach,[1] encouraging multiple strategies for extending aural skills development to reading pitches, rhythms, dynamics, and articulations. Peer teaching assignments were at first 3 to 4 minutes long, beginning with leading echoes of rhythmic movement patterns ("feels like") and sung rhythmic syllables ("sounds like"), then adding flashcards ("looks like"). The preservice teachers gradually extended their lessons, and applied a variety of rote-to-note strategies to teach students to read songs in a beginning instrumental method book. Then they designed a number of 10-minute lesson segments that extended the same principles to rehearsals at the middle and high school levels, including warm-ups, repertoire, and activities based on the national standards in music (National Association for Music Education [MENC], 1994). At several points in the year, after practicing these lessons on their peers, the preservice teachers taught some of the same lessons to children in local elementary, junior high, and high school bands or orchestras. Throughout the year, we encouraged frequent modeling with voice, movement, or instrument, and consistently reinforced the use of complete sequential patterns of instruction (Price, 1992).

Data Collection and Analysis

During their first year of full-time teaching, I observed each teacher in his or her schools five times, approximately every 6 weeks, videotaping as each taught two different 30- to 40-minute classes each time, and attended two concerts given by each. I audiotaped our postobservation discussions (five for each teacher), transcribed those discussions verbatim, and kept notes of our informal conversations. As I collected data throughout the year, I conducted on-going analysis, focusing on the methods these teachers used to teach songs in their method books and formulating questions for subsequent interviews and observations (Glesne, 1999). All three used the same two books, *Essential Elements 2000* (Allen, Gillespie, & Tellejohn-Hayes, 2000) and *Concert Tunes for Strings* (Brubaker, 1992).

When data collection was complete, I compared interview and observation data, and created a case record for each teacher, identifying major elements of each one's approach to song-teaching. Cross-case comparisons then led me to develop four categories for further data analysis (Merriam, 1988; Yin, 1989), based on the strategies the teachers used to develop their students' aural and music reading skills, as reported in the data analysis section of this paper.

My involvement with these participants began with their first year in the university program. All three enrolled in my string techniques class, and two served as teachers in our String Project, an after-school program where preservice teachers under my supervision offer classes and private lessons for area children. I also supervised all three in student teaching. In all these settings, I demonstrated and encouraged applications of the aural approach to teaching. Although this background data was not the focus of this study, I recognize that my prior relationships with the participants undoubtedly affected my analysis of this study's data. However, the long-term nature of our relationship also permitted a depth of analysis possible *because* of my extended involvement with their growth (Jansen & Peshkin, 1992). To increase the credibility of my findings, I actively sought disconfirming evidence and negative cases (Creswell, 1998). Addressing alternative explanations, documenting the influence of my interactions with the teachers, and peer review of early versions of this paper by five experienced researchers, helped me identify points of researcher bias (Huberman & Miles, 1994; Jansen & Peshkin, 1992).

DATA PRESENTATION: SAMPLE CLASSES

To examine processes by which these three teachers applied song-teaching routines from Practicum, I have constructed three vignettes, descriptions of a typical class. Each shows the entire process the teacher used to present a new song to their fifth-grade (first year) string students. In addition, I provide background information on each teacher.

Karen

Karen began string bass in elementary school and enjoyed attending a local arts-focused charter school, even though she "wasn't one of the top students there." At the university, she taught classes and private lessons in the String Project during its first full year of existence. Karen's work in Practicum was inconsistent—she often demonstrated enthusiastic and well-organized instruction, but at other times, confessed to be unprepared. She worked all year to develop a more authoritative look and voice, and to reverse her tendency to make faces and apologize for mistakes she noticed as she taught. She student taught with one cooperating teacher in a large district with both urban and suburban school populations, traveling to three elementary schools and a high school. She grew in confidence, authority, and organizational skills as a student teacher and, the following summer, accepted a job in that district as her cooperating teacher moved to a different district. Karen began the year teaching at two of the four schools where she student taught (the high school and one elementary) as well as two new-to-her elementary schools. A few weeks into the school year, she was offered extra pay to add a daily class at a middle school that had no orchestra teacher, and began traveling to four different schools on most days. Following is an account of one of Karen's classes, most of which are heterogeneous. The 18 fifth-grade violinists and violists at this Title I school may only use their instruments at school, so they are not able to practice at home. This sequence took 14 minutes to go through eight measures in 4/4 meter, using five different pitches.

Karen: Watch. How many D's do I play? *[She plays four D's, the students call out both "three" and "four." Without responding, she plays again. Most say "four."]*

One, two, ready, play. *[Karen gives a cue with her head, and the students echo her.]*

Listen. *[She plays D-E-F#.]* What notes did I play? Lydia? *[Lydia doesn't answer. Karen plays the pattern again, and calls on another student who answers, "D-E-F."]*

Listen. *[The students echo the same pattern twice.]*

Pretty good. Make sure your fingers are on your tapes. Listen–I'm on F, listen. *[She plays "F# F# F# rest, F# F# F# rest."]* How many F's did I play? *[It takes a few guesses before one student answers, "Three notes and a rest, three notes and a rest."]*

Let's play it. *[They play.]*

Let's do it again. I heard some people playing on the rests. *[As they play, she says "Shh" on the rests. Some are looking around the room or at Karen while they play.]*

Now listen–this is a tough one. *[She plays.]* Listen again–count how many G's and how many F's. *[The students call out answers–it sounds to me like they're guessing. She keeps demonstrating and eventually tells them it is five G's and four F's. Then she has them play while she counts out loud.]*

That's tough! Take out "Jingle Bells" on page 13. *[A student says, "I don't want to play "Jingle Bells."]* You just played half the song! *[He says, "I did?"]*

Who can tell me where you see this? *[She plays "F# F# F# rest, F# F# F# rest." A student calls out the answer.]* Yes! First and second measure. It goes like this. *[She plays.]* What's the first note? *[I hear "G" and "F" called out.]* F! Let's play this. Second finger. *[They play. Karen no longer says "Shh" on the rests.]* We have to do it again. I had somebody play on a rest. *[They play.]* Do you see measures 3 and 4? No? *[She holds up her book and points.]* Maria, will you show José where measure 3 is? Tell me the name of the first note. *[Most of the students call out "F."]* F! The next note? *[Most say "G."]* G! Tell me the note names. *[Karen plays the notes very slowly one by one, loudly singing the note names on pitch. Most students sing too, with varying degrees of accuracy. I think some are watching Karen or their neighbor, waiting to hear what others sing first.]* Say it again. *[They sing.]*

Can you pluck it? This measure is the hardest measure in the song. But I think you can do it. *[After a few tries plucking the notes together, Karen goes around the room, having each child pluck those two measures alone. She responds to

each one with, "Excellent job!" "What's the last note? You tell <u>me</u>." "Good sound!"
"José, I'm going to come back to you."] Everyone, third and fourth measures.

Students: With our bows?

Yeah, let's play it with our bows. *[They play those two measures.]*

Let's play that entire line. From the beginning. Sit up stra-a-aight. *[They played three notes.]* Augh! I saw at least half the class play on the rest. *[They play the line.]*

Next line. Listen. Tell me where you see this. Watch. *[She continued in a similar vein for about four minutes with the second line. It seems to me that some students aren't looking at the music or focusing on playing the correct notes.]*

Second line. Let's play it. Play it with your bows. *[They slowly play the line.]*

OK. On Friday we're going to keep looking at this.

Jing-Wei

Jing-Wei, originally from Southeast Asia, came to the university to earn a DMA degree in guitar performance, having taught band in his home country and private and class guitar in the Southern United States while earning a master's degree. A sensitive classical guitarist, he performed regularly in local restaurants. He decided to earn a teaching certificate because it offered the best chance for employment that would allow him to stay in the United States with his wife and young daughter. With no prior bowed string experience, Jing-Wei developed his skills to play bass with the university's nonmajor orchestra. He describes himself as "a little lazy," and for his classes and student teaching, appeared to prepare only as much as he felt was necessary to get by. In Practicum, Jing-Wei showed good energy in front of a group, and regularly used experiential and rote strategies in his peer teaching, focusing most often on musical (rather than technical) concepts, especially dynamics. He often came late to class or neglected to complete assignments, and admitted that he "didn't like" to create detailed lesson plans. He learned best by imitating a model, which might be attributed to an innate ability to imitate, to difficulty with English, or to his desire to avoid what he considered unnecessary work. Perhaps because of his age or his previous teaching and parenting experience, he always seemed very comfortable in front of children. I encouraged his cooperating teachers for his fieldwork and student teaching placements to help him understand American school culture. When junior high students made fun of Jing-Wei's accent and his violin playing, he and his cooperating teacher together decided to have him play his guitar for them and talk to them about his country, and his presentation had the desired effect of creating a more respectful rapport between them. Jing-Wei traveled each day to three different elementary schools in a large suburban district, teaching a fifth- and sixth-grade heterogeneous string class at each school. The students came to class 2 out of every 3 days, on a rotating 6-day cycle. Following is a description of one of Jing-Wei's fifth grade low strings classes, with six violas, three cellos, and one bass. This sequence took 16 minutes to go through 32 measures of dotted-half notes in 3/4 meter, using five different pitches.

Jing-Wei: OK. We're going to learn a new song, Starlight Waltz. *[He goes to the board, where he had drawn a staff and some notes.]*

Cello–Glen–what note is this? *[He answers "G."]* What finger plays it? *[Another student says, "It's open G." Jing-Wei writes in the next higher note.]*

Katelyn, what note is this? This is G, right? So the note above the G is? The note after G? *[She doesn't answer.]* Play me the G. *[She plays G, then A.]* So the note after G is what letter? *[She finally says "A."]* After G you go back to A. You don't have an H. So this is the new note today.

Bass–Jeremy, how about this one? *[He points at the board. Jeremy doesn't answer.]* Look at "Serenata." Do you remember this one? Play it. Very good. Now, what note is this? *[He writes an "A" and Jeremy responds.]* That's the new note for this song. Can you try to search for this new note in your music, cellos and bass, while I show violas their note? *[Students start to call out answers.]* Don't tell me yet.

[He directs his attention to the violas, and writes their open G on the board.] Viola, tell me what is this note. Laura, what note is this? This is G in "Serenata," right? And what finger is it? And what note is this next one? Play it. *[She plays timidly.]* Don't be scared. *[She says she needs rosin on her bow. As he walks over to her,]* OK, I'll fix it. Now find this note in the music and tell me where it is. *[Most students point at the music, one calls out, "Found it." Jing-Wei rosins the bow, tests it, and returns it to the student. While he's taking care of that, several students try playing the song, two mess around with their instruments, and two just sit. Then Jing-Wei claps a four-beat rhythm that the class echoes as a signal for quiet.]*

OK, person on the left [side of the music stand] point [at the notes on the page]. Everyone say the note out loud. *[Most sing the notes reasonably well, as Jing-Wei sings the pitches, speaks the rests, and plays the melody and harmony on piano.]*

Good. Just viola. Now the person on the right point. *[Violas give a very half-hearted effort to name the notes while Jing-Wei plays the tune on piano. After a co-verbal reminder, "Louder, violas," Jing-Wei stops them part way through the song.]*

Cellos and bass. After that we're going to come back to viola. *[Cellos and basses speak the notes loudly.]*

OK, viola, one more time. Let's see if you can say it louder than that. I bet you can. *[Violas do better. I think a couple of them aren't reading the notes, but are waiting to hear what the person next to them says. Jing-Wei has everyone pluck the song. After an announcement interrupts from the loud speaker, he starts them again at the beginning, plucking the entire song of 32 measures.]*

Bowing. *[The students cheer and bow the song.]*

One more time. Longer bows, use more bow. And mouse house *[a reminder to check left wrist position. They play, still using six to eight inches of bow as before.]*

Very good. *[Jing-Wei then asks me for suggestions. The class turns to look at me. I suggest, "I would air bow it once and see if you can get the correct bow directions," something Jing-Wei hadn't yet mentioned. Jing-Wei writes the down-bow sign on the board, asking the students what the "monkey bar" sign means, and they play the whole song twice more, with Jing-Wei calling out "Lift" for each lifted bow.]*

Jennifer

Jennifer, a fine violinist with well-developed performance skills, grew up in the area and spent 1 year at a small Christian college that had no orchestra program. When she realized that she wanted to teach music, she transferred to the university. She participated in the String Project for her first three semesters, assisting with a class and teaching several private students. Jennifer prepared assignments for Practicum thoroughly and presented them with command, although she claimed to always feel nervous and uncertain. She much preferred to know her teaching assignments well ahead of time, but in student teaching she learned to adapt to her two cooperating teachers, who often decided a few minutes before class who would teach which parts of the lesson. Her cooperating teacher at the middle school used many aural and rote strategies along with a rigorous music reading program. Jennifer used similar strategies at the middle school, but also followed her other cooperating teacher's model of asking elementary students, with little step-by-step preparation, to sight-read each new line in the method book. As a new teacher, as she had in Practicum, Jennifer planned her classes thoroughly. She taught in the same district as Jing-Wei and, like him, traveled each day to three different elementary schools. Here, I present a representative fifth grade class, 22 violins. This sequence took 13 minutes to go through 24 measures in 4/4 meter, using four different pitches.

Jennifer: I would like you to put your instruments in a safe place and look up at the board. You're not going to need your bow. And you're looking up at the board, and we're going to clap. And when you see these guys *[she points to the quarter rests]* what are you going to do? *[A student shows a waving gesture.]* Because, what are they called? *[A student answers and Jennifer repeats,]* Quarter rests.

I'll point and you clap and you wave and do all that good stuff. *[They clap eight measures as Jennifer points and says "rest, rest, rest" where appropriate. She then asks them to notice the difference in note-stem directions.]*

Jason, do they look different? How? *[He answers that some go up and some go down.]* Are they both notes? *["Yeah."]* Yes, they're both notes. All right, now you're going to say *[she demonstrates how they will clap and speak the note names. While they do that, she plays the melody line on the piano.]*

OK, guitar pizzicato. *[They pluck the measures while Jennifer points at the board and sings letter names.]*

I'm going to play piano while you rest, but you still have to wait for the rest. It's going to sound like this. *[She demonstrates, and then they play.]*

Very nice. You rested exactly the amount of time you were supposed to rest. I would like you to pizz. on your shoulder. Instruments nice and tall. *[To one student:]* I'll get your question later. You're pizzing, I'm bowing. *[As they play, she speaks the rests.]*

What did I do with my bow in the rests? *[She repeats the answer a student gives:]* I circled my bow. I'd like you to open your *Concert Tunes* book to page 3. This is the beginning of a song called "Marching Along." Does it sound like a march? *[She sings a little and marches.]*

Go to your first note. I want you to check with your neighbor, whisper to them to see if it is actually an A. I want you to go to the next measure where the pitch changes and check that with your neighbor. Does it look familiar? *[The students notice it's the same as what they played on the board.]* Yes, it's the same as what we played.

All right, I want you to look at your music this time, and you're going to pizzicato where you start, right on it. Up on your shoulder, no bow. *[They pluck eight measures.]*

And stop right there. Are you at circle 1? *[Students answer that they are.]*

OK, grab your bow. And don't forget the circle bows. I should have had you circle when you were plucking, but you guys are so good at circle bows. *[They play that part of the song, with most students getting the correct notes and bowing. Jennifer has them review the last two measures of that section, because some aren't changing notes correctly. She has the class sing the note names several times, then bow it, then play row by row, reviewing the note changes if students seem unsure. Then everyone plays the two measures three more times.]* What note is that, Alicia?

D, right, we know that from our note test. *[Using leading questions, she prepares them to sight-read the next eight measures.]*

Give me a thumbs up if you think it's the same, thumbs down if you think the rhythm is not the same. I'm seeing mostly thumbs up. If you said thumbs up, you are correct. *[She points on the board to the first eight measures, singing the new notes, to show that it's the same rhythm. Then she gives them time to practice that section with their neighbor and circulates through the room, helping individual students for 60 seconds. She asks partners to volunteer to play for the group while the class points at the notes to check the volunteers. Then everyone plays that section together. She asks if the last section of the song looks familiar. A student says it's the same as the beginning.]*

So could you take it home and learn the whole song tonight? Now let's play "Serenata," [a favorite song, to end the class].

DATA ANALYSIS: LINKING AURAL SKILLS AND MUSIC READING

These three lessons are representative of the approaches these teachers used to introduce a new song. It was encouraging that all three seemed to use many of the strategies we presented in Practicum. For example, each asked students to echo melodic and rhythmic patterns without reference to notation, and modeled melodies and rhythms on an instrument and/or with their voices. All three used piano to demonstrate and to accompany the class. Jennifer is the only one who consistently modeled patterns using violin. I observed Karen use violin to demonstrate only in this lesson; at her other schools she sang or played the string parts on piano. Jing-Wei used only piano in the lessons I observed, although he sometimes borrowed a child's instrument briefly to demonstrate a point he was trying to make. This may simply have been because Jennifer owned a violin. When I asked Karen, a string bass major, and Jing-Wei, a guitarist, about modeling on a string instrument, both told me there were no extra school instruments available for them to use. Therefore, it is difficult to know whether their use of piano to model was a deliberate choice or a practical consideration.

Although all three of them used strategies we recommended, they did so with varying degrees of effectiveness, as they struggled with how to help students simultaneously develop both aural and music reading skills. Because this was a focus of the Practicum class, I organize my analysis around four aspects of these teachers' strategies for transitioning from rote to note: the ways they appeared to link aural skills with reading pitches, their methods for connecting aural skills and rhythm reading, their strategies for using aural warm-ups to prepare for reading the music, and some of their thoughts about the process of transitioning from rote to note.

Linking Aural Skills and Pitch Reading

I saw all three teach sections of a new song by rote or with alternate notation on the board before asking students to read the notated song in the book. When Jing-Wei graduated, he took over another teacher's position in the middle of the year. He initially taught songs by having students read the finger numbers from the board as he pointed, and seldom had them read notation from the book. I offered my opinion, that using the finger numbers did not facilitate transfer to reading standard notation. This year, Jing-Wei was convinced that, due to his own neglect, the second-year students' "note reading is a lot of problem" *[sic]*, because he had "to write all the fingerings and everything" for them. He often introduced songs using a notation system with letters for pitch names, although I am not sure whether it was because he recognized that the finger-number approach was not successful, or due to his district supervisor's or my encouragement. He said he tried to be "more consistent," as he knew he could no longer blame the previous teacher if his students could not read. He "always lets them say the notes first, then pizzicato, and then bow. Although they hate it, I want to make sure they learn to read music."

In this lesson, Karen taught by rote the exact sequence of pitches used in the song, "Jingle Bells," proceeding in two-measure chunks. For each two-measure phrase, she then asked the students to identify the measures in the book, sing the note names, and then pluck the notes. Once most were able to pluck a two- or four-measure chunk, Karen had them add their bows, considerably below a tempo that might be expected for performance. In this lesson, the students never heard, sang, or played the entire song.

Jennifer used the same steps as Karen and Jing-Wei, singing, plucking, and bowing. However, she added additional steps in anticipation of student errors. For example, in this lesson, she prepared the students to read and follow the bow directions before they bowed the song. She also used specific strategies ("check with your neighbor," "thumbs up," "Are you at circle one?") to assess whether the students were actually reading the music. Jing-Wei prepared students to avoid some common errors, but was less systematic in his process. Rather than anticipate student errors, Karen responded to them (Duke & Madsen, 1991).

Jennifer was the only one of the three who took an elementary general music methods course at the university, and I noticed that she was careful to distinguish between asking students to "speak" or "sing." Karen and Jing-Wei often asked the students to "say" the note names. At first, I saw Jing-Wei sing note names on pitch, but the students tried to match the octave he was singing, so he may have decided speaking was more effective. Jing-Wei usually played both melody and accompaniment on piano as he spoke the note names; Jennifer provided a melodic model on violin or piano as she and the students sang the pitches, and played accompaniment when the students plucked or bowed; and Karen tended to both speak and sing note names even though she usually asked the students to "say" them, using piano to play melody with only occasional chordal accompaniment.

Linking Aural Skills and Rhythm Reading

In Practicum, we had particularly emphasized the "feels like-sounds like-looks like" approach for teaching rhythm reading. All three teachers had students echo rhythmic patterns by rote with clapping, pizzicato, air bow, and bow. They also used rhythm flashcards or wrote rhythm patterns on the board, at least on occasion, but each used them differently. Karen less frequently linked written rhythm patterns on either the board or flashcards with just-echoed aural patterns. She reported that she kept the flashcards in a tub of organized equipment in her car, so that she could "run out and get them," if there were a day when students could not or did not bring their instruments; however, I never observed her using them. When Jing-Wei first started teaching, he used the flashcards the way we practiced in Practicum; I did not see him use them during the study. However, he applied the same principle, using aural exercises, followed by reading notation on the board. Jing-Wei frequently asked students to echo on their instruments rhythmic patterns he played on piano, and often modeled the rhythm of a new song on piano before the students played it. He and Jennifer both had the students read entire phrases or songs from alternate pitch notation, while they pointed at the board in rhythm. Jennifer consistently used flashcards or the board to have the students echo-sing, read, and play rhythm patterns on open strings, her own variations of the "feels like-sounds like-looks like" approach. Later in the year, Jennifer began to have students clap, count, and play complete phrases, as opposed to one-measure patterns, from the board and from rhythm worksheets.

Jing-Wei often played on piano or clapped rhythmic patterns for the students to repeat, and also used rhythm pattern echoes as a signal for the class to get ready to listen. All three notated on the white board and/or demonstrated rhythm patterns to be played on scale pitches by playing, singing, or speaking word rhythms (e.g., "long, short-short," "down, up-up," "Mississippi River," or "1, 2, 3, lift"). I saw them also apply word rhythms to reading songs in the book, sometimes connected with having students clap or move their bows in the air as they spoke the rhythms or pitches of the song. Jennifer also used rhythm worksheets to assess each individual student's ability to write rhythmic counts.

Linking Aural Warm-ups and Music Reading

Jing-Wei began each class with the same structured aural warm-up, with various scales and major/minor fingering drills cued by the piano. I did not see him use a warm-up activity that seemed relevant to the material he intended to teach that day, a concept I thought we had stressed frequently in Practicum. For example, in the lesson described in this paper, nothing he did in the previous 16 minutes of the class seemed in any intentional way to prepare for the new note and meter of the song he planned to introduce: all the scales and finger patterns he had the students do were in 4/4 meter, although the new song was in 3/4, and he made no particular mention of note names on the G string to prepare the students for playing or reading the new note. He used the board to ask students to identify the song's new note, also shown in a box on the page in the book. He then took the students through his usual steps for reading from the music: pointing at the notes and saying the note names, plucking the notes and saying the note names, and then bowing.

In the lesson described above, Karen taught short phrases from the song by rote, then went back over them, asking the students to identify those same phrases in the printed music, as we had demonstrated in the class. Although we discouraged expecting beginners to successfully sight-read music containing new concepts, later in the year Karen more often asked students to read directly from the page with little aural preparation.

In the lessons I observed, Jennifer seemed to make the most direct connections between her warm-up activities and the song to be learned. As we had encouraged in Practicum, Jennifer, unlike Jing-Wei and Karen, seemed to begin some aural preparatory exercises for a new concept several class periods before she introduced that concept in notation. She spoke to me more often of specific long-term goals she had for the students, and she worried that her students were "behind" where others in the district are. For example, Jennifer was bothered by having to prepare students on music for the district honor orchestra auditions that included slurs and other skills she had not yet taught them. Noting that the district mentor "said, for two weeks before she introduces slurs, she has them do hooked bows," Jennifer lamented that she "didn't have time for" preparatory exercises and instead "just had to slam [the students] into it." This indicated to me that she usually did intend to prepare new skills several weeks in advance, and was disappointed in herself for being in a spot where the students had to read notated slurs the same day that she first introduced the aural preparatory exercises.

Thoughts About Transitioning From Rote to Note

Jennifer, although still uncertain that she was doing the "correct things," most clearly articulated her ideas for helping students learn to read music. She explained that "this year, [she] just didn't know what [she] wanted to do" to teach note reading, although she felt that the class "picked up on it pretty well."

> *Essential Elements 2000* is great because it has the notes in the front. And I give them flashcards [to take home in a plastic sandwich bag]—I think I showed you those. I tell them to practice them. Some of them do, and some of them just lose them. I didn't have them sing the notes very much today, but that's a daily thing, to sing while looking at it. And I'll play piano so they hopefully get it.

Jennifer also gave her students the timed tests provided by the district. Each of the ten levels consisted of a page of whole notes that students had to label with note name, string, and finger number in 3 minutes. By February, Jennifer also had her students do counting worksheets supplied by the district, writing the counts and clapping the lines using the standard "1 and 2 and" system. She assigned one eight-measure line each week, modeling in class how to practice it at home. Her goal was to have each child individually pass off each line in sequence, checking them as they brought their instrument to her to be tuned at the beginning of each class.

Jing-Wei described similar understandings of the rote-to-note transition but, although the district mentor offered him the same flashcards, time tests, and rhythm worksheets that Jennifer used, he did not use any of them regularly. In the fall, before I knew about the district resources, I had suggested that some worksheets might help him assess whether *every* child really knew note names but, after doing it once, Jing-Wei "didn't feel like it was helping." Later, I again asked what he thought about doing the tests. He replied that they were "good," and that perhaps he was kind "kind of scared" after his first attempt because he had to ask his wife for help grading the papers. At the time, it seemed like "there were so many things to do and [he was] not used to" all the required paper work. He admitted—when I suggested it—that although in the first semester his record keeping "took forever," he had learned to "do this kind of thing really fast, so probably now [he] could do" the time tests, grading them in the time he had between schools. However, Jing-Wei was satisfied with the students' skill development.

> I have to [give it to] every student, then they take [the test]. I come back, I have to check if they do it right, and they have to retake it. I'm lazy—I was thinking if I could come up with an easier way. That's why—with this fifth grade I was doing a lot of plucking, singing, things like that. It seems to help. I feel like they really read it.

When I asked Karen if she had any particular ideas or strategies for helping students progress from rote to note, she replied, "No. It's *so* big!" and seemed to hope that I could give her some answers. This imprecision in her thinking appeared to be reflected in her somewhat unfocused strategies which, as in this "Jingle Bells" lesson, often showed no particular sequence of moving the students from rote echoes to reading the notation. Karen believed that, although her schools had a high percentage of English-language learners on free or reduced lunch, they could learn to read music, but worried that her students "relied on" writing the note names under every note in every song. Karen's students were not unique; I have noticed that this common student-initiated strategy often emerges, once the *Essential Elements* book changes from noteheads that contain the pitch names to standard notation. "Jingle Bells" is the first song in the book without these note names, although in this lesson Karen did not point that out to the students.

DISCUSSION

Although I wanted to focus on song-teaching methods in this study, it proved to be difficult to discover the teachers' beliefs on that specific topic. In our discussions, the teachers consistently circled back to a multitude of other issues: problems with individual students' behavior, concerns about individual students' learning, problem parents, concert preparation and logistics, and a host of issues related to classroom management, record keeping, and time management. This sense of overload and of being on an emotional roller coaster ride is commonly described in the beginning teacher literature (Conway, Micheel-Mays, & Micheel-Mays, 2005; Knowles & Cole, with Presswood, 1994).

I asked each what he or she specifically remembered learning in Practicum. Karen and Jing-Wei mentioned primarily activities and teaching strategies, such as leading the group with flashcards, having the students pluck and air bow, and writing lesson plans. As they named these things, both somewhat sheepishly said that, although they were not using them frequently, they knew they "should." For example, Karen remembered that writing "unit lessons," making a long-range plan for introducing a new piece to an ensemble and preparing it over 6 weeks for a concert, "was a good specific thing that we did [in Practicum], even though it's a pain in the butt…. It's something that I need to do…. [I know it would help], because right now, I'm running around in circles." Although Jing-Wei was required to turn in lesson plans every week to his principal, he "just writes what [the class is] going to work on," rather than writing out step-by-step instructions, as we required in Practicum. In addition, he justified not writing lesson plans because his district mentor said *she* "didn't write lesson plans" either.

In contrast, Jennifer clearly articulated a number of activities she learned in Practicum, but she also described concepts she used, such as "the complete teaching cycle," and using flashcards or piano as "teaching tools." Jennifer could describe not only *activities* to promote music reading, but an entire *process* of teaching music literacy. I asked if the Gordon theory had been a new idea for her when she took the class.

> It was. Because I had taught [both private students and String Project classes], but you were putting words to what I had tried to do before. So when you talked about it in Practicum, it just made so much sense. Hear it, feel it before you play it. Of course the kids just want to play songs. So sometimes maybe I do overkill with the activities, like the D scale, *[she sings and air bows]* 3, 3, 3, or whole-whole–but to me, I feel like I have to make sure everything is there before they go to [read] it, and then at least they have a chance…. I do remember first learning about it in Practicum. And now I *hope* it's just a natural thing–I don't really think about it.

This study's data, however, do not explain *why* Jennifer seemed to learn more than the other two teachers about principles and processes, in addition to activities, in Practicum.

There are several possible explanations that could, individually or in combination, account for these observed differences. Level of musicianship is unlikely as a primary reason as, although Jennifer's musical skills are quite solid, Jing-Wei's guitar playing identified him as the most skillful musician of the three. It is also possible that these teachers adapted their teaching methods or conversations to try to please me when I came to observe; however, their teaching practices were so consistent that it seems unlikely they could radically change them for the entire time I was there.

Some research has suggested that the amount of prior teaching experience is correlated with the development of teaching performance (e.g., Paul et al., 2001; Standley & Madsen, 1991). In this study all three teachers had similar experience in the classroom and in private lessons before and during Practicum, suggesting that the quality and content of those experiences, rather than the amount, may be more important in teachers' development (Dewey, 1938/1963). To better understand the impact of early field experience, in a future study, I plan to revisit notes and videos from these teachers' student teaching and university course work.

Karen traveled to five schools a week, often arriving just as class is beginning, and taught students in grades 5 to 12. Jing-Wei and Jennifer traveled to three schools daily, with adequate travel time between, and taught only Grades 5 and 6, so they had both more preparation time and fewer types of lessons and materials to prepare. Their district mentor was a string teacher, and the music teachers in their district met often; Karen's mentor was a math teacher. This meant that Karen worked much more in isolation than Jing-Wei and Jennifer; she commented often that she liked having me come to observe her because I could offer suggestions specific to string teaching. Yet Jennifer and Jing-Wei had the same district mentor (who is skilled in teaching both aural and music reading skills), so it is unlikely that mentoring accounts for all the difference.

In addition, Jennifer's statement above that, at the time we introduced Gordon principles in Practicum, "it just made so much sense," suggests that perhaps she had a greater "need to know," or readiness to learn (Bridges, 1993; Paul et al., 2001) at that point, than the other two. Both Karen and Jennifer had taught in the String Project, where they received suggestions from me to use an aural approach, but neither mentioned a connection between those experiences and the concepts presented in Practicum. Jennifer had, from the beginning, shown more interest in—and ability to—ask for and apply teaching advice from other mentors and from me. In the summer following the study, Karen asked me to continue working with her during her second year, specifically to develop long-term goals for all her groups and strategies for teaching beginners. This suggests that readiness to learn may happen at different times for different people, including in the first years of teaching. Effort also certainly made a difference: Jennifer readily admitted her own tendencies toward perfectionism, and she clearly worked more diligently at both schoolwork and at most aspects of her teaching than the other two, with a concomitant desire to implement her mentor's and my advice.

IMPLICATIONS FOR PRACTICE AND
RECOMMENDATIONS FOR FURTHER RESEARCH

Without question, all three teachers implemented elements of an aural or rote approach to teaching new songs in elementary string classes. Although it is difficult to know with certainty how strong that tendency was before they entered Practicum, it is likely that instruction in Practicum did make a lasting impact on them. They also demonstrated differences in the strategies they chose to use, and in the appropriateness and depth of understanding with which they applied them. This study illuminates those differences, but does not completely explain them, raising a number of questions for practice and for further research.

Readiness to learn and individual effort appeared to be important influences in this study. What part do preservice teachers' effort and investment in both methods courses and initial job placements play in their retention of learning? What is the role of a "need to know" in making learning relevant, meaningful, and memorable? Can these learner characteristics be fostered during preservice teachers' college years to improve their understanding and application of course-based learning in their future classrooms? The complex relationships among existing beliefs, readiness to learn, effort, course work, and initial teaching practices suggest that continued study of individuals, from their preservice years into the first years of teaching, may help unravel the varied processes and time lines by which novices implement, modify, or reject practices presented in university-based courses and student teaching.

Every year as my colleague and I teach the Practicum course, we struggle with ways to clarify the difference between teaching strictly by rote and an aural approach that leads logically to music reading (Haston, 2007). These teachers' incomplete learning of concepts and strategies I thought we taught, even with the relative luxury of time available in a year-long 6-hour-a-week course, highlights the need for teacher educators to frequently make explicit connections between specific teaching strategies and the principles or theories that help teachers develop knowledge of how and when to use them. Novices need extended practice with new techniques to become fluent with them and convinced of their usefulness (Berliner, 1995; Clift & Brady, 2005), particularly if methods course approaches are different from their own experiences as students or do not fit easily into their "lay theories" of teaching (Holt-Reynolds, 1991). Context-rich studies of individuals' interactions with the explicit and hidden curricula (Eisner, 1994) of a variety of teacher education programs may suggest more effective ways to develop knowledge of—and fluency with—specific skills, and also understanding of the principles that undergird them.

Most beginning teachers identify deficiencies in their preparation in a number of areas that are difficult to learn in a college classroom, including experiences such as dealing with parents and managing paper work (Conway, 2002; Veenman, 1984). These three teachers, like many other novices, desired instructional assistance, as well as psychological support and validation, from knowledgeable and caring mentors (Fredrickson & Neill, 2004; Gold, 1996). In a large-scale survey study, Smith and Ingersoll (2004) highlighted the importance of discipline-specific mentors and of mentors experienced with high-poverty school populations. Karen's math-teacher mentor very effectively helped her with school policies and techniques of classroom management, but Karen also appreciated my help with specific questions about string class teaching. More studies of novice teachers are needed, particularly to document ways that beginners in music, art, and physical education cope with specific challenges, such as large numbers of students, multiple grade levels, travel between schools, and lack of respect for the subject they teach (Conway, 2003; Hebert & Worthy, 2001; O'Sullivan, 1989).

This study suggests, as does an increasing body of research, that it is "possible, but not predictable" for methods courses to influence preservice teachers' beliefs "and in some instances actual teaching practices" (Clift & Brady, 2005, pp. 319, 329). Several case studies besides this one (e.g., Bullough with Baughman, 1993; Conway, Micheel-Mays, & Micheel-Mays, 2005; Ryan et al., 1980; Schmidt & Canser, 2006) suggest the potential value of opportunities beyond graduation for novice teachers and teacher educators to continue learning together, both to assist the new teachers in refining their practices and to permit university faculty to assess their own teaching. The logistical and financial challenges are many, but well worth exploring, because of the mutual benefits for both.

NOTES

1. We present Gordon's (1993) eight-stage music learning theory, and frequently refer to a similar and less complex approach advocated in James Froseth's workshop presentations. Froseth suggests students need to first experience a musical concept ("feels like"), then what it "sounds like," with the notation ("looks like") presented last.

REFERENCES

Bauer, W. I., & Berg, M. H. (2001). Influences on instrumental music teaching. *Bulletin of the Council for Research in Music Education, 150,* 53-66.

Berliner, D. C. (1995). Teaching expertise. In L. W. Anderson (Ed.), *International encyclopedia of teaching and teacher education* (pp. 60-83). London: Cassell Educational.

Bridges, M. S. (1993). What our graduates wish we had told them. *The Quarterly Journal of Music Teaching and Learning, IV*(1), 68-72.

Brubaker, D. (1992). *Concert tunes for strings* (Vol. 1). Mesa, AZ: JLJ Music.

Bullough, R. V., with Baughman, K. (1993). Continuity and change in teacher development: First year teacher after five years. *Journal of Teacher Education, 2*(4), 285-298.

Campbell, M. R. (1999). Learning to teach music: A collaborative ethnography. *Bulletin of the Council for Research in Music Education, 139,* 12-36.

Clift, R. T., & Brady, P. (2005). Research on methods courses and field experiences. In M. Cochran-Smith & K. M. Zeichner (Eds.), *Studying teacher education: The report of the AERA panel on research and teacher education.* Mahwah, NJ: Erlbaum.

Conway, C. (2002). Perceptions of beginning teachers, their mentors, and administrators regarding preservice music teacher preparation. *Journal of Research in Music Education, 50*(1), 20-36.

Conway, C. (Ed.). (2003). Part V: Listening to music teachers. In C. Conway (Ed.), *Great beginnings for music teachers: Mentoring and supporting new teachers* (pp. 167-187). Reston, VA: The National Association for Music Education.

Conway, C. M., Micheel-Mays, C., & Micheel-Mays, L. (2005). A narrative study of student teaching and the first year of teaching: Common issues and struggles. *Bulletin of the Council for Research in Music Education, 165,* 65-77.

Creswell, J. W. (1998). *Qualitative inquiry and research design: Choosing among five traditions.* Thousand Oaks, CA: SAGE.

Dewey, J. (1963). *Experience and education.* New York: Macmillan. (Original work published 1938)

Duke, R. A., & Madsen, C. K. (1991). Proactive versus reactive teaching: Focusing observation on specific aspects of instruction. *Bulletin of the Council for Research in Music Education, 108,* 1-14.

Eisner, E. W. (1994). The three curricula that all schools teach. In *The educational imagination: On the design and evaluation of school programs* (3rd ed., pp. 87-107). New York: Macmillan.

Ferguson, K. (2003). Becoming a string teacher. *Bulletin of the Council for Research in Music Education, 157,* 38-48.

Fredrickson, W. E., & Neill, S. (2004). "Is it Friday yet?" (Perceptions of first-year music teachers). *Bulletin of the Council for Research in Music Education, 161/162,* 91-98.

Fredrickson, W. E., & Pembrook, R. (2002). "When you pinpoint incorrect notes and they still miss them, what do you do then? (Perceptions of field experience students). *Bulletin of the Council for Research in Music Education, 153/154*, 8-11.

Froseth, J. O. (2002). *Do it! Play violin, viola, cello, bass*. Chicago: GIA.

Gillespie, R., Allen, M., & Tellejohn-Hayes, P. (2000). *Essential elements 2000, Book 1*. Milwaukee, WI: Hal Leonard.

Glesne, C. (1999). *Becoming qualitative researchers: An introduction* (2nd ed.). New York: Addison Wesley Longman.

Gold, Y. (1996). Beginning teacher support: Attrition, mentoring, and induction. In J. Sikula (Ed.), *Handbook of research in teacher education* (pp. 548-594). New York: Macmillan.

Gordon, E. E. (1993). *Learning sequences in music: A music learning theory*. Chicago: GIA.

Gore, J. (1990). Reflecting on reflective teaching. *Journal of Teacher Education, 38*(2), 33-39.

Grossman, P. L., & Richert, A. E. (1988). Unacknowledged knowledge growth: A re-examination of the effects of teacher education. *Teaching & Teacher Education, 4*(1), 53-62.

Harwood, E., & Wiggins, J. (2001). Composing a lesson: Examining our metaphors. *The Mountain Lake Reader*, 32-41.

Haston, W. (2007). Teacher modeling as an effective teaching strategy. *Music Educators Journal, 93*(4), 26-30.

Hebert, E., & Worthy, T. (2001). Does the first year of teaching have to be a bad one? A case of success. *Teaching and Teacher Education, 17*(8), 897-911.

Holt-Reynolds, D. (1991, February). *Practicing what we teach*. Paper presented at the annual meeting of the Association of Teacher Educators, New Orleans.

Huberman, A. M., & Miles, M. B. (1994). Data management and analysis methods. In N. K. Denzin & Y. S. Lincoln (Eds.), *The SAGE handbook of qualitative research* (2nd ed., pp. 428-444). Thousand Oaks, CA: SAGE.

Jansen, G., & Peshkin, A. (1992). Subjectivity in qualitative research. In *The handbook of qualitative research in education* (pp. 682-725). San Diego, CA: Academic Press.

Knowles, J. G., & Cole, A. L., with Presswood, C. S. (1994). *Through preservice teachers' eyes: Exploring field experiences through narrative and inquiry*. New York: Merrill/Macmillan.

Lawes, J. S. (1987). The relationship between non-verbal awareness of self and teaching competence in student teachers. *Journal of Education for Teaching, 13*(2), 145-154.

Leglar, M., & Collay, M. (2004). Research by teachers on teacher education. In R. Colwell & C. Richardson (Eds.), *The new handbook of research on music teaching and learning* (pp. 855-873). New York: Oxford University Press.

Madsen, C. K., & Duke, R. A. (1985). Perception of approval/disapproval in music. *Bulletin of the Council for Research in Music Education, 85*, 119-130.

Madsen, C. K., Standley, J. M., & Cassidy, J. W. (1989). Demonstration and recognition of high and low contrasts in teacher intensity. *Journal of Research in Music Education, 37*(2), 85-92.

Merriam, S. B. (1988). *Case study research in education: An introduction*. San Francisco: Jossey-Bass.

Miranda, M., Robbins, J., & Stauffer, S. L. (2006, April). *Seeing and hearing music teaching and learning: Transforming classroom observations through ethnography and portraiture.* Paper presented at the annual meeting of the American Educational Research Association, San Francisco.

National Association for Music Education. (1994). *The school music program: A new vision.* Reston, VA: Author.

Nierman, G. E., Zeichner, K., & Hobbel, N. (2004). Changing concepts of teacher education. In. R. Colwell & C. Richardson (Eds.), *The new handbook of research on music teaching and learning* (pp. 818-839). New York: Oxford University Press.

O'Sullivan, M. (1989). Failing gym is like failing lunch or recess: Two beginning teachers' struggle for legitimacy. *Journal of Teaching in Physical Education, 8,* 227–242.

Paul, S. J., Teachout, D. J., Sullivan, J. M., Kelly, S. N., Bauer, W. I., & Raiber, M. A. (2001). Authentic-context learning activities in instrumental music teacher education. *Journal of Research in Music Education, 49*(2), 136-145.

Pembrook, R., & Fredrickson, W. E. (1999). "I got to teach all day!" (Perceptions of student music teachers). *Bulletin of the Council for Research in Music Education, 141,* 36-40.

Price, H. E. (1992). Sequential patterns of music instruction and learning to use them. *Journal of Research in Music Education, 40*(1), 14-29.

Robbins, J. (1993). Preparing students to think like teachers: Relocating our teacher education perspective. *The Quarterly Journal of Teaching and Learning, IV*(1), 45-51.

Robbins, J. (1999). Getting set and letting go: Practicum teachers' in-flight decision-making. *The Mountain Lake Reader,* 26-32.

Ryan, K., Newman, K. K., Mager, G., Applegate, J., Lasley, T. Flora, R., et al. (1980). *Biting the apple.* New York: Longman.

Schmidt, M. (1998). Defining "good" music teaching: Four student teachers' beliefs and practices. *Bulletin of the Council of Research in Music Education, 138,* 19-46.

Schmidt, M. (2006, April). *Experience meets experience: Dewey's theory and preservice music teachers' learning.* Paper presented at the annual meeting of the American Educational Research Association, San Francisco.

Schmidt, M., & Canser, J. (2006). Clearing the fog: Constructing shared stories of a novice teacher's success. *Research Studies in Music Education, 27,* 55-68.

Smith, T. M., & Ingersoll, R. M. (2004). What are the effects of induction and mentoring on beginning teacher turnover? *American Educational Research Journal, 41*(3), 681-714.

Stake, R. E. (2005). Qualitative case studies. In N. K. Denzin & Y. S. Lincoln (Eds.), *The SAGE handbook of qualitative research* (3rd ed., pp. 443-466). Thousand Oaks, CA: SAGE.

Standley, J. M., & Madsen, C. K. (1991). An observation procedure to differentiate teaching experience and expertise in music education. *Journal of Research in Music Education, 39*(3), 5-11.

Thompson, L. K., & Campbell, M. R. (2003). Gods, guides, and gardeners: Preservice music educators' personal teaching metaphors. *Bulletin of the Council of Research in Music Education, 158,* 43-54.

Veenman, S. (1984). Perceived problems of beginning teachers. *Review of Educational Research, 54*(2), 143-178.

Yin, R. K. (1989). *Case study research: Design and methods.* Newbury Park, CA: SAGE.

CHAPTER 5

MUSIC EDUCATOR AS CHANGE AGENT

A Personal Narrative

Melissa Natale Abramo

ABSTRACT

Amidst conservative education policies, educators today are faced with increased impositions on their daily work. Recent scholarship in music education is also urging music educators to address the growing divide between school music programs and the broader culture of music in society. This study is the personal narrative of a progressive music educator who employs alternative pedagogies in an attempt to resist the conservative and traditional practices of the profession and address the growing divide in music education. Positioned in a discussion of the self as change agent, influenced by the work of Bourdieu (1977), Foucault (1979), and Butler (1999), this study examines the social and cultural hindrances to transformation as well as the degree to which a socially constructed self can act as a change agent.

Diverse Methodologies in the Study of Music Teaching and Learning, pp. 91–109

INTRODUCTION

In the midst of conservative political education policies as in the No Child Left Behind Act and the American Competitiveness Initiative (Bush, 2006), educators are faced with increased imposition on their daily work. Informed by agenda-laden concepts of accountability and high stakes testing, this political climate becomes, as described by Barone (2006), "a deep intrusion into the once public space of the classroom for the purpose of managing the transactions between those who live and work here" (p. 214). It is particularly difficult for music educators to situate themselves among such agendas emphasizing math, sciences and technology (Bush, 2006), and still locate a space of possibility in arts education.

Recent scholarship in music education has contended that our field is at a point of crisis and in need of transformation (Jorgensen, 2003; Reimer, 2003). Writes Reimer, "we are facing a growing crisis of dispensability as music in our culture thrives while music education faces constant uncertainty as to its value" (p. 281). Jorgensen calls for music educators to position themselves as agents of transformation in the broader field of education. She writes that music educators should not be passive in this world and must commit to transforming education.

> given the nature of their subject matter, musicians and artists are especially positioned to create a powerful model of a humane and holistic music education that can help to transform education generally and those who undertake or undergo it. (p. xii)

As music educators are increasingly aware of the growing options of how and where music can be taught, and as students are seemingly less tolerant of traditional pedagogies, music educators have finally started to take a look at the gulf between school music programs and the broader culture of music in society. There are some who are seeking out alternatives to the traditional practices of the field, looking to create music classrooms that are more relevant to the diverse musical cultures of the larger community, and take into account the subjectivities of teachers and students (Allsup, 2002; Allsup, 2004; Folkestad, 2006; Green, 2002; Stalhammar, 2003). For teachers seeking such alternatives, the classroom becomes a place of tension between theory and practice, tradition and innovation, between their musical experiences and those of their students, between musical traditions and educational research.

Thiessen and Barrett (2002) address the lack of reform-minded music educators, call for more research involving such educators, and propose a design for music teacher education programs to cultivate teachers who can create change in the profession. They account for specific issues in the field of music education that complicate a reform-minded teacher's work such as, "the view of music teaching as a specialized form of practice, the balance of identity between musician and teacher, the prominence of performance in music programs, and the pressing advocacy needs of music programs in schools" (p. 774). The present study is intended to add to the body of research on reform-minded music educators, uncovering facets of one teacher's work for change in the classroom.

There has been considerable debate on the degree to which one can change oneself and one's environment, or to what degree individuals have social agency. Foucault (1979) and Bourdieu (1977) argue that the environments and social factors in which we live and work not only constrain us, but also dictate who we become. According to these philosophers, an individual's capacity for social change is limited because that individual may be constrained by the same social factors she wishes to change. On another side of the debate, critical and feminist pedagogues argue for the power of pedagogy to "create social transformation in a world of shifting and uncertain meaning" (Weiler, 1991, p. 450). Butler (1999) believes that, although we are constrained, we can recreate our environments, and therefore enact change. Maxine Green (1986) proposes that we "find out how to open such spheres, such spaces, where a better state of things can be imagined" (p. 441).

Whether one is constrained or confined there is always a place for music educators to contest the ossification of traditional practice, and there are music educators working toward transformation of their classrooms and the field at large. Understanding the daily experiences of such a music educator can provide invaluable insight for both the practicing music teacher and those preparing to enter the field. In order to better address the need for transformation we must better understand the experiences of the music teacher working toward that transformation. What I have chosen to uncover through this study is the *experience* of agency, through the lens of the change agent, in this case a music educator. Using narrative inquiry this study will examine the following:

1.   How does the progressive educator define herself as progressive in her professional context? What experiences brought her to define herself as such?

2.   What social, cultural and political factors hinder a progressive educator? In what ways does she perceive herself as constrained, and in what ways is she successful?

3.   What is the progressive music educator's relationship with agency?

THEORETICAL FRAMEWORK

Theoretically, this inquiry is situated in the debate concerning human agency. Agency refers to the capacity of individuals to decide among options and make their own free choices (Honderich, 1995). The debate occurs among those who believe our agency is severely limited by social constraints, and those who believe we can construct and reconstruct ourselves among those constraints. Foucault (1979) and Bourdieu (1977) would argue that human capacity for agency is limited because the environments and social factors in which we live create and dictate our choices. When one chooses among options that are determined by society at large, one is not really choosing at all. For Foucault, levels of power that are created by our societal structures and policies in large part determine who we become.

The structuring of a teacher's work can illustrate this point. When in the classroom, an individual teacher has a particular position in relation to daily practice with students. These individuals are also part of a larger group of faculty within a school, who are positioned in relation to administrators who oversee their work. That school is situated in a local community with particular expectations. Beyond that community, the school is positioned within state and national structures of education, with its own particular expectations and policies. These examples of power structures (here the classroom, school, community, state, and national policy) at the very least play a large part in who the teacher becomes, and how that teacher shapes her practice. In relation to agency, Foucault might say that a teacher working for change would be severely limited by these examples of embedded power structures, since it is those structures that in large part determine that teacher's role, identity and practice.

Bourdieu (1977) has a similar position in relation to agency. For him, the socially constructed self is created "in deeply ingrained habits of behavior, feeling, thought" (Lovell, 2000, p. 12). His concept of *habitus* refers to the daily routines and practices that are not only a result of our beliefs, but also dictate our beliefs. For Bourdieu, the self is produced, and maintained, by repeated daily social practices, and those everyday practices determine our truth, how we view reality. He refers to how this reality is not seen as malleable or constructed, but misrecognized as taken for granted, normal and "the way things are".

An example in music education might be the performance ensemble as an instructional model. For most teachers, instrumental music education is situated in a performance ensemble of the Western tradition. Therefore, instrumental music classrooms are based on the structure of the ensemble, and teacher education emphasizes conducting skills, instrumental technique, and a deep knowledge of performance practice and core pieces of literature in the ensemble tradition. The idea of the large ensemble as a classroom structure is taken for granted, or misrecognized. Our practices surrounding that classroom model are not only determined by that taken for granted belief, but also create that belief as we continue to practice instrumental music teaching in the large ensemble. This *habitus* makes it more difficult for alternative options to become part of our practice. In this example, the use of popular music, instruments other than those of the traditional concert band or orchestra, or an instrumental music classroom structure not based on a particular performance ensemble, are less likely to become part of the possibilities of instrumental music education, when the daily practices of the profession itself maintain the large ensemble as "the way things are." Both Foucault (1979) and Bourdieu (1977) propose that even when attempting to change ourselves or our environments, we are severely limited by the structures and habits with which we live.

Feminist scholars have disagreed with Foucault and Bourdieu, arguing that they leave little room for autonomy, and do not adequately account those who work to resist and subvert the dominant culture. Lovell (2000) explains, "Bourdieu's 'reflexive sociology'... is so successful in identifying the embeddedness of agency in institutional practice that there is no denying that it induces at times a strong sense of political paralysis" (p. 16). Weedon (1997) argues that as we bring the factors that shape us into consciousness, we have the ability to resist and question their influence.

> Having grown up within a particular system of meanings and values, which may well be contradictory, we may find ourselves resisting alternatives. Or, as we move out of familiar circles, through education or politics, for example, we may be exposed to alternative ways of constituting the meaning of our experience which seem to address our interests more directly. The collective discussion of personal problems and conflicts, often previously understood as the result of personal inadequacies and neuroses, leads to a recognition that what have been experienced as personal failings are socially produced conflicts and contradictions shared by many women in similar social positions. This process of discovery can lead to a rewriting of personal experience in terms which give it social, changeable causes. (p. 33)

Butler's (1999) concept of *performativity* provides another perspective on agency, where the individual is viewed as *performing* the self. Butler posits that gender is a series of acts, or performances, that are not linked to a biologically determined self. Gender is rather a series of repeated acts that create the semblance of a fixed, preexisting entity that has a gendered identity. For Butler, "there is no gender identity behind the expressions of gender; that identity is performatively constituted by the very 'expressions' that are said to be its results" (p. 33). In other words, one's actions are not the result of the stable and habitual self described by Bourdieu, but in fact one's actions create the *illusion* of an identity. The question then becomes not how the self is created, but how one *creates the self.* This provides a position seemingly counter to that of Foucault and Bourdieu, proposing a capacity for us to create ourselves, choosing among many options.

It could also be argued that creating a binary between these two positions of agency is artificial (Kopelson, 2002). Describing Foucault and Bourdieu's idea of self as overdetermined self versus Butler's position of the free self, could be seen as an oversimplification and does not address the nuances that exist between. In his later work, Foucault (1984, 1990) begins to discuss the space of possibility of agency, writing that his work

> is not about what it is impossible for us to do and to know, but it will separate out, from the contingency that has made us what we are, the possibility of no longer being, doing, or thinking what we are, do, or think. (Foucault, 1984, p. 46)

He begins to acknowledge the human capacity for resistance to domination and the capacity for self-creation, although still amidst social and political limits. For the purposes of this study, the question of the music educator's sense of agency as she works for change is situated in this tension, and theories of agency and their interpretations will frame my analysis.

NARRATIVE INQUIRY

This study adopts a narrative mode of inquiry, more specifically personal narrative (Personal Narratives Group, 1989; Witherell & Noddings, 1991). Although relatively new to the field of music education, narrative inquiry has received much attention in social sciences over the past 10 to 15 years and is flourishing in education (Casey 1995; Chase 2005; Clandinin & Connelly, 2000; Riessman 1993). Interdisciplinary in its approach, narrative grew out of early life histories and the second wave of feminist movement in the 1960s where "by listening to previously silenced voices, feminist researchers challenged social science knowledge about society, culture, and history" (Chase, 2005, p. 654). Interpretive in its analysis, narrative is not only the telling of one's story, but the interpretation of *how* that story is told. Narrative researchers can take various approaches, as the term is continually redefined and rewritten, and resists a fixed methodology. For this study I adopt what Chase describes as identity work where "sociologists highlight the 'identity work' that people engage in as they construct selves within specific institutional, organizational, discursive, and local cultural contexts" and therefore "treat narratives *as* lived experience" (p. 658, italics in original).

What is particularly important for this study is the connection of narrative inquiry to social agency. As described by Casey (1995), "narrative inquiry *is* a mode of social action and "dares to announce 'I am' ('we are') and in so doing deliberately defies the forces of alienation … authoritarianism … fragmentation" (p. 213). Situated in postmodern thought, where there is the rejection of a unified subject or identity, narrative celebrates human agency through the telling of personal story and life history. With narrative inquiry, the personal is political and is particularly relevant to this study in that I seek to document my personal struggle with agency, as someone who seeks to create a space of possibility in the classroom. I hope that through the telling and analysis of my own story, I not only provide insight into the research questions stated above, but also provide a space for the voices of progressive music educators to be heard; stories which I believe are integral to transformation of the field.

DATA COLLECTION AND CONTEXT

I am currently in my eighth year of public school music teaching. After working for 2 years in an elementary band position, I attended a university as a full-time masters degree student, where I focused on research, composition, and creative thinking in the music classroom. The position I took upon graduation is where I have remained for the past 6 years; a small middle/high school, comprised of Grades 6 through 12, located in a middle-upper class suburb of New York City. I direct four concert bands as well as teach eighth grade general music, high school general music, and high school composition electives. I began doctoral work in July of 2004, and have since been both teaching full time and pursuing doctoral work part time.

Over the course of 2 years I have been documenting my experiences in a journal. Initially used as a way to keep a running log of questions and topics of interest for my doctoral work, it became the primary source of data for this project, as I would write about various experiences ranging from interactions with colleagues, to classroom events, to my feelings of success, frustration, doubt and curiosity. I also conducted interviews with students, and documented conversations with students, colleagues, and administrators.

ANALYSIS

Although there are various perspectives on narrative analysis and technique, I have based data collection and analysis on the work of Riessman (1993) who discusses techniques and approaches to transcription and analysis. Several readings of the journal allowed me to uncover significant events in both my teaching experiences and my professional biography that related to research questions. As I reread and reflected upon what I had written, I added more to my narratives to expand on particular events or emotions involved at the time. I read the data for emotional responses, significant events and recurring topics. I analyzed the interactions described between myself and students, parents and colleagues, as well as how I interpreted those interactions.

In relation to the research questions, emotional themes emerged, ranging from feelings of failure and success, frustration and hope. Stories related back to either my professional biography, or events and experiences that I perceived as barriers to change, or as fostering success. Tradition and the expectations of those that surround my work were uncovered in relation to hindrances I experienced. Discussion of my perceived successes involved definitions of what it meant to be successful, as well as the particular people or situations in which I experienced feelings of success.

PROGRESSIVE EDUCATOR

I identify as a progressive music educator, and I have done so since my first year in the classroom. Progressive in its most general term implies a forward looking and forward thinking philosophy. In this context it also implies a certain dissatisfaction with status quo, and is forward thinking in the sense that it doesn't allow traditions to remain unquestioned.

The term progressive also has various meanings in political and historical contexts. Politically, the progressive movement in American history began in the late nineteenth century in response to the large gaps in wealth and poverty resulting from industrialization (Berube, 1994; Cuban, 1993). Progressivism in education, an outgrowth of political progressivism, viewed the education of children as a means to rectify the growing differences of class in America (Berube, 1994; Cuban, 1993). Derived from European philosophers and pedagogues, progressive educators believed in educating the whole child socially, morally, and intellectually. The educational philosophy of Dewey (1944) steered the progressive education movement in the United States, calling for students to learn through experience, through the process of discovery rather than rote learning. This movement has taken on various forms throughout the twentieth century, and is most formalized in Progressive schools which are based on such philosophies (Berube, 1994; Cuban, 1993).

Although the term progressive also has various meanings in political and historical contexts, it is the more broad definition first described, with which I identify; one who is unafraid to question the status quo and sees her role as a change agent and not someone who replicates unquestioned practice. I take a critical stance to my classroom, one where concepts, understanding, ideas and practice are not given, but must be created and recreated, justified and critiqued.

I attribute this approach to a pivotal moment early in my teaching career. Graduating with an undergraduate degree in music education, I secured a teaching position working with beginning band students at a suburban elementary school in New York. I made the transition into teaching with ease. My lessons were well planned and consistent. My students progressed systematically through the method book. My band rehearsals were efficient, controlled, and productive. The students were quiet, respectful, followed my direction, and progressed. My administration and fellow music colleagues were impressed with my work. Yet with all that "success" I was bored, frustrated, and confused. What I was doing with students felt like neither music nor teaching. I gave direction and they followed. I was doing music *to* them rather than *with* them. It is this crystallizing moment in my first year of teaching that I credit with my transformation as a teacher. Those feelings of frustration and intuition set me on a path of questioning the traditional methods and structures of music teaching and learning, and seeking alternatives for a more meaningful, student-centered classroom.

HINDRANCES: TRADITION

As I worked to put my philosophy into practice, I found that an overwhelming tension existed between my experience of the concert band tradition and my pedagogical beliefs. Much of my own education had focused primarily on instrumental music teaching, and I found that the traditional practices and structure of band classrooms limited my ability to create a student-centered music classroom. One of my students illustrated this tension quite clearly in an interview. Anna, an eleventh grade student, participated in my band classes for 5 years, and had also taken a "Foundations of Music and Composition" class with me. These second set of courses occurred in a music laboratory setting, and were steeped in student-centered pedagogies. In an interview, Anna compared her experience in band with her experience in the other music electives.

Anna: In band you don't really stand out in the class you can't
        always speak your mind and there isn't really anything to
        speak about. It's not like in Composition or Foundations
        where we can have thorough discussion and where like
        everybody has their input and then you can basically grow
        on each others ideas. Like there is none of that in band and
        basically we just get handed the music and we learn the
        rhythms and that's it.

Anna's statement described band as a place where she was limited in
both her musical experience and in the lack of opportunity to "speak her
mind." Not only did she feel it inappropriate to engage in discussion, but
she perceived a kind of silencing, that "there isn't really anything to speak
about." She compared her experience in band to that of other music
classes grounded in student-centered pedagogy, and she saw the two
experiences as very different. This tension she described mirrored my
daily experience as I moved between the two classroom settings. As a
pedagogue and educator I felt silenced within the traditions of the band
classroom, and freed in the classroom outside of ensemble tradition.

In particular, I found the band classroom limiting in the musical
experiences it allowed me to provide students, and the imbalance
between teacher and student voice. The typical teacher-student ratio in
an ensemble class was much different than most other classes, and I found
it almost impossible to use a student-centered pedagogy in a class of more
than 60 students, with only one teacher.

In my attempts to create a new type of band classroom, I found the
music, instrumentation, and focus on traditional music notation to be
limiting in not only the experiences I could provide, but the types of
students I could involve in the program. Incorporating students who play
instruments not typical of the concert band, or who do not read
traditional notation proved difficult in such a large classroom. It was also
more complicated to engage with music outside of the concert band
tradition, when the instruments used in the traditional band classroom
were confined to that tradition.

As I tried to integrate creative and analytical activities into our rehearsal,
for example journaling, composition and improvisation, and student
critique and rehearsing, I found myself in a juggling act between the time
these activities took, and concert preparation. Regularly scheduled
concerts became even more of a stress as I tried to find a balance between
the time needed for a class of sixty students to engage in student-centered
activities, and the pressure of a polished concert performance. As concerts
were approaching I found myself leaning more toward the conductor, and
then feeling inadequate as a student-centered pedagogue. As I tried to be

both, I did not feel successful at either. In a sense, my attempts to work around tradition, left me feeling successful at neither.

Out of frustration (or impatience) with the slow rate of change I was able to enact in the band classroom, I proposed high school general music and composition classes. These classes were also music electives, but held in a laboratory setting which included live instruments, digital recording studios, and music composition and recording software. This setting allowed for student-centered, collaborative music classrooms, and set the stage for what seemed to be an immediate transformation of a music learning environment as well as my own pedagogies.

As I wrote about the inspiring successes and opportunities in these transformed music classrooms *outside* of the band tradition, I was equally as frustrated at my inability to enact change *inside* the band classroom. Here, the idea of tradition emerged in reference to my undergraduate training, as I felt unsuccessful at creating change. The training I received in the band tradition in my undergraduate program, as do most pre-service teachers, did not provide pedagogical models other than that of the exemplary conductor. In fact, in my experience, pedagogy itself was never discussed, but rather substituted with rehearsal techniques. As a result I was equipped to carry on a tradition, and ill-equipped to incorporate competing discourses surrounding education. This training itself, which intended to prepare me for a successful career, became a structure that confined and limited my practice. As a teacher, that tradition (no matter how harmful I found it to be) was what I was most comfortable doing. I had been provided with numerous models and resources with which to maintain this tradition.

Student Perspective

I conducted interviews with students who had diverse experiences in our school music program to gain insight into how tradition might play a role in their interest in music classes. Bryan, a senior, had been in my band classes for 5 years and planned to become a band or orchestra teacher. Anna was a junior and had also been in band classes for 5 years. Both students had also taken "Foundations of Music," and "Composition and Improvisation," the two music electives described earlier. I was interested specifically in why these students signed up for band year after year and how that tradition played a role in their experience.

      M: Why do you sign up for band?

  Bryan: 'Cause I know it will look good on my college application when I go to become a music teacher and because I enjoy band. I enjoy making music. I always like the sound of a lot of music playing at once, like when all the people go to Mecca to pray and they have their whole prayer. That sound so cool with so many voices and I know band isn't the same thing but it will take me there when I am a teacher in front of a band or orchestra.

Interestingly Bryan used another tradition, the pilgrimage to Mecca, as a metaphor for his experience in band. He also cited musical reasons, the aesthetic experience those in music often speak of; the fulfillment and enjoyment of being part of a greater musical experience. This might have also been a factor in Bryan's desire to study music in college, to continue to experience such satisfaction from musical performance. He also referred indirectly to the benefits of how band can increase status for acceptance into an undergraduate program.

When asked the same question, Anna gave a very different response that posed interesting questions.

> Anna: It is more relaxed than my other classes. I don't have any free periods—and my Mom wants me to have a free period—but I like doing it. I've been playing clarinet since I've been in fourth grade. So I just do it. It's a no-brainer and I just do it every year. I don't look at it as a required class, it is just what I do every year … it is just a time where I don't have to worry about anything, I don't have homework due. I don't have to stress about it and I can at least relax for 40 minutes.

Anna did not think much about signing up each year, exposing a tradition of her own. She played clarinet since fourth grade and saw it as something she must continue. What I found most intriguing was the welcomed passivity that she described. She saw it as a time without pressure, a time to relax. Situated in her school day, band was juxtaposed against classes that placed stressful demands on Anna, and her passive role in band class was a relief. This passivity that I wished to rid her of was part of why she signed up for band, and a factor in the reproduction of this tradition. This called into question my assumptions about the negativity of passive students, and also called into question other school structures that leave students needing an outlet, or a place where they can "relax for 40 minutes."

When asked which setting they would choose if they could only take one music class, both chose music electives outside of band.

Bryan: There is less people for one and it is easier to work with. With band you have a path set ahead for you to do and in classes like Foundations it is more open ended and you can do what you want. Instead of playing something someone else has composed you can compose something on your own. There's no real guideline for what you have to do, it is good for creativity. That effect that I can get with a big group of people in band, why wait on fifty people when I can use technology and get the same effect myself in a few hours?

Being that Bryan's career choice was to become a music teacher, his interview provided a look into another aspect of why this tradition is not at a loss for members.

M: Why did you decide to go into music education?

Bryan: I got to know you and got to see what you do in your job and I thought "Wow, that's a pretty neat job." It seems like sometimes to be a lot of fun, and it seems that you have a goal that you work for as well, not just working up a ladder in a system of an office. And its not also like a desk job. You have a lot of freedom than your own little cubicle.

Bryan's perception of a music educator, or the profession in general, was of one that embodied autonomy and independence. He perceived the job of a music teacher to involve more freedom, independence and creativity when compared to other alternatives. When juxtaposed with my narrative it presented an interesting commentary. I described feeling confined where Ryan perceived me as independent. This is evident in his next response.

M: So now you're the teacher. If you were offered two jobs, one as a band or orchestra conductor and one as a composition teacher, which would you choose?

Bryan: I would rather do an orchestra because I like the sound of it overall, with decent students who can play the instruments and play decent pieces that aren't bad. And just like the product you get and the sound of a whole orchestra coming together. It is something that's like, you're the car driver for the world's largest car when you're doing that. You're in control, you can do it how you want. If you say we're going to play it faster because it will sound cooler like that, then you can do it because you're in control.

As a student Bryan would rather be in a composition class because he has control over the musical experience, yet as a teacher he would choose the ensemble conductor for similar reasons. For him, having control over the musical decisions was enticing, exciting, and possibly empowering.

HINDRANCES: EXPECTATIONS

The second theme in reference to hindrances revolved around sets of expectations and assumptions, whether my own, or someone else's. For example, as I first tried to create new experiences in the band classroom I experienced resistance from students who were uncomfortable with the activities. One very frustrated student approached me after one of his peers had led a rehearsal. "Why are you making us do the work? You're trying to make band class something else. We are supposed to come to class, play music, and have fun. This isn't fun." My classroom was clearly in conflict with his expectations of band. This student, consequently, dropped the class mid-year. Similar comments were frequent from parents. On open house night in October I was told, "What we really need is a jazz band or a marching band." One parent suggested, "Instead of doing all that composing stuff you should get the kids ready to play at the basketball games." Their set of expectations of what band should be was often in conflict with what I envisioned those classes might be.

I perhaps found the most conflict of expectations from within the field of music education. Most of my colleagues did not share a similar vision of the music classroom. I did not meet their expectations as a band teacher, for my ensembles were not at the highest level of performance and were not performing music solely from the traditional canon. I did not bring my students to competitions, nor did many students qualify for all-county and all-state performing groups. When I was looking to replace concerts with curriculum demonstrations, they were looking to add more performances. This juxtaposition of approaches created conflict.

Interestingly, this conflict created a sense of paralysis in that I could neither fulfill my own vision, nor meet the expectations of my peers in the greater field. Through deconstructing race perception, DuBois (1903/2005) coined the term "double-consciousness" to mean how one views oneself through the eyes of others. He described, "it is a peculiar sensation, this double-consciousness, this sense of always looking at one's self through the eyes of others, of measuring one's soul by the tape of a world that looks on in amused contempt and pity" (p. 7). Berger (1977/2003) describes a similar concept in relation to how women are forced to view themselves through two lenses simultaneously.

To be born a woman has been to be born ... into the keeping of men. But this has been at the cost of a woman's self being split into two. A woman must continually watch herself ... and so she comes to consider the *surveyor* and the *surveyed* within her as the two constituent yet always distinct elements of her identity as a woman. She has to survey everything she is and everything she does because how she appears to others, and ultimately how she appears to men, is of crucial importance for what is normally thought of as the success of her life. Her own sense of being in herself is supplanted by a sense of being appreciated as herself by another. (p. 46)

As I was teaching and reflecting, I found myself caught between two perspectives of myself. I was viewing myself through the expectations of my colleagues and at the same time through the expectations of a progressive educator, two seemingly incongruent identities. As I tried to enact ideals into practice, I simultaneously viewed those practices as weak when held up to the ideals of my colleagues. I was both proud and ashamed of my program when standing in their judgment; proud of my innovative approach, hoping to engage them in discussion of new possibilities, yet shameful as a result of how they as traditionalists might judge me as an educator. It was perhaps in my interactions with them that I felt the most hindered and the least successful.

These themes of tradition and expectation come together in relation to structural hindrances. When proposing structural change, for example smaller class size to allow for different pedagogy, those who have the power to allow for such changes were informed by the same concert band tradition from which I was trying to break. This tradition created expectations that not only informed my own practice, but the perception of those who made decisions around my practice, and therefore provided a structural barrier to change.

SUCCESSES

Interestingly, the experience to which I attributed most feelings of success in practice occurred outside of the band classroom. The music electives described earlier flourished, and became the most popular courses in our high school music program. Not only was my vision of pedagogy realized, but I was able to involve many different types of students in those musical experiences.

Success also occurred when I discussed experiences removed from school, in conversations with colleagues from my doctoral program, or through other experiences tied to my doctoral work. In those situations I did not feel that I needed to validate or explain my position. I worked to learn more and expand my experience, free in these contexts to explore possibility. Either through coursework, participation in conferences, or involvement in projects with fellow students and professors, feelings of success and fulfillment were frequent.

The most successful collegial interaction in my school involved my principal. Although her expectations of my program were informed by traditional band classes, she engaged in dialogue with me about my vision for the program and my educational justifications. On several occasions she acknowledged that my ideas were not typical, but she allowed me the space to put them into practice. As she has allowed me this space, and observed my ideas in practice, her own vision of what was possible in music classrooms had shifted. She began to see my approach as one other possibility among the traditional music programs. This perhaps is the most important type of success, in that it truly shifted the dominant practice to allow for other possibilities.

CONCLUSION: AGENCY AND IDENTITY

My experience of agency involved shifting identities of minority and majority, hindrance and success. I viewed myself often in terms of being in a minority position, and situated myself in opposition to that majority. Whether it was progressive versus traditional, student-centered versus teacher-centered, mainstream music education versus cutting edge of music education, I perceived and described myself in a minority position. As a result, many of my experiences were reactions to that positioning. Tradition, for example, by its very nature is something that is perceived as unchanging, as reproductive rather than productive. Reflecting on Bourdieu's (1977) concept of *habitus*, tradition can easily be seen as something that is taken for granted or misrecognized, particularly in the case of concert band classrooms. In many ways, tradition became a barrier to my ability to transform my classroom.

Yet, tradition at the same time also *created* agency. As I resisted traditional practice, particularly in terms of band class, my reaction to that tradition propelled me forward to find new possibilities. In a sense, tradition was a springboard for change. My reaction and resistance to that barrier created a need for me to find new ways of practice. Where I could not completely remove the hindrances I experienced, at the same time I recreated the role of music teacher in relation to those hindrances, which was in part informed by a reaction to those barriers. In this case, it might be said that tradition both hindered and created agency. Perhaps by creating an alternative, I created a space to engage with others. As I presented situations which did not meet another's expectations of a band teacher, program, or classroom, I created a predicament which could very easily lead to dialogue, with administrators, colleagues, parents, students. Through that engagement and hopeful dialogue, I provided the possibility of acceptance by others. As Butler (1999) might argue, willingly calling into question societal or professional norms, and proposing an alternative in itself is a subversion of the status quo or the dominant culture, and is an example of agency. As other alternatives became valid options through dialogue, I have in a sense created a new accepted alternative, amidst and among the hierarchies of which Foucault (1979) writes.

While traditions and norms still exist, it is nihilistic to believe that one can never move beyond them, but also unrealistic to believe that a progressive alternative could replace and remove those norms. What I found through my experience is that the creation of an alternative provides the possibility to not only call into question those norms, but to engage in dialogue about what other options might exist, and broaden the possibilities of what is seen as acceptable and possible.

Interestingly, this hopeful look at agency in the classroom brings the discussion back to my self-described, progressive identity. As I positioned myself as a minority in the field, as one who was hoping to push the greater field in a new direction, I was also ultimately seeking acceptance. This identity of un-acceptance, of being on the progressive edge of music education, propelled me forward in transforming my practice, yet I wished to have my practice then accepted by those in the field who may not have thought beyond the tradition. My identity existed in tension with itself. As a progressive, I ultimately desired to have my vision validated and accepted by those that I resisted, in order to create new possibility. My experience of agency involved the balancing of these identities, as I negotiated the tension of creating new alternatives and finding a place for them among tradition.

REFERENCES

Allsup, R. E. (2002). *Crossing over: Mutual learning and democratic action in instrumental music education*. Unpublished doctoral dissertation, Teachers College, Columbia University, New York.

Allsup, R. E. (2004). Imagining possibilities in a global world: Music, learning and rapid change. *Music Education Research 6*(2), 179-190.

Barone, T. (2006). Making educational history: Qualitative inquiry, artistry and the public interest. In G. Ladson-Billings & W. F. Tate (Eds.), *Education Research in the Public Interest: Social justice, action, and policy* (pp. 213-230). New York: Teachers College Press.

Berger, J. (2003). *Ways of seeing*. New York: Penguin. (Original work published 1977)

Berube, M. R. (1994). *American school reform: Progressive, equity and excellence movement 1881-1993*. Westport, CT: Greenwood Press.

Bourdieu, P. (1977). *Outline of a theory of practice*. Cambridge, England: University Press.

Bush, G. (2006). *President's letter on the American Competitiveness Initiative*. Retrieved July 24, 2006, from http://www.whitehouse.gov/stateoftheunion/2006/aci/index.html

Butler, J. (1999). *Gender trouble: Feminism and the subversion of identity* (10th anniversary edition). New York: Routledge.

Casey, K. (1995). The new narrative research in education. *Review of research in education, 21*, 211-253.

Chase, S. E. (2005). Narrative inquiry: Multiple lenses, approaches, voices. In N. K. Denzin & Y. S. Lincoln (Eds.), *The SAGE handbook of qualitative research* (3rd ed., pp. 651-679) New York: SAGE.

Clandinin, D. J., & Connelly, F. M. (2000). *Narrative inquiry: Experience and story in qualitative research*. San Francisco: Jossey-Bass.

Cuban, L. (1993). *How teachers taught: Constancy and change in American classrooms 1880-1990* (2nd ed.) New York: Teachers College Press.

Dewey, J. (1944). *Democracy and education*. New York: Simon & Schuster.

DuBois, W. E. B. (2005). *The souls of Black folk*. New York: Simon & Schuster. (Original work published 1903)

Folkestad, G. (2006). Formal and informal learning situations or practices vs. formal and informal ways of learning. *British Journal of Music Education, 23*(2), 135-145.

Foucault, M. (1979). *Discipline and punish*. New York: Vintage Books.

Foucault, M. (1984). What is enlightenment? In P. Rabinow (Ed.), *The Foucault Reader* (pp. 32-50). New York: Pantheon Books.

Foucault, M. (1990). *The history of sexuality: An introduction* (Vol. 1). New York: Vintage Books.

Green, L. (2002). *How popular musicians learn: A way ahead for music education*. London, England: Ashgate.

Greene, M. (1986). In search of critical pedagogy. *Harvard Educational Review, 56*(4), 427-441.

Honderich, T. (Ed.). (1995). *The Oxford companion to philosophy*. Oxford, England: Oxford University Press.

Jorgensen, E. R. (2003). *Transforming music education*. Bloomington, IN: Indiana University Press.

Kopelson, K. L. (2002). *Teaching trouble: Performativity and composition pedagogy-composing connections* Doctoral dissertation, Purdue University, Indiana.

Lovell, T. (2000). Thinking feminism with and against Bourdieu. *Feminist Theory, 1*(1), 11-32.

No Child Left Behind Act of 2001, Pub. L. No. 107-110 (2002).

Personal Narratives Group. (Eds). (1989). *Interpreting women's lives: Feminist theory and personal narratives*. Bloomington, IN: Indiana University Press.

Reimer, B. (2003). *A philosophy of music education* (3rd ed.). Englewood Cliffs: Prentice Hall.

Riessman, C. K. (1993). *Narrative analysis*. Thousand Oaks, CA: SAGE.

Stalhammar, B. (2003). Music teaching and young people's own musical experience. *Music Education Research*, *5*(1), 61-68.

Thiessen, D., & Barrett, J. R. (2002). Reform-minded music teachers: A more comprehensive image of teaching for music teacher education. In R. Colwell & C. Richardson (Eds.), *The New Handbook of Research on Music Teaching and Learning* (pp. 759-785). Oxford, England: Oxford University Press.

Weedon, C. (1997). *Feminist practice & poststructuralist theory* (2nd ed.). Malden, MA: Blackwell.

Weiler, K. (1991). Freire and a feminist pedagogy of difference. *Harvard Educational Review, 61*(4), 449-474.

Witherell, C., & Noddings, N. (Eds.). (1991). *Stories lives tell: Narrative and dialogue in education*. New York: Teachers College Press.

CHAPTER 6

TEACHING IN AN UNFORGIVING PRESENT FOR THE UNKNOWABLE FUTURE

Multicultural Human Subjectivity, Antiracism Pedagogy and Music Education

Deborah Bradley

ABSTRACT

This paper describes a critical ethnographic study conducted with members of a community youth choir in Mississauga, Ontario, Canada. Interviews with choristers suggest that a world choral music repertoire taught within an antiracism pedagogy may contribute to an emerging sense of self-understanding referred to herein as *multicultural human subjectivity*. This theoretical construct derives from a cosmopolitan sociology that suggests globalization impacts the moral life worlds of individuals, significantly transforming everyday consciousness in communities such as Mississauga that are marked by transnationality and cultural hybridity. Choir members' descriptions of a concert before an international audience provide evidence

Diverse Methodologies in the Study of Music Teaching and Learning, pp. 111–136

of emerging multicultural human subjectivity. For some students, however, such musical experiences reify stereotypes or reiterate rigid concepts of identity. The paper argues for an antiracism approach to multicultural music education to counter liberal multiculturalism's tendencies to reiterate power relations and stereotypical notions of the other.

INTRODUCTION

This paper describes a critical ethnographic research study of the Mississauga Festival Youth Choir (MFYC), a community youth organization for children aged 9 to 19, located in a racially and ethnically diverse Canadian city. The study seeks to bring to light the ways in which an antiracism music education, taught in an unforgiving present—a time in which racial constructs and racism remain deeply embedded within society and in the education systems produced by those societies—may influence the unknowable future. Britzman's (1998) assertion that "learning occurs in belated time" (p. 26) suggests that what we teach today may only become part of students' meaning-making much later, perhaps when some event provides a rich context for the knowledge. My interest in this unknowable future stems from a curiosity about how our practices of multicultural music education may influence students' self-understanding. I questioned how engaging with music of many cultures might bring meaning to other experiences students have beyond the choral rehearsal, experiences that also influence how they understand themselves and others. Because students do not enter the choir rehearsal as "empty vessels," I wanted in the research to acknowledge that discourses of globalization, official multiculturalism in Canada, and antiracism pedagogy may also influence students' self-understandings towards the disposition I have termed *multicultural human subjectivity.*[1]

The abstraction, multicultural human subjectivity, suggests a potential outcome of the intersection of antiracism pedagogy (critical multiculturalism) in music education with those discourses influencing the social complex or habitus (Bourdieu, 1977) in which education takes place. Multicultural human subjectivity within this paper is posited as a form of self-understanding (Brubaker & Cooper, 2000) rather than as a political or cultural identification, that may emerge in locations characterized by transnational populations, cultural heterogeneity, and cultural hybridity—sites where antiracism pedagogy and praxis offer significant and uniquely powerful opportunities for students to develop self-understanding through other-understanding.

This paper is drawn from my doctoral dissertation (Bradley, 2006). The following research questions framed this large study: (a) How does the global song with which the MFYC engages enable choir members to locate themselves in the world, and what type of selves in relation to others do they create as a result; (b) how, if at all, does engaging in global song within MFYC's antiracism, multicultural choral music education praxis, contribute to the possibility for an emergent, socially and discursively constituted "multicultural human subjectivity?" and (c) how might multicultural human subjectivity emerge within the particular context of the MFYC in relation to the performativity of that context? The data and findings presented herein derive primarily from questions two and three, and relate to the intersections of world music (global song), antiracism pedagogy, and various performative discourses that influence the way students understand themselves and the world around them.

Discursive Framework for Multicultural Human Subjectivity

Official Multiculturalism

Canadian education, including that in community education settings such as the MFYC, is strongly influenced by *official multiculturalism*, the political doctrine first established in 1972 and signed into federal law in 1988. The policy promotes cultural diversity as an intrinsic part of the social, moral, and political order of the nation (Dei, 2000, p. 21). While a complete history of how multiculturalism came to be official policy in Canada is beyond the scope of this paper, it is important to note that multiculturalism has become entrenched as ideology in the national imaginary of what it means to be Canadian. Dei and others (Bannerji, 2000; Mackey, 2002), have critiqued official multiculturalism for its failure to disrupt systemic racism in Canada, and for the ways ethnic and cultural groups are reified as discrete entities despite the realities of Canada's cultural hybridity. Mackey writes that although multiculturalism differs greatly from the overt racism and assimilationist policies of earlier Canadian governments, it evolved from patterns that became entrenched during colonial times and earlier national projects. Even as cultural diversity was allowed to proliferate under policies of official multiculturalism, the power to "define, limit and tolerate differences still lies in the hands of the dominant group. Further, the degree and forms of *tolerable* differences are defined by the ever-changing needs of the project of nation-building" (Mackey, 2002, p. 70, italics in original).

Multicultural Music Education and Global Song

The need to recognize difference in North American education probably began in the early twentieth century with the work of scholars

W. E. B. DuBois and Carter G. Woodson, and gathered more interest in the 1940s as a way to reduce prejudice. It gained greater momentum during the 1960s Civil Rights movement, and eventually led to the metadiscipline we now refer to as multicultural education (Campbell, 2002). This metadiscipline has been formulated, however, "from a variety of constituencies, and its principles have been sometimes vague and its policies multifarious" (p. 28). Multiculturalism within music education is likewise a somewhat amorphous concept, meaning different things to different practitioners. Some practitioners seek to separate the locally "multicultural" from global or international education. In my own choral praxis, I consider all music other than western art music to be a form of *global song*, a concept I will address shortly.

Current music education discourse suggests that one purpose for multicultural and/or global music education is to "develop in students an understanding of the cultural thought and practices of populations across the globe" (Campbell, 2002, p. 28). While this goal is important, "understanding" does not automatically guarantee acceptance of difference, nor does it challenge hierarchical value systems against which the diverse musical cultures outside of the canon are judged. As Campbell argues, too few students really know music for its global and cross-cultural manifestations, an understanding that develops only by discarding "the west is best" perspective (Campbell, 2004, p. xvi). In addition, multicultural music education discourses frequently utilize language that frames cultures as monolithic, static entities, rather than "dynamic, productive, and generative material and immaterial practices" (McCarthy, Crichlow, Dimitriadis, & Dolby, 2005, p. xix).

The term *global song* describes the choral repertoire of the MFYC. Global song acknowledges that culture is dynamic, productive, and generative. The term also acknowledges the fusion of musical practices from around the world with the predominantly European notion of "choir" and "choral music." The choir's repertoire de-centers the Western canon to provide students with opportunities to come to know a wide range of musics for their global and cross-cultural manifestations. MFYC's multicultural repertoire includes music from aural traditions, taught aurally with respect to the practices of its originators. Many of the published choral arrangements in our repertoire, however, utilize rhythms, melodies, and harmonies representing musical cultures from around the world, notated as choral arrangements for which the teaching-learning process is dependent upon western notation. Occasionally, characteristics from several musical cultures are incorporated into a single choral arrangement, a musical enactment of the hybridity characteristic of globalization. While one might argue that such music does not "authentically" represent the musical cultures involved, my position is that such arrangements function as cultural entanglements, or those cultural formations marked by multiple intersections of engagement in the absence of a single or unique location of origin (Hesse, 2000, p. 22). I use the term global song (rather than "world music") to acknowledge the hybridity and creolization that multicultural choral music education represents, even as official educational discourses often invoke museum perspectives of discreet, static, "other" cultures.

Antiracism as Counternarrative to Multiculturalism

Multiculturalism is a dominant ideology that to date has done little to disrupt systemic racism in Canada or within educational systems. In fact, the policy is utilized in ways that mask racist practices, thus allowing most Canadians the illusion that they live in a relatively nonracist country (Bedard, 2000, p. 43). This does not mean that Canada's multicultural policies have been completely ineffective, however, and later in this paper I provide evidence that the discourse may contribute as a catalyst for change. Multiculturalism, though, in both governmental and educational policy, operates on the notion of "traditional" cultures that are monolithic and static, slipping into the cultural discourse of tradition versus modernity. In this slippage, color signals "traditional cultures, in a constellation of invented traditions" (Bannerji, 2000, p. 33).

Because multiculturalism has become part of the dominant ideology in Canada and in many school systems across North America, I believe antiracism, sometimes referred to as *critical multiculturalism*,[2] offers greater promise for change. The term *antiracism* makes an important distinction between liberal ideologies and critical theories of multiculturalism. Liberal multiculturalism works on the notion of human commonalities and simultaneously downplays human differences, leading to the erasure of difference or color-blindness, a perspective that minimizes the material realities of racism in North America. In contrast, antiracism

> shifts the talk away from tolerance of diversity to the pointed notion of dif-
> ference and power. It sees race and racism as central to how we claim,
> occupy and defend spaces. The task of antiracism is to identify, challenge
> and change the values, structures and behaviors that perpetuate systemic
> racism and other forms of societal oppressions (gender, class, ability, and so
> forth). (Dei, 2000, p. 21)

Challenging structures and behaviors includes acknowledging that singular, identifiable cultures are increasingly "elusive" (Yon, 2000), particularly in transnational spaces such as Mississauga, Canada, and wherever the local population embodies global migration. Therefore, the concept of multicultural human subjectivity posits a different way for thinking of the self. It acknowledges shared human commonalities but resists unitary identities articulated as race, ethnicity, nationality, gender, ableism, and heterosexism. Multicultural human subjectivity is an abstraction useful for questioning "how identities continue to be produced, embodied and performed, effectively, passionately, and with social and political consequence" (Bell, 1999, p. 2).

Musicking

Christopher Small's (1998) concept of *musicking*, which he defines as "to take part, in any capacity, in a musical performance, whether by performing, by listening, or by rehearsing or practicing, by providing material for performance (what is called composing), or by dancing" (p. 9), provides the entry point for a question this study likewise seeks to illuminate about musical performances: "*What's really going on here?*" (p. 10, italics in original). As he argues, the act of musicking stands as a metaphor for ideal relationships as the participants in the performance imagine those to be. It is in those relationships that the meaning of the act resides. The ideal relationships created through musicking—between people, between individuals and society, and between humanity and the natural world—are, as Small puts it, "perhaps the most important in human life" (p. 13). My research sought to illuminate how, in the context of performing global song within a community marked by transnationality and cultural heterogeneity, multicultural human subjectivity might emerge as a metaphor for ideal relationships.

Performativity

In *Performativity and Belonging*, Bell (1999) posits identity as related to theories of "the subject," and that investigations into identity require that attention be turned to "the production of selves as effects" (p. 1). In this she calls upon Foucault's notion of the subject as the product of discourse (Foucault, 1970, p. xiii). The discourses implicating multicultural human subjectivity are dynamic and fluid; thus multicultural human subjectivity as discursive product is always in flux and continually emerging. Brubaker and Cooper's (2000) concept of "situated subjectivity" (p. 17) is useful here as well, given the particularity of this study of one community group situated in racially and ethnically diverse Mississauga, Canada.

From a performative viewpoint, the term multicultural human subjectivity acknowledges that there are multiple understandings through which we may "perform ourselves" in response to discourses of race, ethnicity, nationality, gender, and so forth. These discourses along with others (family or religious discourses, and so forth) wield subtle, sometimes unconscious influences on an individual's self-understanding. Like Christopher Small, I believe that "something is going on" within transnational, glocalized[3] (Robertson, 1992) communities affecting how individuals understand themselves. Thus multicultural human subjectivity refers to an individual-level sense of identity as self-understanding, influenced by the multiple discourses at work both locally and beyond the immediate community. From this perspective, multicultural human subjectivity suggests resistance to the oppressions articulated through socially and discursively constructed, over-determined concepts of race, ethnicity, nation, gender, ability, and so forth. The term also acknowledges the fluidity and dynamism of boundaries as discursive concepts that result in continually shifting understandings of what it means to be human. My concept for multicultural human subjectivity borrows from Britzman's (1998) stated interest in education practices that "unhinge the normal from the self" as a way to prepare the self to encounter its own conditions of alterity. While Britzman refers specifically to reading practices, I think multicultural music education may similarly provide

> an imaginary site for multiplying alternative forms of identifications and pleasures not so closely affixed to—but nonetheless transforming—what one imagines their identity imperatives to be. Then pedagogy may be conceived ... as a technique for acknowledging difference *as the only condition of possibility for community.* (pp. 85-86, italics in original)

Along this line of thought, multicultural human subjectivity emerges as a way for individuals to think of themselves as members of a community where difference is their common bond.

Cosmopolitanism

Walcott (2003) writes that "local cultures beget expansive questions" (p. 26); DeNora (2000) argues that it "is probably impossible to speak of music's 'powers' abstracted from their contexts of use" (p. x). These perspectives suggest that music education research needs to explicate the social contexts within which the research takes place. The study in question argues that potential for multicultural human subjectivity depends upon the performativity (Butler, 1990) of the *habitus* (Bourdieu, 1977) within which individuals live; thus to focus only on the immediate music rehearsal context of MFYC to the exclusion of wider social conditions misses the point that music is a performative social phenomenon within a particular habitus. Tastsoglou (2000) writes that it is crucial for educators to have well-grounded understandings of the borders and the intersections of the large social structures likely to be encountered in the classroom (pp. 98-99). The discourse of official multiculturalism in Canada influences these larger social structures, interacting with antiracism pedagogy within the context of MFYC rehearsals and performances. Multiculturalism as official government policy in Canada usually finds support among those who are also influenced by discourses of cosmopolitanism. These two discourses may work in tandem within the local habitus, which I argue, is performative in constituting the self-understandings of individual MFYC members.

Cosmopolitanism is a complex concept, and space here does not permit a detailed exploration of the term's lengthy history and various nuanced connotations; however, my use of the term in this paper relates it to the economic and social conditions of globalization and glocalization (Robertson, 1992). Glocalization, or what Beck (2002) calls *cosmopolitanization*, is an internal globalization that "transforms everyday consciousness and identities significantly. Issues of global concern become part of the everyday local experiences and the 'moral life-worlds' of the people" (p. 17). Roudometof (2005) posits that individuals living in transnational, glocalized communities can adopt either open, encompassing attitudes, or closed, defensive postures (p. 121). Open and encompassing attitudes are characteristic of and necessary for emerging multicultural human subjectivity within specific musical contexts.

For purposes of this paper, *cosmopolitanism* as discursive framework indicates an outward-looking, interculturally sensitive moral and ethical standpoint whose corollary is glocalization (cosmopolitanization), a process that transforms everyday consciousness and identities by bringing global concerns into the moral life-worlds of individuals. When this occurs, multicultural human subjectivity may be constituted through particular musical experiences. Multicultural human subjectivity within this framework shares conceptual terrain with various "post-race" discourses; that is, "planetary humanity" (Gilroy, 2000), "color-blind future" (Williams, 1997), and "human solidarity" (Rorty, 1989). As a White, middle-class female academic, I am cognizant of the tenuous position in which I place myself by drawing upon post-race theory, as it could easily be misconstrued as an ideology of Whiteness. However, post-race perspectives do not deny the impact of racialization and racism, and despite Williams' use of the term *color-blind*, do not promote the color-blind perspectives typically employed within educational discourses. Rather, post-race perspectives acknowledge the injury created by what Gilroy (2000) refers to as *raciology*, or the lore that brings the damaging impact of race as virtual reality to life (p. 11). Within a post-race outlook, "it is important to ask what critical perspectives might nurture the ability and the desire to live with difference on an increasingly divided but also convergent planet" (Gilroy, 2004, p. 3). It is my belief that antiracism, as a form of critical pedagogy, offers the sort of critical perspective that may nurture not only the ability, but also the desire to live with difference. When antiracism is integral to music education practice, it may be particularly potent as a pedagogy for nurturing such desire. Multicultural human subjectivity, then, offers a possibility for not only accepting difference, but living with it in ways that enrich us all.

The cumulative effect of official multicultural policies in Canada, cosmopolitanism and globalization as influencing discourses, and an antiracism pedagogy guiding learning and performing global song, suggests the potential for a space from which multicultural human subjectivity may emerge. Figure 6.1 depicts the relationships between these spheres of discourses, showing where their intersections may allow

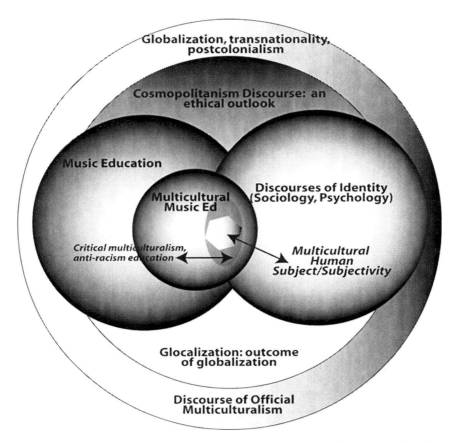

Figure 6.1.   Social Complex of Mississauga and Discursive Spheres: Locating the Potential for Emerging Multicultural Human Subjectivity.

for an emerging multicultural human subjectivity within the rehearsal context of the MFYC.

Design of the Study

Location

The study took place in Mississauga, Ontario, Canada, a community characterized by transnationality and cultural hybridity. Mississauga, the sixth largest city in Canada, bordered by Toronto to the east and Lake Ontario to the south, is the fastest growing major city in Canada. According to the 2001 Canada Census, Mississauga's population was 612,925. Current road signs (in 2007) marking the city boundaries cite the population as 704,000. Residents of Mississauga represent cultures from around the world.[4] The 2001 census revealed that over 40% of Mississauga's population consider themselves to be other than racially White; Statistics Canada projects that by the year 2017, people of color will be the majority population in Mississauga and the greater Toronto area. Cultural diversity and cultural hybridity form the lived realities of most students in Mississauga.

Mississauga is predominantly suburban, with a growing downtown core of high-rise offices and residences. As the busiest entry point for new immigrants who settle in the local area, it is perhaps the most diverse city in Canada. As of 2001, the "visible minority" (non-White)[5] population of Mississauga comprised 40.32% of the total. Fifty-two percent of Mississauga's current population was born in Canada. Of the 48% of Mississauga's total population who immigrated to Canada, 40% of those did so between 1991 and 2001.

Another statistics Canada table on religion also speaks to the diversity of the local population. This table names nine distinct religions represented in Mississauga: Catholic, Protestant, Christian Orthodox, Christian not included elsewhere, Muslim, Jewish, Buddhist, Hindu, Sikh, and two amalgam descriptions, "Eastern religions" and "Other religions." Thirty-six percent of the population claimed an affiliation with a religion other than Christianity.

According to the Mississauga Economic Development Office Web site,[6] in 2004, 54.5% of Mississauga's population claimed English as their first language; French speakers made up 1.3% of the total. The balance represents a wide range of "mother tongues." The Web site offers the following annotation to the statistics: (a) *Mother tongue* is defined as the first language learned at home in childhood and still understood by the individual at the time of the census; (b) Mississauga has a diversity of linguistics and a high degree of integration without any one dominant minority language; (c) Persons whose mother tongue is other than English or French make up 17.6% of Canada's total population, 39.0% of Toronto's population, and 41.8% of Mississauga's population.

Items (b) and (c) hint at an interesting aspect of life in Mississauga. Unlike Toronto and some other major Canadian cities, Mississauga's diverse population groups tend to integrate within neighborhoods rather than settle into ethnic enclaves. This has led to great diversity in most of Mississauga's public schools, and within the MFYC membership. Many members of the MFYC, therefore, come to the choir with a considerable amount of knowledge and experience with persons of different religions, ethnicities, and first languages.

Participants and Recruitment

At the time of the study, the MFYC was comprised of two instructional levels: Level I was designated for beginning singers in Grades 4, 5, and 6, and Level II was for singers in Grades 7 and higher. Both levels of the MFYC were racially and ethnically diverse, and as a result, the choir frequently received invitations to perform for events seeking to "celebrate diversity." Because the questions involved in this research required that participants be able to articulate answers about their developing sense of self, only members of the Level II division of the MFYC were invited to participate in the study.

In order to determine how global song in the context of an antiracism pedagogy may function to constitute multicultural human subjectivity, I wanted to interview enough Level II choir members to capture the potential range of viewpoints. My supervisor and I determined that twenty interviews would provide a representative sampling of Level II choir members' voices. An initial informal recruitment letter was sent to the parents or guardians of all 45 members of the Level II choir and to the choir members. I had initially planned to do a random draw to determine the final participants if the response to the informal recruitment letter exceeded 20 potential interview candidates. This proved unnecessary, as only 21 students replied indicating their willingness to take part in the study. A formal information letter was then sent to these 21 choir members and their parents to determine willingness to participate in the study. One choir member subsequently elected not to proceed with the project and withdrew. There were no further withdrawals from the pool of potential participants, and all twenty[7] of these choir members took part in the study.

It is important to acknowledge here that some MFYC members may have joined the choir because of its reputation for performing world music, or because of its visible racial and ethnic diversity. Thus the participants in this study were to some degree self-selecting. The study sought to recognize the insidious and pervasive ways in which globalized and transnational cultural artifacts influence our lives in North America, consciously and unconsciously predisposing some of us to the malleability of identity formation. Some of the participants in this study, therefore, may have already been open to the possibilities of multicultural reformation as a central aspect of who they are, while others may not have been so insightful about their identity constitution. For the latter, joining a choir such as the MFYC would have held potential for a significant life transforming experience. For those who already had some understanding of the way discourses work to constitute identities, MFYC membership reinforced possibilities for multicultural reformation. In making this statement, I want to reiterate that my intent is not to imply that multicultural human subjectivity is possible only within the context of MFYC, but rather to posit the MFYC context as one possible site for its emergence.

Table 6.1 lists the participants (by their self-chosen pseudonyms), their ages, countries of birth as well as their parents' birthplaces, the number of years they had sung with MFYC at the time of the study, and the terminology each used to describe themselves ethnically or nationally.

Mode of Inquiry: Critical Ethnography

While the primary focus for this paper is the theoretical construct *multicultural human subjectivity* as a form of self-understanding, it is important to note how the research supported this concept. Critical ethnography guided the collection of data and its analysis. Critical theorists question the assumption that societies such as the United States, Canada, Great Britain, and others are unproblematically democratic, instead recognizing that individuals in these societies have become "acculturated to feel comfort in relations of domination and subordination" (Kincheloe & McLaren, 2000, p. 281). Their research interests seek to disrupt or change this inequitable power relationship. Critical theorists work within the premise that individual social and historical forces profoundly influence individuals' understandings of self and the world. One goal of critical ethnography, therefore, is to "rethink subjectivity itself as a permanently unclosed, always partial narrative engagement with text and context" (p. 301), and for this reason is an appropriate methodology to research the theoretical concept of multicultural human subjectivity. My choice of this methodology follows from Britzman's (2000) assertion that:

> Ethnographic narratives should trace how power circulates and surprises, theorize how subjects spring from the discourses that incite them, and question the belief in representation even as one must practice

Table 6.1.   MFYC Participants in the Study

Name	Sex	Age	Year in MFYC	Country of Birth	Parents' Country of Birth	Self-Identity Terminology
Aileen	F	16	4	Canada	Philippines and Canada	Filipino-Austrian-German-British
AJ	F	17	6	Canada	Canada	Canadian-Scottish
Alicia	F	14	3	Canada	Jamaica	Jamaican-Canadian "but probably just Canadian"
Ally	F	12	1	Canada	United States and Canada	Canadian—wasn't sure
Amber	F	15	4	Canada	Canada and United States	Canadian and Norwegian
Diana	F	16	3	Canada	Canada	Celtic
Dominique	F	14	2	Canada	Trinidad and Barbados	French
Emily	F	15	1	Canada	Canada	Ukrainian-Canadian
JoAnne	F	15	4	United States	United States and Italy	Mixed: Italian, American, French, Polish
Kate	F	16	7	United Arab Emirates	Sri Lanka	Singhalese (Sri Lankan)-Canadian
Katrina	F	10	1	Canada	United States and Germany	Canadian-American-German
Kristen	F	14	5	Canada	Philippines and Canada	Filipino-Austrian-German-British
Lauren	F	16	1	Canada	Canada	Italian-French but "just Canadian"
Madison	F	13	3	India	India	Indian-Canadian
Michelle	F	17	4	Canada	Canada	Canadian
Raka	M	14	4	Canada	Canada	Canadian-Scottish-Irish
Renée	F	13	4	Canada	Canada and Italy	Italian-Canadian
Ricky	M	19	6	Canada	Trinidad and Jamaica	Canadian-Trinidadian-Jamaican
Roxy	F	15	3	Canada	Canada	Canadian-Irish-Spanish
Stefanie	F	13	1	Canada	Uruguay	Spanish (Uruguay)

representation as a way to intervene critically in the constitutive constraints of discourses. (p. 38)

My research into an emerging multicultural human subjectivity is likewise an attempt to theorize how subjects spring from discourses, in this case from official multiculturalism in Canada, from discourses of cosmopolitanism and globalization, and from antiracism pedagogy as it frames and informs the MFYC rehearsal context. As an intervention into constitutive constraints of discourse, critical ethnography seeks to bring to participants' consciousness how cultural identities are represented within multicultural discourse, enabling them to question those representations that may be overdetermined.

Data Sources and Analysis

Data for this study consists of videotaped interviews with 20 Level II choir members ranging in age from 10 to 19. These interviews occurred between February and April 2004. Other data sources include a reflexive journal of my teaching and research maintained for the duration of the study (Aug. 2003-June 2004), and video recordings of the choir's public performances. In addition, a focus group of five senior choir members[8] was selected. All interviews and the two focus group meetings were fully transcribed and coded with themes that emerged from the interviews, using the QDA (qualitative data analysis) software program HyperResearch. Theme codes were not predetermined but were drawn from the language employed by choir members during the interviews. The first five interviews I transcribed served to establish a list of 122 codes, by which all remaining interviews were coded. I reexamined those five interviews to ensure that similar types of statements made by different participants were coded consistently. The codes were analyzed and supported the development of a grounded theory of multicultural human subjectivity. The focus group met twice over the course of the study to discuss my interpretation of the findings, and to offer their input into that interpretation, consistent with the concepts of face validity and reciprocity within critical ethnography.

Face Validity and Reciprocity

Negotiating the meaning of data resonates with Britzman's (2000) call for ethnography to trace the circulation of power, and suggests the need for what Lather (1986) has termed *face validity*. Face validity is achieved by going back to the research participants with data and tentative results, to allow them the opportunity to participate in the interpretation of the data, or to question the researcher's conclusions. Such negotiation of meaning between the researcher and the participants results in a text that provides "a click of recognition and a yes, of course, instead of a yes, but experience" (p. 271).

Lather (1991) also identifies *reciprocity* as an important characteristic of critical ethnography. Reciprocity operates at "the juncture between researcher and researched and between data and theory" (p. 263). In this juncture, the researcher uses the research to help participants understand and change their situation through an approach of collaborative interviewing and interactive research. Lather asserts that the goal of critical research is to encourage self-reflection and deeper understanding on the part of the persons being researched (p. 266). It calls for "empowering approaches to research where both researcher and researched become, in the words of feminist singer-poet, Cris Williamson, 'the changer and the changed' " (p. 56). This requires that participants in the research be involved in the negotiation of meaning or interpretation of the descriptive data or the construction of empirically grounded theory (p. 58). Reciprocity in this sense contributes to collaborative texts that lead to "sharing privilege, sharing literacy, sharing information—which in our world is power" (Behar, 1995, p. 263).

Because I was the artistic director for MFYC at the time of the study, reciprocity provided a process through which to minimize the inherent power imbalance between the researcher and the researched. Throughout the project, reciprocity was ongoing: the focus group of five senior members of the choir had input into the interview questions before they were finalized. Their suggestions helped ensure that all the participants could understand the language of the interview questions. All participants (some with help from their parents) reviewed and approved the transcripts of their own interviews. The approval process enabled participants to restate any responses that they felt did not accurately represent their thoughts, and some of the older participants took advantage of this opportunity. In general, though, most participants approved their transcripts without requesting changes. The focus group met twice to discuss themes emerging from the interview transcripts and offered their suggestions for interpreting data as it related to the concept of multicultural human subjectivity. They also reviewed a draft of the penultimate chapter of the dissertation, which was based upon those themes. The meetings provided an opportunity to share information and to further discuss the implications of the research for them as individuals and for the choir as a whole. As Lather (1986) writes, an interactive approach to research invites reciprocal reflexivity and critique, which guard against the "central dangers to praxis-oriented empirical work: imposition and reification on the part of the researcher" (p. 265).

Evidence of the Potential for Emerging Multicultural Human Subjectivity

According to Butler, performativity operates through the "reiterative power of discourse to produce the phenomena that it regulates and constrains" (Butler, 1993, p. 2). While discourses of official multiculturalism, cosmopolitanism, and antiracism pedagogy predispose some individuals to the potential for emerging multicultural human subjectivity, musical performances may in particular circumstances produce it, or appear to do so. For example, in August 2003, MFYC performed for the Prison Fellowship International (PFI) Quadrennial Convocation held in Toronto. The audience numbered nearly 1,000 people representing over 180 countries. Many of the convocation delegates were former political prisoners, including some from South Africa who had been imprisoned under apartheid. MFYC's performance for PFI included two South African freedom songs. Our rehearsal preparation for this performance included discussions of apartheid in South Africa, the struggle against it, and the role of the freedom songs in that struggle. When we began to sing the second of the freedom songs at the PFI concert ("Haleluya! Pelo Tsa Rona"), the entire South African delegation jumped to their feet and sang and danced along with us. The energy of this moment spread throughout the audience, who by the end of the song were also taking an active part in our performance.

The moment was so powerful that most of the choir members who were involved in this performance raised it voluntarily during their interviews several months later as their "most meaningful choir experience." For example, fifteen-year old Amber[9] described the moment in such a way that it appears to have been transformative for her:

Amber: The Prison Fellowship—I always go back to that. I loved that—I loved seeing people who knew it (the song)—that was so cool. Now I want to go to like Ghana and do Bobobo and everyone will know it—that would be so cool…. And they just started cheering and they got up dancing, and it felt *very powerful*, because they knew what it was, and we knew what it was. Like we're so used to our parents going, "oh, that was an interesting, fun piece" but they don't understand—but this was like—they are dancing and we know the dance! It was so cool! I can't really describe it but it was like that barrier was just gone (Interview, March 29, 2004).

Singing "Haleluya! Pelo Tsa Rona" created an epiphany moment for Amber with a profound depth of understanding. Her exclamation, "they knew what it was and we knew what it was!" suggests to me that this was a moment of recognition that transcended race, ethnicity, and nationality. Gilroy (1993) argues in *The Black Atlantic* that these moments of recognition, "produced in the intimate interaction of performer and crowd," are actually signifying practices mediated through the body. In Gilroy's argument, this musical recognition produces "the imaginary effect of an internal racial core of essence" (p. 102). I would like to co-opt Gilroy's argument for my purposes here. Although I, too, reject notions of essential internal cores, racial or otherwise, is it not possible that in Amber's moment of recognition, she realized a possibility for emerging multicultural human subjectivity, where despite discourses of race, ethnicity, and nation, there was, at least briefly, only humanity? In that particular space, for those two minutes as MFYC sang Haleluya! Pelo Tsa Rona, it seemed as though such barriers truly were gone—that briefly we experienced multicultural human subjectivity.

Other choir members also described this sense of recognition that occurred as MFYC sang at the PFI event. Some offered emotional accounts of how the moment affected them:

> Kate: Yes! And all the Africans started dancing as we sang—because I think they hadn't heard it ("Haleluyah! Pelo Tsa Rona") since they left…. And they were *so* happy … it was amazing to see their faces just light up—and even the people around them—they didn't know what was going on but they were happy to see these people happy—and I think—well, myself and another girl, we were both talking about it for *days* afterwards, how they were just (puts her hands to her face in a gesture that implied a sort of joyous radiance but adds no words).
>
> D: Yes, that was a pretty special moment, I think, for all of us.
>
> Kate: It was a really big moment. I think we weren't expecting that—we were definitely not expecting that (Interview, February 8, 2004).

Raka's narrative of the same event is perhaps less poetic than Amber's or Kate's; at the time of the interview he was 14 years old and tended to offer two or three word answers to the open-ended interview questions. His description of the PFI event, however, speaks to the impact this moment had on him as a moment of realization, the flash of recognition that the song was "real" and carried meaning for "real people:"

Raka: I nearly broke down in tears because nobody ever does that at our concerts, and it just made me very very happy—them doing that.

D: What did you think about the people in the audience who were doing the dancing and the cheering?

Raka: I thought that they were very joyous because … they were all smiling and happy—they all definitely recognized the song!… I just basically thought—wow! They recognize this song! (Interview, March 20, 2004).

Counternarratives: Reiterating Stereotypes and the Construction of Racial Identity

The foregoing descriptions of the PFI event suggest that in this particular performance, a new sense of self-understanding developed, indicative of the potential for multicultural human subjectivity to resist oppressions articulated as categories of race, ethnicity, gender, and so forth. The sense of mutual recognition described by many choir members suggests one of the ways that multicultural human subjectivity might emerge in particularly powerful musical moments. For some individuals, however, these same musical moments may reify stereotypes, and there were examples of such reification in the interviews. For example, Diana, a 16-year-old who had been a member of the choir for 3 years, and who was on stage at the PFI concert, indicates in that her experiences learning and performing various African musics with MFYC may have reinforced preexisting stereotypes:

Diana: I could tell that Africans were a more primal society than a sophisticated society like Victorian, because I can hear that in the music. Like when I hear the Bobobo stuff—it's the kind of thing that makes everyone in the audience want to sing right along, even if they don't know the words. But in a sophisticated society, like with Mozart and stuff, people in the audience will just go quiet and listen to it. I personally think music from a sophisticated society is like—it's more the music you listen to, you don't sing to. Whereas societies like West Africa, Ghana, that kind of thing, the songs they make up—they are meant to be sung by everyone. They're meant to be shared by the whole gathering (Interview, April 6, 2004).

Diana's comments show interesting insight into the benefits of performing world music as a way to encourage understanding across cultures. She has captured a glimpse of one purpose of music in Ghanaian culture and contrasted that with her experiences listening to Mozart. However, her choice of the terms "primal" and "sophisticated" makes me squirm. Even though Diana also took part in the PFI concert, and as a 3-year choir member had twice been involved in intensive study of West African music, the imagined cultural narrative (Frith, 1996) that she constructed for herself when she performed that music was based on a racist, colonial discourse that neither Canada's official multiculturalism nor the antiracism pedagogy of MFYC rehearsals had disrupted. Later in the interview she told me that she enjoyed reading Victorian novels. I suspect that these books, written at the peak of Britain's colonial period, influenced her use of the terms *primitive* and *sophisticated* in our discussion about music. Thus the literary discourses to which our students are exposed, either by choice or as required reading in English literature courses, also influence what and how students construct their images of others.

Likewise, although the Haleluya! Pelo Tsa Rona moment at the PFI concert may be interpreted as opening a space for emerging multicultural human subjectivity, for Ricky, a 19-year-old Black male, the same space allowed for a differently nuanced meaning. His description of the event suggests a multidimensional learning experience that both converges with and diverges from the concept of multicultural human subjectivity:

> D: I wanted to go back because you talked about the sense of pride from ... doing African music. Can you talk about that a little bit more?
>
> Ricky: Oh! It was when we sang at ... The Prison Fellowship. And we started singing Bobobo—no, we started singing "Haleluya! Pelo Tsa Rona." I started smiling and people started looking at me and going (he points and nods), and people started jumping up and carrying on and all. It just felt really cool that I could sort of be in Africa, sort of, mentally, for that little bit of time.
>
> D: So, were people in the audience actually pointing at you?
>
> Ricky: Well, I could see them looking at me going (nods his head as if trying to get someone to look in a particular direction).
>
> D: You mean making eye contact as if, "you're one of us, brother?"
>
> Ricky   Yes, exactly. That's what it felt like (Interview, March 6, 2004).

In this excerpt, Ricky's description articulates the recognition of self through the recognition of others. His mental trip to Africa is one indicator of how our engagement with world music can disrupt boundaries of time and space, allowing him in this instance to envision himself in an elsewhere, perhaps with those audience members who were sharing their joy in our music through their spontaneous dance. It is another example of creating what Frith refers to as an imagined cultural narrative. This moment for Ricky points to the multidimensional nature of a potentially emerging multicultural human subjectivity. It contributed to his sense of belonging (collective identity) as an MFYC member,[10] reinforced by singing in a language not native to him, in a performance that created a powerful moment of connection between the choir and the audience,. There is also an obvious reference to his own evolving racial identification as a young Black man (Tatum, 1997). From the excerpt above, one cannot tell which level of learning may be dominant, if any, in his self-understanding. I would like to think there is no hierarchy, since my own antiracism perspective calls for the end of racialization, but I recognize that at 19 years old, Ricky's developing racial identity is also an important aspect of his self understanding.

Conclusions and Importance of the Study to Music Education

As the above interview excerpts indicate, it is crucial to remember that pedagogical practice cannot guarantee meaning (Simon, 1992, p. 61). Thus there is an ongoing need for pedagogies such as antiracism (critical multiculturalism) within music education to subvert liberal multiculturalism's tendencies to reify stereotypes, instead opening the spaces from which multicultural human subjectivity may emerge as a metaphor for ideal relationships (Small, 1998). When I reflect upon MFYC's performance of "Haleluya! Pelo Tsa Rona," before an international audience who shared a common vision for social justice through prison reform, Small's words are both poignant and potent in their suggestion that the possibility for a fragile, emerging multicultural human subjectivity does exist. I believe that during that performance, even if only for a few seconds, we collectively experienced what it might feel like to live in a world where all humans understand themselves as multicultural human subjects.

Our students are exposed on a daily basis to many discourses that confound the opportunities for multicultural human subjectivity. Media images and sound bites reiterate hour after hour the racialized stereotypes of poverty, inner cities, illiteracy, and violence worldwide.

Discourses of liberal multiculturalism promote color-blind attitudes that deny the material consequences of racism in North America. Nation-building projects in both Canada and the United States rely on the myth that "we are all immigrants"—but such statements deny the forced migration of hundreds of thousands of Africans to the Americas under colonial economic systems built upon human slavery. Educational literature drawing upon the so-called "classics" reinforces the racist attitudes upon which the era of empire and colonialism justified conquest and domination. Within music education, continued reliance on concepts of traditional cultures reiterates notions of *primitive* and *sophisticated*, ignoring the reality that all cultures are dynamic and in continual flux from the influences of globalization and cultural creolization.

Despite the obstacles to multicultural human subjectivity that such discourses present, the kernel of hope for its potential is present throughout most of the interviews with MFYC members. In the "Haleluya! Pelo Tsa Rona" moment, the students recognized, some for the first time in their lives, the real people beyond the media images. In the 2 or so minutes when the boundaries blurred between performers and audience, a space opened for the ability to understand those who are different from ourselves, to see each person as human; in that space we also come to understand ourselves.

As North American society becomes increasingly multicultural, students have increased contact with those of different races and cultures. The meaning they bring to and take away from that contact cannot be predicted, but it has significant influence on society's future. In educational settings such as the MFYC, where antiracism pedagogy informs the learning process, I believe opportunities for multicultural human subjectivity exist. The performative power that learning and performing global song can wield, particularly when cultural context is richly understood, will present itself more frequently as those "unique situations" of cultural entanglement become more commonplace in society. I believe that as teachers, our job is to prepare students for those moments, so that when they occur, through musical performances or other events, students have sufficient cultural understanding to experience them as moments within which multicultural human subjectivity may emerge.

Small (1998) puts it this way: *"How we like to music is who we are"* (p. 220, italics added). MFYC's experiences with global song suggest that our musical border crossings allow for continued blurring of the boundaries of race, nationality, ethnicity, ability, sexual orientation, and other labels that humans have created to separate "us" from "them." Our musicking offers potential for "who we are" to approach the ideals of multicultural human subjectivity. Moments such as "Haleluya! Pelo Tsa Rona" open the space for its emergence, and I am confident that such spaces exist elsewhere, too, created by other musickers who allow for its possibility.

When we teach students in the here and now to interrogate biases and critique power relations, we also work to shape a future no longer reliant upon raciology, "the lore that brings the virtual realities of 'race' to dismal and destructive life (Gilroy, 2000, p. 11). This paper is a call, therefore, to move away from music education practices that ignore context in their overemphasis on musical technique, to pedagogies that situate music within the local habitus, and in doing so conscientize (Freire, 1970) the power relationships that reiterate oppressions and reproduce biases. Our students deserve to understand that music of all genres, including music of the Western canon, is inherently social, emerging within contexts often formed from inequitable power relationships, or during historical periods of conquest and domination. As teachers, we have choices: we may help our students understand how power operates in the world, or we may choose to ignore these issues and continue to reproduce inequities in our classrooms, thus disenfranchising many students while differentially rewarding those who conform to the White, middle class norms around which education in North America is most often centered (Apple, 1995, 2004; Bedard, 2000; Bourdieu & Passeron, 1977; Dei, 2000; Dei & Kempf, 2006; Giroux & Simon, 1989; hooks, 1994; McLaren, 1997; Simon, 1992).

Finally, the study addresses the importance for educators to understand music as a constitutive technology of the self (DeNora, 2000). Through musical experiences, we interpret the world to construct our individual and collective identities or self-understandings. This viewpoint resonates with Small's statement that how we like to music is simultaneously indicative of who we are as people, of the relationships that we value as ideal. This raises a question with which music educators have wrestled for some time. Music as constitutive of the self implicates the question, "what repertoire?"—a question that is always-already one of "whose repertoire?" In an increasingly globalizing world, what we teach and how we teach it becomes crucially important if one task of education is to help students understand their classmates, their future work colleagues, the neighbors whose religious or cultural values may be different from their own, or the people they may encounter in unanticipated situations like the "Haleluya! Pelo Tsa Rona" moment. These realities of life in the world today urge us as music educators to engage ethically (Bowman, 2002) with music as diverse human practice (Elliott, 1995), through performative pedagogies such as antiracism that are designed to foster self-understanding through other-understanding.

In closing, I would like to return to Britzman's (1998) arguments for educational reading practices, which I believe hold particular importance for music education. Music as diverse human practice provides a potent means through which we may engage and interrogate both text and context with learners as they develop self-understandings. In doing so, we help our students encounter their own conditions of alterity and transform what they imagine their identity imperatives to be. By helping students encounter their own conditions of alterity, we also prepare them for a future where difference is the *only* possibility for community, a future in which multicultural human subjectivity is fundamental to understanding what it means to be human.

NOTES

1. The term *subject* is used in the Foucauldian sense of an identity (self-understanding) brought into being within and influenced by discourses of multiculturalism globalization, and cosmopolitanism. The abstraction *multicultural human subjectivity* seeks to acknowledge this relationship to discourse as a condition of its formation. Despite tendencies within discourses to create rigid categorizations, subjects' agency enables them to remain dynamic and fluid, just as the conditions of their subjectivities are also dynamic and fluid. Although the term *subject* is sometimes associated with positivist research paradigms, this is not the meaning I seek to convey in the abstraction *multicultural human subject or subjectivity*; indeed, such meaning would be antithetical to the critical ethnographic method integral to this research. At the same time, however, subjects and subjectivities are sometimes constrained by the discourses leading to their formation. The term *multicultural human subject*, therefore, acknowledges that along with its fluidity and dynamic possibilities, the risk of hegemonic appropriation also exists.

2. In the United States, the term "critical multiculturalism" is more common. However, I prefer the terminology of antiracism to distinguish it from the bland forms of multiculturalism that this paper critiques.

3. Robertson (1992) defines *glocalization* as the condition that emerges when local economic interests become dependent upon global issues. While his definition was developed specifically to describe economic conditions, the term has become part of the vocabulary within both social science disciplines and the humanities as indicative of the integration of global concerns into local living conditions, language, and individual thought.

4. http://www.mississauga.ca/portal/discover/aboutmississauga

5. In 2007, the United Nations declared the term *visible minority* to be racist (reported in *National Post*, March 08, 2007), hence the use of scare quotes around the term in the text.

6. Retrieved August 13, 2005, www.city.mississauga.on.ca/edo

7. Of the 20 participants, 19 were aged 13 or older; one participant was 10 years old. Her admission to Level II was based upon considerations other than her age or grade in school.

8. The five focus group members had each been with the choir for at least 3 years. Their selection for the focus group was based upon their prior choir

experience, and my confidence that they would be able to maintain the confidentiality associated with ethnographic research.

9. All students' names in this paper are pseudonyms.

10. See Bradley (2006), chapter 6 for explanation of how MFYC members formed a collective identity.

REFERENCES

Apple, M. W. (1995). *Education and power* (2nd ed.). New York: Routledge.

Apple, M. W. (2004). *Ideology and curriculum* (3rd ed.). New York: Routledge Falmer.

Bannerji, H. (2000). *The dark side of the nation: Essays on multiculturalism, nationalism, and gender.* Toronto: Canadian Scholars' Press.

Beck, U. (2002). The cosmopolitan society and its enemies. *Theory, Culture & Society, 19*(1-2), 17-44.

Bedard, G. (2000). Deconstructing whiteness: Pedagogical implications for anti-racism education. In G. S. Dei & A. Calliste (Eds.), *Power, knowledge, and anti-racism education: A critical reader* (pp. 41-56). Halifax, Nova Scotia: Fernwood.

Behar, R. (1995). Introduction: Out of exile. In R. Behar & D. Gordon (Eds.), *Women writing culture* (pp. 1-32). Berkeley, CA: University of California Press.

Bell, V. (Ed.). (1999). *Performativity and belonging.* London: SAGE.

Bourdieu, P. (1977). *Outline of a theory of practice.* New York: Cambridge University Press.

Bourdieu, P., & Passeron, J. C. (1977). *Reproduction in education, society and culture.* London: SAGE.

Bowman, W. (2002). Educating musically. In R. Colwell & C. Richardson (Eds.), *The new handbook of research on music teaching and learning* (pp. 63-84). New York: Oxford University Press.

Bradley, D. (2006). *Global song, global citizens? Multicultural choral music education and the community youth choir: Constituting the multicultural human subject.* Unpublished doctoral dissertation, Ontario Institute for Studies in Education, University of Toronto, Toronto, Ontario, Canada.

Britzman, D. P. (1998). *Lost subjects, contested objects: toward a psychoanalytic inquiry of learning.* Albany, NY: State University of New York Press.

Britzman, D. P. (2000). The "question of belief": Writing poststructural ethnography. In E. St. Pierre & W. Pillow (Eds.), *Working the ruins: Feminist poststructural theory and methods in education* (pp. 27-40). New York: Routledge.

Brubaker, R., & Cooper, F. (2000). Beyond "identity." *Theory and Society, 29*(1), 1-47.

Butler, J. (1990). *Gender trouble.* New York: Routledge.

Butler, J. (1993). *Bodies that matter: On the discursive limits of "sex."* New York: Routledge.

Campbell, P. S. (2002). Music education in a time of cultural transformation. *Music Educators Journal, 89*(1), 27-32.

Campbell, P. S. (2004). *Teaching music globally: Experiencing music, expressing culture*. New York: Oxford University Press.

Dei, G. J. S. (2000). *Power, knowledge and anti-racism education*. Halifax, Nova Scotia: Fernwood.

Dei, G. J. S., & Kempf, A. (Eds.). (2006). *Anti-colonialism and education: The politics of resistance* (Vol. 7). Rotterdam, the Netherlands: Sense.

DeNora, T. (2000). *Music in everyday life*. Cambridge, England: Cambridge University Press.

Elliott, D. J. (1995). *Music matters*. New York: Oxford University Press.

Foucault, M. (1970). *The order of things: an archaeology of the human sciences*. New York: Vintage Books.

Freire, P. (1970). *Pedagogy of the oppressed*. New York: Seabury Press.

Frith, S. (1996). Music and identity. In S. Hall & P. du Guy (Eds.), *Questions of cultural identity* (pp. 108-127). London: SAGE.

Gilroy, P. (1993). *The Black Atlantic: Modernity and double consciousness*. Cambridge, MA: Harvard University Press.

Gilroy, P. (2000). *Against race*. Cambridge, MA: Belknapp Press of Harvard University Press.

Gilroy, P. (2004). *After empire: Melancholia or convivial culture?* London: Routledge.

Giroux, H. A., & Simon, R. I. (1989). *Popular culture, schooling, and everyday life*. Toronto, Canada: OISE Press.

Hesse, B. (Ed.). (2000). *Un/Settled multiculturalisms: Diasporas, entanglements, "transruptions."* London: Zed Books.

hooks, b. (1994). *Teaching to transgress: Education as the practice of freedom*. New York: Routledge.

Kincheloe, J. L., & McLaren, P. L. (2000). Rethinking critical theory and qualitative research. In N. Denzin & Y. Lincoln (Eds.), *Handbook of Qualitative Research* (2nd ed., pp. 279-314). Thousand Oaks, CA: SAGE.

Lather, P. (1986). Research as praxis. *Harvard Educational Review, 56*(3), 257-276.

Lather, P. (1991). *Getting smart: Feminist research and pedagogy with/in the postmodern*. New York: Routledge.

Mackey, E. (2002). *The house of difference: Cultural politics and national identity in Canada*. Toronto, Canada: University of Toronto Press.

McCarthy, C., Crichlow, W., Dimitriadis, G., & Dolby, N. (2005). Introduction: Transforming contexts, transforming identities: race and education in the new millenium. In C. McCarthy, W. Crichlow, G. Dimitriadis, & N. Dolby (Eds.), *Race, identity, and representation in education* (2nd ed., pp. xv-xxix). New York: Routledge.

McLaren, P. (1997). Unthinking whiteness, rethinking democracy: Or farewell to the blonde beast; towards a revolutionary multiculturalism. *Educational foundations, 11*(2), 5-39.

Robertson, R. (1992). *Globalization: Social theory and global culture*. London: Newbury Park, CA: SAGE.

Rorty, R. (1989). *Contingency, irony, and solidarity*. New York: Cambridge University Press.

Roudometof, V. (2005). Transnationalism, cosmopolitanism, and glocalization. *Current Sociology, 53*(1), 113-135.

Simon, R. I. (1992). *Teaching against the grain: Texts for a pedagogy of possibility.* Toronto, Canada: Ontario Institute for Studies in Education.

Small, C. (1998). *Musicking: The meanings of performing and listening.* Hanover: University Press of New England.

Tastsoglou, E. (2000). Mapping the unknowable: The challenges and rewards of cultural, political and pedagogical border crossing. In G. J. S. Dei & A. Calliste (Eds.), *Power, knowledge, and anti-racism education: A critical reader* (pp. 98-121). Halifax, Nova Scotia: Fernwood.

Tatum, B. D. (1997). *Why are all the Black kids sitting together in the cafeteria?and other conversations about race* (1st ed.). New York: Basic Books.

Walcott, R. (2003). *Black like who?: Writing Black Canada* (2nd rev. ed.): Toronto, Canada: Insomniac.

Williams, P. J. (1997). *Seeing a color-blind future: The paradox of race.* New York: The Noonday Press.

Yon, D. A. (2000). *Elusive culture: Schooling, race, and identity in global times.* Albany, NY: State University of New York Press.

CHAPTER 7

DISCOURSE IN
THE BAND ROOM

The Role of Talk in an
Instrumental Music Classroom

Teryl L. Dobbs

ABSTRACT

Language is a primary vehicle for imparting knowledge and information in education and other settings where teaching and learning take place (Cazden, 1986, 2001; Edwards & Furlong, 1978). The instrumental music classroom functions similarly. The performance of discourse and spoken language has its place within the context of music teaching and learning yet problematically, talk is often treated structurally as a transparent vehicle for conveying information. Through the combination of ethnomethodological inquiry and a discourse analysis grounded in Austin's (1962) speech act theory, the purpose of this study was to investigate the role of talk within an instrumental music performance classroom, how it shaped the teaching and learning of music and assisted the young musicians in creating a social cohort.

Diverse Methodologies in the Study of Music Teaching and Learning, pp. 137–160
Copyright © 2008 by Information Age Publishing
All rights of reproduction in any form reserved.

PROLOGUE

It is a warm day and we all have a touch of spring fever. Addison[1] and Claire compare and contrast 3/4 and 4/4 meter signatures embedded within an exercise based on the folk song, Shenandoah. As I ask the girls what they notice about the meter signatures, Addison yawns and stretches, answering, "It's 4/4 time." "No it's not!" exclaims Claire, who proceeds to list every meter signature in the exercise.

In an attempt to re-focus their energies, I interject: "What does andante mean?" "Walking speed," replies Claire. I press for more information: "What kind of walking speed?" Without any preamble, Addison jumps from her chair and proceeds to demonstrate, walking in front of us in a slow and steady manner. "Right," I tell them, "SLOW walking speed." Not to be left out, Claire makes slow undulating gestures with her arms as she explains that this particular tempo "glides." We agree to perform the final two measures of the exercise. "Ready—here we go." They play it beautifully. As Claire and Addison perform Shenandoah, I sing and gesture rhythmically with them. (vignette from Intermediate Flute Small Group Technique Class, field notes May 2001)

The setting was a band room in a public middle school located in a suburb of a large Midwestern city, my former teaching position. Imagine a brightly lit rehearsal space filled with the sounds and talk of a sixth grade flute lesson. The students and I were seated in a semicircle at the front of the classroom, a band room filled to capacity with the array of equipment necessary for an instrumental music curriculum: chairs, music stands, musical instruments, a percussion battery, and stacks of music texts and band compositions.

This study began as a journey into the uncharted territory of the familiar: the everyday discourse that occurs within the music classroom. The specific territory to which I refer was that of the world of the middle school band room, a place that I inhabited for several years as band director. Because of the mundane nature of classroom talk and its perceived transparent, ephemeral yet pervasive nature, I believed that talk within the instrumental music classroom was and is an aspect of the musical experience worthy of further investigation. I chose to study classroom talk in this specific venue because of my curiosity with words, what they do, and the seemingly commonplace nature of those words. My interest was heightened in this area by my readings in gendered language, discourse analysis focusing on speech act theory, and relevant literature discussing verbal data within the field of music education.

Language's role in music research can be viewed as problematic; Reimer (1997) discussed the role that language plays in "both our understandings of music and our cultivation of musical understandings in others" (p. 1), maintaining that the use of language as a teaching tool is so commonplace that researchers and practitioners alike quite understandably accept it as a matter of course. When listening to or performing a particular piece, however, the listener or performer is sometimes moved to a place where language cannot sustain the import of the musical experience: that experience becomes, in essence, ineffable. However, in describing those moments of intense perception and in communicating those experiences to others, the perceiver often resorts to language. This is also the case in the music performance classroom, in which language is deeply embedded in the teaching and learning process: "Language, evidently, is required in all music instruction whether primarily or secondarily" (p. 2).

Language however, is the primary vehicle for imparting knowledge and information in education and other settings where teaching and learning take place (Cazden, 1986, 2001; Edwards & Furlong, 1978). Throughout my readings in this area, I grappled with the growing perception that language was often viewed through a structuralist lens as a transparent vehicle for conveying and communicating information. It appeared that the use of language as a teaching and research tool was so commonplace that this transparency was a matter of course, and it was my discomfort with this structuralist perspective on language and discourse that has led me to explore the thinking of those who propose alternate viewpoints. The instrumental music classroom functions in similar ways to other classrooms, in which spoken language coupled with sonic production, have currency. Forms of talk, discourse, and spoken language have their place within the context of music teaching and learning: "Spoken language is the medium by which much teaching takes place, and in which students demonstrate to teachers much of what they have learned" (Cazden, 2001, p. 2).

Purpose and Research Questions

I constructed this investigation into music classroom discourse similar to a *logic of inquiry* (Gee & Green, 1998), an ethnomethodological study wherein a discourse analysis is guided by an ethnographic perspective. That perspective in this case was my immersion in the study as a fully active participant (Creswell, 1998). The purpose of my study was to investigate the pedagogical role of language, how the talk within an instrumental music performance classroom shaped the teaching and learning of music as well as how that talk assisted the musicians in creating a social cohort. I examined how our classroom discourse functioned within two curricular situations: (a) our small group technique lessons and (b) our full ensemble classes. Over the course of this study, I came to understand that our classroom discourse conveyed not only content-based knowledge, but it also fostered evolving social relationships within the instrumental ensembles.

Five assumptions guided the research questions: (a) language usage is a means for expressing musical understanding; (b) through language, knowledge of music is transmitted via social contexts, such as classes, rehearsals, and lessons; (c) the use of language influences the manner whereby people think about music, shaping their musical reality; (d) language usage acts as a cognitive mediator in structuring musical understanding and one's musical experience; and (e) the music classroom is a setting where young musicians build social relationships. Because of my active role in this study and the emergence of new themes, three overarching research questions evolved over time and distilled into the following:

1. How does the classroom discourse that occurs between music students and their teacher within a specific music performance classroom shape teaching and learning? What types of discourse patterns emerge? What types of physical gestures emerge that convey meaning? How do discourse patterns and meaningful physical gestures converge in shaping music teaching and learning?

2. How does classroom discourse serve to induct these young musicians into a music community, shaping a collaborative social cohort?

3. What themes emerge from the data that impact or constrain the teaching and learning of instrumental music within the context of this particular classroom?

Theoretical Foundations

In constructing the theoretical framework for this investigation, I assumed that language and cognition were linked and turned to literature addressing language and its relationship to thought and reality. The notions that (a) higher order thinking is language dependent and (b) how one's comprehension of the world depends upon one's habitual language use underscore Sapir's (1951) and Whorf's (1956/1959) concepts of linguistic relativity. Both claimed that language and thought were irrevocably entwined with culture and context: the language one utilized structured cognition and was therefore an integral psychological component of being human. More recently, language has been considered to be a mediating tool of social action, a concept incorporating intention and action on the part of the participants and as a mechanism through which we solve problems within specific sociocultural contexts (Rogoff, 1990; Wertsch, 1991). Because of language's relationship to culture and context, it has been argued that language is a primary tool for sharing and transmitting cultural knowledge, particularly when children apprentice themselves within social situations (Rogoff, 1990). Learning is thus contextually situated, requiring specific sets of skills and language uses that vary according to the situation.[2] The relationship between context, language, and cognitive structuring is dynamic and recursive and within this relationship, language is a cultural tool that mediates human action, particularly in understanding human mental action as related to communicative processes (Wertsch, 1991).

Researchers in music education have investigated and treated verbal data in myriad ways, utilizing it transparently to communicate stated or requested information; parsing talk itself as a primary research focus is relatively new to the field. Studies have relied upon verbal data by employing verbal descriptors in the form of adjective checklists when listening to music (Nierman, 1985a, 1985b) and in examining responses to aural discrimination tasks (Hair, 1987), in expressing comprehension of music terminology (Flowers, 1983), and in demonstrating singing tasks (Addo, 1998). Investigations examining effective rehearsal techniques paid close attention to teachers' spoken language (Buell, 1990; Goolsby, 1997; Sang, 1987), while other studies employed verbal data to detect teacher effectiveness (Froehlich, 1981; Yarbrough, Price, & Hendel, 1994) and to better understand student-teacher interactions (Kennell, 1992; Munsen, 1986). Additional studies employed verbal data in seeking to understand preservice teachers' delivery of their instructional language (Schleuter, 1994; Yarbrough, Price, & Hendel, 1994) and in exploring the verbal interplay occurring within the applied music studio (Abeles, Goffi, & Levasseur, 1992; Kennell, 1992, 2002).

Written or spoken verbal responses have been utilized to describe and define the musical experience (Cassidy & Speer, 1990; Flowers, 1983; Zerull, 1993) and when investigating children's and adult language use in music listening (Costa-Giomi & Descombes, 1996; Flowers & Costa-Giomi, 1991; Hair, 1987). Researchers attempted to parse aspects of musical listening through a variety of methods employing language as a means of description and data capture. Bundra (1993) and Kerchner (1996) employed verbal responses as a means of examining cognitive understanding of music listening processes, whereas Richardson (1996) investigated the verbal responses children produced concurrently while listening to music. In the ensemble rehearsal context, Williams (1997) parsed student verbal responses recorded during instrumental rehearsals in examining their music listening processes. Berg's (1997) investigation of the verbal interactions occurring within high school chamber ensemble rehearsals uncovered various patterns of musical thought and action, including the types and frequency of verbal and nonverbal activity utilized by the participants. In addition to these studies, researchers utilized verbal data as a means of data capture in seeking to unpack children's music compositional processes (DeLorenzo, 1989; Hickey, 1995; Kratus, 1989; Wiggins, 1994; Younker, 1997), and adolescents' music improvisation strategies (Fodor, 1998). Throughout the literature, researchers have employed a variety of data collection and analysis methods, including the *Flanders System of Interaction Analysis* (Erbes, 1972; Pontious, 1992) and protocol analysis types (Kerchner, 1996; Richardson, 1996; Williams,1997).

Researchers in music education have begun to reach across disciplinary boundaries, employing methodologies adapted from sociology, anthropology, and linguistics to collect and interpret verbal data. Through an analysis of musicians' and students' language, particularly the analogies and metaphors they employed to describe musical sounds and actions, a hypothetical link has been established between a musician's musical vocabulary and that person's ability to perform musically (London, 1982). Within music classrooms, the discourse itself has been investigated to examine the construction of transition moments within a rehearsal and how these moments enable rehearsal effectiveness (Naddeo, 1992), as well as exploring and parsing discursive conversation patterns enacted between teacher and students (Rohwer, 1997). Research linking student conductors' musical thinking and their use of verbal language suggests the interconnectedness of verbal language to musical concept formation and knowledge (Russell, 1995).

In order to scrutinize and parse the verbal data that emerged in this study, I turned to speech act theory for the discourse analysis. Discourse analysis is utilized to study verbal interaction processes within a particular social context, the result being an investigation that is both pragmatic and situated.[3] Definitions of discourse analysis or as some term *discourse-centered methods* appear to be purposely fluid and somewhat elusive. Implicit within a definition of discourse analysis is the investigation of spoken or written language use as being both socially and culturally constructed, its purpose for exploring the ways in which social and cognitive domains are united through speech (Cazden, 1986). Such an analysis acknowledges that speakers bring their backgrounds and experiences to any spoken conversation or textual interchange, such as their social histories, beliefs, intentions, actions, and experiences, as well as their embodiments and constructions of gender, race, and power (Levinson, 1983). A discourse analysis that is sensitive to such subtleties has the potential to create a more complete portrait of a discursive event and provide a more trustworthy, complex representation. It is for these attributes that I chose to undertake a discourse analysis approach in this study rather than submit the data to another analytical treatment such as a *Flanders Interactional Analysis*. A discourse analysis employing speech act theory relies on the notion that words function as performances, that they *do* something within a particular context (Austin, 1962). I derived the coding categories employed in this study directly from the concept of speech events as performances, including questions, assertions and directives, expressives, reactives, and acknowledgments.

To gather the data for this study, I chose to immerse myself within its social setting as a fully active participant (Creswell, 1998; Kemmis & McTaggart, 2000). This decision was replete with challenges, among them the seeming necessity to accomplish a sense of balance and distance as a researcher while being completely engulfed within the classroom and teaching milieu. What I experienced has been described as a "melting of the horizons" (Kemmis & McTaggart, p. 574), a perceiving of events from both the *inside* and the *outside* (Kemmis & McTaggart, 2000). Choosing a fully immersed researcher stance allowed me to facilitate data collection and formulate emergent themes into sensible questions, as well as providing me with a deeper understanding of the heuristics inherent within the world of this particular classroom (Bernard, 1994).

Methods

The research setting was the middle school band room where I had taught instrumental music for several years; 113 of my students Grades 5-8 in advanced, intermediate, and beginning concert bands participated in the study. Primary data sources for the study included 90 videotapes and 45 audiotapes of small group technique classes and large group ensemble classes; this data were taken from each level of the band curriculum. The videotapes provided the platform for my inscription of field notes and each audiotape was transcribed. I pursued the analysis of both large ensemble and small group lesson contexts in order to obtain as complete an understanding as possible of the classroom discourse from across the band curriculum. Supplemental data sources included field jottings taken during the teaching day, student concert reflections, and ancillary materials of a curricular nature.

Following collection of the data, I viewed the videotapes and inscribed the field notes concurrently, coding the field notes once the entire viewing and inscription process was completed. The coding categories emerged from a line-by-line reading of the entire corpus of field note data and a re-reading of data sets several times. This recursive process produced a set of five codes that I employed in analyzing the field note data: (a) teacher talk and actions, (b) student talk and actions, (c) talk and actions related to music, (d) talk and actions related to social/community building, and (e) talk and actions related to school/administrative business.[4] Two coding categories were pivotal to my answering the research questions: (a) talk and actions related to music and (b) talk and actions related to social/community building. The field note coding structure informed the discourse analysis of the classroom transcripts, providing necessary contextual meaning and depth. Analyzing both the field notes and the classroom transcripts was a recursive process in that my interactions with one data source would inform and clarify my thinking with the other, and vice versa.

In contrast to the emergent coding structure that I employed with the field note data, I applied an a priori coding structure to the audiotape transcripts for the discourse analysis. Each of the 45 audiotapes produced was first transcribed verbatim then reshaped into a transcript that followed a comprehensive set of transcription conventions (Bracewell & Breuleux, 1994; Edwards & Lampert, 1993; Gumperz & Berenz, 1993). The transcripts presented a textual portrait of our classroom interactions and included both spoken language and descriptions of physical and musical gestures germane to our classroom discourse. In addition to speech events, phenomena such as turn taking and interruptions among speakers, pauses in talk, music conducting gestures, music performance gestures, and transcriber uncertainty were accommodated.

Once the transcripts were produced and formatted, I coded each utterance according to performance categories adopted from speech act theory (Austin, 1962). Each speech act nested within a taxonomic category: *representatives* (speech that commits speaker to the truth of the expressed proposition), *directives* (attempts by the speaker to get the addressee to do something), *commissives* (speech that commits a speaker to some future action, such as promises or threats), and *expressives* (talk that reveals the speaker's current psychological state, such as expressing gratitude) (Searle, 1976).[5] Transcribed and coded discourse transcripts were then matched with their corresponding field notes that specifically addressed the curricular and social components embedded within the classroom talk: the talk and actions that related to music and to building social and community relationships. Field note exemplars referencing such talk and actions, matched with the codable cases[6] taken from the corresponding discourse transcripts, allowed me to answer the research questions. Figure 7.1 depicts the study's data analysis process.

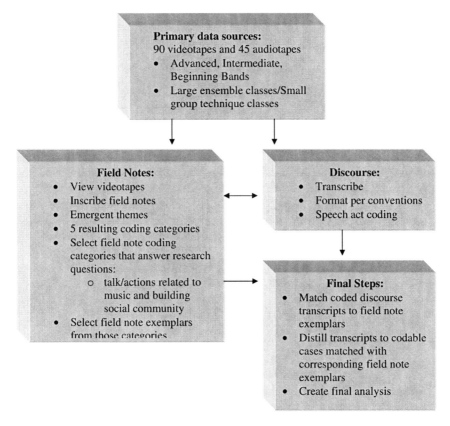

Figure 7.1.   Data analysis procedure for the present study's investigation of band room discourse.

Results and Conclusions: Major Findings

Throughout the study, talk was abundant within our particular instrumental music classroom whether large ensemble or small group lesson context. A caveat exists: whereas the information that emerged from this study was fruitful and filled with nuance, I must place that data within the wider concentric contexts of talk and culture. The public middle school where this study took place is located in an upper middle class suburb of a major Midwestern city; the preponderance of the student population continues to be Caucasian and socioeconomically advantaged. The discursive patterns and behaviors presented within this study embody enculturated community speech behaviors reflective of upper middle class socioeconomic status.

How does the classroom discourse that occurs between music students and their teacher within a specific music performance classroom shape teaching and learning? What types of discourse patterns emerge? What types of physical gestures emerge that convey meaning? How do discourse patterns and meaningful physical gestures converge in shaping music teaching and learning?

From the data and the discussion that follows, it is clear that the classroom discourse in this study assisted in the shaping of music teaching and learning through discursive patterns, physical gestures, and the convergence (that is, concurrent performance) of both. Two discursive patterns emerged from the data that shaped music teaching and learning, each bearing particular import for music teaching and learning in general and within the music performance classroom specifically: (a) *musical uptake* and (b) *repetition framing*. I termed musical uptake[7] as a discursive phenomenon wherein the students demonstrated their knowledge and understanding of music concepts via their musical performance (Figure 7.2).

Musical uptake would "sound" like the following discourse example taken from a small group technique class:

```
                    | rep/assert  | dir/require/sof  |rep/assert/inf
Dobbs: = Nice and light. Let's go to the pick up .. entrance to measure
 | rep/assert                   | dir/require | rep/assert
*MODELS* (singing using vocables). Here we go. Three,
                               | dir/require      |
four, five, (counting prep measure and cueing in students). =
                 | rep/assert
Students: =*PLAY*=
         | ack                     |dir/require
Dobbs: = Huh uh (indicating dissent). Don't put a slur into 17
              | rep/assert                        |
measure 17). *MODELS* (singing measure using vocables). Here
dir/require | dir require  | dir/require |
we go .. slow it down (cues in group). =


              | rep/assert
Students: =*PLAY*=
            | rep/assert/inf                  | rep/assert
Dobbs: = I'm hearing a slur in measure seventeen *MODELS*
                          | dir/require
(singing measure using vocables). Take the pick-up into measure
     |dir/require                     | rep/assert
17 and play over to count one in measure 18. Three, four,
     | dir/require                |
five (counting in 5/4 meter and cueing in students). =
        | rep/assert
```

MANAGERIAL TALK
(Teacher Instructions or Directions)

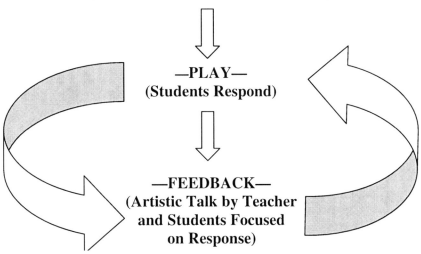

Figure 7.2.   Musical uptake feedback structure.

```
Students:  =*PLAY*=
            | ack | rep/react/eval  | rep/react/eval    | dir/require |rep/assert
Dobbs:  = Yeah, that was perfect. Good articulation. Do it again. One,
          |dir/require                                            |
two, three, four, play (counting in 5/4 meter and cueing in students). =
          |rep/assert|
Students:  =*PLAY*=
```

This looping of musical uptake created its own sense of ensemble within the rehearsal structure, serving to shape music teaching and learning within our classroom through the use of verbal feedback and assisting the students in constructing their perception of their music performances. Managerial talk and actions at the beginning of the example scaffolded the students' understanding for what they were about to rehearse or perform, whereas artistic talk and actions throughout included feedback on the students' performances and error detection, addressing musical concerns. I coded the students' responses (denoted above as *PLAY*) as *representative-assertives* (Austin, 1962; Searle, 1976): the students' musical responses to my feedback *asserted* specific information as enacted in their performance. As depicted in Figure 7.2, the feedback looping within this architecture was recursive and continued for as long a time as we chose, clarifying and refining the music teaching-learning process.

The second emergent discourse pattern, that being a repetition framing device (Tannen, 1989) occurred when I verbally affirmed a student's opinion, answer to a question, or comment by repeating a portion of that student's utterance as portrayed in Figure 7.3. This discursive pattern created an involvement strategy that reinforced the student's curricular knowledge and affirmed the social dynamics of the teacher-student relationship. Linguists maintain that repetition of talk among speakers is a powerful discursive move, providing a basis for creating a bond among the speakers and affirming their right to actively engage in the discourse (Tannen, 1989). The repetition frame simultaneously enacts the curricular goals and objectives of the teacher by scaffolding the students' construction of music understanding while enhancing a sense of collaboration. This has the potential to become an empathic process, one in which the teacher offers both emotional and musical support to the student by attending to the social-musical nature of their relationship.

Physical gestures emerged from the data that embodied meaning, often taking the place of talk within this particular music performance classroom; because of the situated meaning conveyed, I coded and denoted these as paralinguistic gestures.[8] Three gestural types emerged from my investigation: (a) conducting gestures, (b) vocable performance gestures, and (c) instrumental music performance gestures. Employing nonverbal activity through a variety of physical gestures imbued with meaning is thought to structure student cognition (Rogoff, 1990). Regardless of large ensemble or small group context, the use of conducting gestures was pervasive in embodying the musical concepts of pulse, tempo, rhythm, expressiveness, and style; the importance of

Student Assertion: Ira: = **Stayed together.** =

Teacher Acknowledgment/
Repetition of Student Assertion: Dobbs: = **Stayed together.** OK. (Looking at raised hands to select next speaker.) Tony?

Student Assertion: Tony: = **Dynamics.** =

Teacher Acknowledgment/
Repetition of Student Assertion: Dobbs: = **Dynamics.**

Figure 7.3.   Discourse repetition frame.

conducting gestures cannot be overstated. The following example taken from an advanced band rehearsal demonstrates the coding of conducted cues and cut-offs as directive-requirements (Austin, 1962; Searle, 1976):

> | dir/require | dir/require | dir/require | dir/require|
> **Dobbs: (Cuts off ensemble) Mark that whole note. Here we go. Do it**
> | dir/require |dir/require/int |rep/assert | ack | dir/require/ref
> **again … Don't talk, <u>come on</u>.** This is hard stuff.… Percussion, **are you all**
> **together**
> |
> **back there?** =
> | ack |
> Student: = Yes =
> | exp | mg | dir/require | dir/require | dir/require |
> Dobbs: = Thank you. Okay**, here we go. Try again.** (???) **(cues ensemble**
> **in)**.
>
> |rep/assert|
> *PLAY*

In coding cut-offs and cues as directive-requirements, I treated these physical gestures paralinguistically, that is, as gestures performed in the place of verbal instructions. As directives, cut-offs and cues provided musical and behavioral information that was contextually situated within the music performance and physically enacted: when to stop and start playing. I intentionally added the secondary code of requirement, which acknowledged the hierarchical relationship between teacher-conductor and students; the student musicians were expected or required to begin and discontinue playing as directed—this expectation was nonnegotiable.

Our performance of vocables to model and make music emerged as a second set of paralinguistic gestures through which we shaped our music teaching and learning. The students and I would often sing a musical line or phrase using nonsense syllables or words to articulate concepts such as melody, phrasing, style, or rhythm. These sequences of vocalized sounds, noted as *MODELS* below, were not meant to convey denotative meaning but rather to embody musical meaning, provided us with information that we could not articulate adequately through spoken language, for example:

> | rep/assert/inf | rep/assert
> Dobbs: = I'm hearing a slur in measure 17 **MODELS** (singing measure
> |
> using vocables).=
> | rep/assert/inf | | rep/assert |
> Dobbs: = Somebody's missing **MODELS** (sings motif using vocables).

because we wanna move on down the scale, but the composer
       |mg| rep/assert |
doesn't want us to .. so *MODELS* (singing motif using vocables). So
dir/require | rep/assert
look at measure 19 *MODELS* (singing measure nineteen using

   | ack |rep/assert
vocables). Yes, the repeated D (pitch).=

Performing with vocables provided the students and me with an instantaneous means of direct modeling, allowing us to represent and assert our musical understanding of how a phrase should be shaped or how a rhythm should be articulated. Because of these performance intentions, I coded vocables as representative-assertives. Our utilization of vocables proved to be an invaluable teaching and student practice tool, a viable means of presenting music information as well as receiving it. With this means at our disposal, vocables enabled us to convey information musically that could not be enacted in any other manner.

The third gestural type, instrumental performance gestures, also functioned paralinguistically in that when the students performed, their musical actions conveyed information and intention:

   | ack |dir/require
Dobbs: = Huh uh (indicating dissent). Don't put a slur into 17
       | rep/assert |
measure 17). *MODELS* (singing measure using vocables). Here
dir/require | dir require | dir/require |
we go .. slow it down (cues in group). =
      | rep/assert
Students: =*PLAY*=
      | rep/assert/inf |rep/assert
Dobbs: = I'm hearing a slur in measure seventeen *MODELS*
         | dir/require
(singing measure using vocables). Take the pick-up into measure
   |dir/require |rep/assert
17 and play over to count one in measure 18. Three, four,
   | dir/require |
five (counting in 5/4 meter and cueing in students). =
      | rep/assert
Students: =*PLAY*=

The students' instrumental performance responses noted as *PLAY* and coded similarly to vocables as representative-assertives, were heuristically replete with musical information embedded within their musical performance. Because of the situatedness of the music classroom setting, verbal articulation of the musical answers depicted by *PLAY* was entirely counterintuitive and inappropriate to the music teaching and learning process. It follows that within this context, musical information could only be delivered adequately through music-making.

Discourse patterns and paralinguistic gestures such as those described above and the concurrent production of talk with these gestures converged to shape music teaching and learning within our music performance classroom. These multimodal presentations enhanced the presentation and understanding of the other. For example, I performed conducting gestures simultaneously with spoken directions, such as counting preparatory beats or measures while conducting or counting-conducting difficult rhythms and tempi:

|dir/require |dir/require |dir/require |rep/assert
Dobbs: = ... Thirty five, here we go, thirty five. **One, two, steady, steady,**
                                    |dir/require |
steady, steady (spoken in 4/4 meter and cues ensemble in 4/4 meter).
|rep/assert|
PLAY
        |dir/req |rep/react/int |dir/require |
Dobbs: Stop. <u>Excellent</u> .. At measure nineteen, pencils required, write
|dir/require/int |rep/assert |
<u>everybody together</u>. Because that's when all the parts come together,
                    rep/assert |dir/require |dir/requir |
and everybody goes *MODEL* . . Everybody at nineteen .. here we
        rep/react/eval|ack |rep/assert | dir/require
go .. this is <u>great</u>, Band. **One, two, ready, play** (spoken in 4/4
                              |
meter/conducting prep measure).
|rep/assert |
PLAY

I coded instructions describing the tempo, "steady, steady, steady" and counting a preparatory measure, "one, two, ready" as representative-assertives: my performance of these speech acts presented the students with information regarding the speed, pulse, and meter of the piece. A simultaneous presentation of aural and visual information, such as conducting while verbally counting preparatory measures or describing tempi ("steady, steady"), provided students with multimodal sensory inputs. The benefits of this practice pose positive implications for shaping the learning of novice musicians. While the ideal in instrumental performance praxis is to move to a primarily visual, that is paralinguistic, presentation of musical information, young novice musicians appear to require information presented in multiple modes that includes verbal instructions.

How does the classroom discourse serve to induct these young musicians into a music community, shaping a collaborative social cohort?

This research question emerged from my fifth assumption regarding the study, that the music performance classroom is not only a place to learn, explore, and make music, but it is also a setting where young musicians construct social relationships. Classroom discourse within this particular music performance classroom functioned on both curricular and social levels, supporting music learning as well as the social roles of the classroom speakers. Music-related talk often fulfilled more than that of its intended curricular objectives; it served a social function as well, resulting in shared meanings of culture and relationships (Rogoff, 1990). Informal discourse including humor, narratives, or story-telling (Ainsworth-Vaughn, 2001; Brown & Levinson, 1987), inducted the young students into the art world of a performing musician whereby they began to identify themselves as musicians. The following field note excerpt presents an example of story-telling as French horn students, David and Will, told of their frustrations at a festival rehearsal:

> I asked the students how the All-City Festival rehearsal went. David tells me it was okay, but there is a student from another junior high who plays both French horn and trumpet; this particular student is both first chair French horn and last chair trumpet. Will says, "Yeah, he's horrible" ... David asks, "Guess how long this guy's been playing French horn? Three weeks," holding up his fingers. Will shakes his head, "Yeah, and he's sitting first chair." Will is technically first chair and he is not happy about this development; he takes his horn duties very seriously.... We talk about the first chair's responsibility to blow through the section and David replies, "Yeah, I looked over there to see if something was wrong with Will and there's this other kid on the other side of him." Will shakes his head with the weariness reminiscent of a seasoned veteran. (field notes, March 2001)

David and Will's narrative was informal and spontaneous, serving to reduce the social distance between our teacher and student roles (Ainsworth-Vaughn, 2001). They took on the role of expert by disagreeing with Will's chair placement and voicing their rough assessment of their new colleague's performing ability: "He's horrible" (Rogoff, 1990). Their discipline-specific parlance served to identify both David and Will as members of a musical community with a shared background of knowledge and values (Brown & Levinson, 1987, p. 124), allowing them to make sense of this experience by demonstrating their sense of sociomusical unity.

Small group lesson classes, typically no more than six students, allowed for a greater amount of such peer-to-peer discourse, particularly at the beginning or the conclusion of class when opportunities arose for class members to talk informally. Within both large ensemble and small group lesson contexts, the students and I largely maintained our social roles; however, the small group lesson context allowed for more informal interaction and discursive overlap:

> |dir/require | rep/react/eval|
> Dobbs: = Stop, the second time you played your (???)
> | rep/assert |
>   [Students: (???)
> | ack| mg |
>   [Dobbs: okay, now,
> | rep/assert |
>   [Students: (???) =
> |dir/require/sof | rep/react/eval
> Dobbs: = Are we set? I think you're all right, actually [disagreement between students].

The bracketed utterances above indicate discursive overlap: the students and I spoke over each other in an effort to assist and support each other in solving a musical problem. The students and I did not intend to dominate each other; rather, we spoke over each other enthusiastically as a result of our making connections (Tannen, 1993). Moments of overlap naturally occurred throughout the small group technique lesson discourse, whereas in the large ensemble context, I actively worked to control and curtail it:

> |rep/react/eval |mg | ack | dir/require/sof
> Dobbs: = Excellent. Now .. everybody, let me hear the same people at measure 13 =.
> | rep/assert
> *PLAY* (chord).
> |ack | rep/assert | dir/require | dir/require | rep/react/eval
> Dobbs: = Okay, that's a chord, and we've gotta tune it … Do it again, that was excellent.
> | ack | rep/react/eval |rep/react/ eval |ack | dir/ques/eval|dir/require|
> Matt, that's terrific. You're right on the money my friend. Ready? Go. =
> | rep/assert|
> *PLAY*
> |ack | mg |dir/require/sof |dir/require|
> Dobbs: = Okay, now .. let's have everybody from the first allegro, measure eight. =
> | rep/assert|
> *PLAY*

The excerpt above is representative of the large ensemble discourse data, in which I drove the turn-taking process due to my traditional interpretation and enacting of the teacher/band director role. Through my classroom management and podium practices, I maintained our social roles by controlling our turn-taking, managing rehearsal pacing, and facilitating topic choice.

The convergence of classroom discourse and musical paralinguistic gestures allowed these novice musicians to absorb a repertoire of gestures and cues that inducted them into music performance practice. These cooperative social skills, often taken for granted, provided a foundation for positive, effective, and ultimately, musical experiences within this particular music performance classroom. These social skills appear to be portable, traveling with the students as they move through middle school into high school and laterally across other music performance experiences. Over time, these behaviors go underground and become internalized as the young musicians continue their music performance experiences. The students will eventually absorb variants to these acquired social behaviors and test them, realigning them according to the musical and behavioral expectations of a new ensemble and a new teacher-director.

What themes emerge from the data that impact or constrain the teaching and learning of instrumental music within the context of this particular classroom?

Two additional themes emerged from the data: (a) time and (b) compliance. Throughout the data, the students and I worked against the clock in preparing for concerts and festivals; time was constant, insidious, and pervasive. Time, either the perceived lack of it or the perceived abundance of it, governed my decisions within the classroom to the smallest degree. In several circumstances, my talk became highly direct:

> Dobbs: = I'm hearing a slur in measure seventeen *MODELS*. Measure 17, three, four, five (counting in 5/4 meter and cueing in students). = *PLAY*
> Dobbs: = Yeah, that was perfect. Do it again. One, two, three, four, play (counting in 5/4 meter and cueing in students). = *PLAY*
> Dobbs: = Yeah .. now start at measure 18. =

Such terse direct talk was often a direct result of my felt race against the clock; because of such talk and my vocal tone, the students sometimes misinterpreted me, believing me to be angry or upset. Their perceptions could also be read as gendered interpretations of their enculturated expectations of a female teacher in the gendered role of band director. Because of our race against the clock, compliance on the part of the students became intrinsic to our musical endeavors, and the discourse data reflects my expectations and assumptions of compliance on the parts of my band students. Discovering my own adherence to traditional expectations of student compliance was deeply troubling to me as were the traditional performance expectations that drove much of our music curricular activities.

Implications for Music Education

This study makes three primary contributions to current research in the field of music education, first by its demonstrating and unpacking the complexity and vitality of instrumental music classroom discourse: talk in any music classroom is more than a transparent conveyance of information—it is complex and multivalent. Verbal language plays a vital role not only in shaping students' musical performance, but it is also a vehicle that students employ to identify, explore, and clarify musical concepts while translating those same concepts into musical actions (Russell, 1995, p. 199). Through opportunities to participate within the framework of classroom discourse, students construct their understanding of music and increase their comprehension of a complex set of culturally and cognitively significant behaviors.

It became clear that both the quantity and quality of our talk factored into the nature of our classroom discourse. More teaching talk occurred with the younger ensembles than with the older groups, implying that novices require more explanation and description in their initiation into musical practices than do their more experienced counterparts. Classroom discourse provides a scaffold for these young learners, in which conducting gestures must be clarified, concepts are explained, and performances are analyzed, assessed, and evaluated. Students in every type of music classroom need the discursive space where their voices can be heard, a space with ample opportunities to articulate and mediate their musical understandings. Students require discursive openings to make their own musical decisions and to act as musical experts so that they may take an active role in their learning processes.

The researcher stance of a fully embedded and immersed participant is a second contribution to the field; it is an effective investigative lens for gaining insight into the teaching, learning, and social facets of music education contexts. Inscribing field notes and memos as a result of this process assists the researcher in negotiating the lived experience of being in the middle of the action, in essence creating a situated third space that is fluid, dynamic, and empathic. Much can be gained both professionally and personally by embracing passionately the embeddedness of the active participant and allowing oneself to become entwined within the study.

The study's third contribution to the field is the effectiveness and utility of discourse analysis types as viable and vibrant vehicles for future research. Through the implementation of a discourse analysis employing speech act categories, a microanalysis of music classroom discourse can illuminate moments of transitions and change, reveal discursive patterns necessary for teaching and learning, and demonstrate levels of social relationships previously unnoticed. Future research settings for extending and refining this type of discourse analysis would include studying music students at various stages of music development in a variety of rehearsal settings, whereas a detailed microanalysis of a single rehearsal or music class, incorporating the analysis of both linguistic and musical properties, would be highly revealing. Future studies employing discourse analysis could unpack issues of race, gender, class, and ability/ (dis)ability and their effects upon students' musical and social experiences within our classrooms.

Within the instrumental music classroom, talk is both similar and dissimilar to classroom talk in other disciplines; it is distinctively contextual, multivalent, and more potent than previously understood. Talk in this milieu serves not only to scaffold musical information so that it becomes understandable and accessible to students, but it also serves to induct those students into a community of musical practice. In addition to its pedagogical purposes, discourse within the music classroom communicates power and expectations for successful membership within that community, imparting to young musicians how they are to function and behave within the culture of the music performance ensemble.

Clearly, discourse in the instrumental music classroom is more than simply a transparent vehicle for conveying information and instructions. Discourse in our music classrooms is a vibrant means for shaping teaching and learning, communicating culture, power, social relationships, musical knowledge, and ultimately, for enhancing and perpetuating our students' musical experiences. With future study, a deeper understanding of music classroom discourse will result in a richer, more complete comprehension of the musical experience and enable music researchers the opportunities to understand that experience more fully.

NOTES

1. All names presented herein are pseudonyms.
2. Rogoff (1990) termed certain situations as *skilled cultural activities* (p. 40), in which learning was highly contextualized and occurred within an accepted community of practice, such as the teaching of music.

3.   The unifying construct in creating a discourse analysis is the focus on the social and cultural contexts of language use (Levinson, 1983). I chose to employ speech act theory in creating this study's discourse analysis because of the context's centrality to the data analysis and its contribution toward the investigation's trustworthiness. Rather than select another analytical method such as a *Flanders Interactional Analysis*, speech act theory proved to be a flexible and performative tool that assisted me in answering the research questions.

4.   I invited an outside expert to review and triangulate several of the field note data and attendant coding structure.

5.   As I did with the field note coding structure, I invited an outside expert, a linguist, to review my discourse coding structures, application of those structures, and interpretation of the results.

6.   The concept of codable cases allowed me to distill the amount of transcript data required for the discourse analysis (Lampert & Ervin-Tripp, 1993), thereby necessitating the coding of only those portions of each transcript that corresponded with its previously analyzed set of field notes.

7.   The term *uptake* originated in the pragmatics linguistics literature and denotes how the participants within a conversation pick up on both subtle and obvious inflections (Levinson, 1983). The utterances and gestures employed within the discourse are used to achieve a certain effect, implying the securing of uptake on the part of the hearer with the purpose of getting the hearer to *do* something. This process takes effect in certain ways and by linguistic convention, inviting a response or a sequel on the part of the hearer (Austin, 1962, pp. 115-116). In this manner, uptake is applicable directly to the teaching and learning of music where the ensemble-like discourse between participants relies upon their knowing, interpreting, and performing of musical gestures, both verbal and physical.

8.   Paralinguistic gestures are physical gestures that embody meaning and stand in the place of spoken words, including nonphonemic components of speech, such as vocal tone (Levinson, 1983).

REFERENCES

Abeles, H., Goffi, J., & Levasseur, S. (1992). The components of effective applied instruction. *The Quarterly Journal of Music Teaching and Learning, 3*(2), 17-23.

Addo, A. (1998). Melody, language and the development of singing in the curriculum. *British Journal of Music Education, 15*(2), 139-148.

Ainsworth-Vaughn, N. (2001). The discourse of medical encounters. In D. Schiffrin, D. Tannen, & H. Hamilton (Eds.), *The handbook of discourse analysis* (pp. 453-469). Malden, MA: Blackwell.

Austin, J. (1962). *How to do things with words.* London: Oxford University Press.

Berg, M. (1997). *Social construction of musical experience in two high school chamber music ensembles.* Unpublished doctoral dissertation, Northwestern University, Evanston.

Bernard, H. R. (1994). *Research methods in cultural anthropology* (2nd ed.). Newbury Park, CA: SAGE.

Bracewell, R., & Breuleux, A. (1994). Substance and romance in analyzing think-aloud protocols. In P. Smagorinsky (Ed.), *Speaking about writing: Reflections on research methodology* (pp. 55-88). Newbury Park, CA: SAGE.

Brown, P., & Levinson, S. (1987). *Politeness: Some universals in language usage.* New York: Cambridge University Press.

Buell, D. (1990). *Effective rehearsing with the instrumental music ensemble: A case study.* Unpublished doctoral dissertation, The University of Wisconsin-Madison.

Bundra, J. (1993). *A study of music listening processes through the verbal reports of school-aged children.* Unpublished doctoral dissertation, Northwestern University, Evanston.

Cassidy, J., & Speer, D. (1990). Music terminology: A transfer from knowledge to practical use. *Bulletin of the Council for Research in Music Education, 106,* 11-21.

Cazden, C. (1986). Classroom discourse. In M. Wittrock (Ed.), *Handbook of research on teaching* (pp. 432-463). New York: Macmillan.

Cazden, C. (2001). *Classroom discourse: The language of teaching and learning.* Portsmouth, NH: Heinemann.

Costa-Giomi, E., & Descombes, V. (1996). Pitch labels with single and multiple meanings: A study with French-speaking children. *Journal of Research in Music Education, 44*(3), 204-214.

Creswell, J. (1998). *Qualitative inquiry and research design: Choosing among five traditions.* Thousand Oaks, CA: SAGE.

DeLorenzo, L. (1989). A field study of sixth-grade students' creative music problem-solving processes. *Journal of Research in Music Education, 37*(3), 188-200.

Edwards, A., & Furlong, V. (1978). *The language of teaching: Meaning in classroom interaction.* London: Heinemann.

Edwards, J., & Lampert, M. (Eds.). (1993). *Talking data: Transcription and coding in discourse research.* Hillsdale, NJ: Erlbaum.

Erbes. R. (1972). *The development of an observational system for the analysis of interaction in the rehearsal of musical organizations.* Unpublished doctoral dissertation, University of Illinois, Urbana-Champaign.

Flowers, P. (1983). The effect of instruction in vocabulary and listening on nonmusicians' descriptions of changes in music. *Journal of Research in Music Education, 31*(3), 179-189.

Flowers, P., & Costa-Giomi, E. (1991). Verbal and nonverbal identification of pitch changes in a familiar song by English- and Spanish-speaking preschool children. *Bulletin of the Council for Research in Music Education, 107,* 1-12.

Fodor, D. (1998). *Critical moments of change: A study of the social and musical interactions of precollegiate jazz combos.* Unpublished doctoral dissertation, Northwestern University, Evanston.

Froehlich, H. (1981). The use of systematic classroom observation in research on elementary general music teaching. *Bulletin of the Council for Research in Music Education, 66-67,* 15-19.

Gee, J., & Green, J. (1998). Discourse analysis, learning, and social practice: A methodological study. In P. Pearson & A. Iran-Nejad (Eds.), *Review of*

Research in Education (Vol. 23, pp. 119-169). Washington, DC: American Educational Research Association.

Goolsby, T. (1997). Verbal instruction in instrumental rehearsals: A comparison of three career levels and preservice teachers. *Journal of Research in Music Education, 45*(1), 21-40.

Gumperz, J., & Berenz, N. (1993). Transcribing conversational exchanges. In J. Edwards & M. Lampert (Eds.), *Talking data: Transcription and coding in discourse research* (pp. 91-121). Hillsdale, NJ: Erlbaum.

Hair, H. (1987). Descriptive vocabulary and visual choices: Children's responses to conceptual changes in music. *Bulletin of the Council for Research in Music Education, 91,* 59-64.

Hickey, M. (1995). *Qualitative and quantitative relationships between children's creative musical thinking processes and products.* Unpublished doctoral dissertation, Northwestern University, Evanston.

Kemmis, S., & McTaggart, R. (2000). Participatory action research. In N. Denzin & Y. Lincoln (Eds.), *Handbook of qualitative research* (pp. 567-605). Thousand Oaks, CA: SAGE.

Kennell, R. (1992). Toward a theory of applied music instruction. *The Quarterly Journal of Music Teaching and Learning 3*(2), 5-16.

Kennell, R. (2002). Systematic research in studio teaching in music. In R. Colwell & C. Richardson (Eds.), *The new handbook of research on music teaching and learning* (2nd ed., pp. 243-256). New York: Oxford University Press.

Kerchner, J. (1996). *Perceptual and affective components of the music listening experience as manifested in children's verbal, visual, and kinesthetic representations.* Unpublished doctoral dissertation, Northwestern University, Evanston.

Kratus, J. (1989). A time analysis of the compositional processes used by children ages 7 to 11. *Journal of Research in Music Education, 37*(1), 5-20.

Lampert, M., & Ervin-Tripp, S. (1993). Structured coding for the study of language and social interaction. In J. Edwards & M. Lampert (Eds.), *Talking data: Transcription and coding in discourse research* (pp. 169-206). Hillsdale, NJ: Erlbaum.

Levinson, S. (1983). *Pragmatics.* New York: Cambridge University Press.

London, M. (1982). *Music and language: An ethnographic study of music learning and interpreting situations.* Unpublished doctoral dissertation, Rutgers State University of New Jersey, New Brunswick.

Munsen, S. (1986). *A description and analysis of an Orff-Schulwerk program of music education.* Unpublished doctoral dissertation, University of Illinois, Urbana-Champaign.

Naddeo, M. (1992). *The New Life Singers: A discourse analysis of street kids "doing" a choir rehearsal.* Unpublished doctoral dissertation, Columbia University Teachers College, New York.

Nierman, G. (1985a). The development of a test of verbal descriptors in music. *Bulletin of the Council for Research in Music Education, 84,* 20-33.

Nierman, G. (1985b). The role of vernacular in assessing students' perceptive/descriptive capabilities of musical components. *Bulletin of the Council for Research in Music Education, 85,* 156-165.

Pontious, M. (1992). *A profile of rehearsal techniques and interaction of selected band conductors*. Unpublished doctoral dissertation, University of Illinois, Urbana-Champaign.

Reimer, B. (1997). Episteme, phronesis, and the role of verbal language in "knowing within" music. *Philosophy of Music Education Review, 5*(2), 101-107.

Richardson, C. (1996). A theoretical model of the connoisseur's musical thought. *Bulletin of the Council for Research in Music Education, 128*, 15-24.

Rogoff, B. (1990). *Apprenticeship in thinking: Cognitive development in social context*. New York: Oxford University Press.

Rohwer, M. (1997). *Talking within music: An ethnographic study of choral instruction, verbal interactions, and the resulting ensemble sounds within a high school choral rehearsal*. Unpublished doctoral dissertation, Ohio State University, Columbus.

Russell, J. (1995). *An investigation of the role of language in student conductors' comprehension and construction of musical meanings in practicum settings*. Unpublished doctoral dissertation, McGill University, Montréal.

Sang, R. (1987). A study of the relationship between instrumental music teachers' modeling skills and pupil performance behaviors. *Bulletin of the Council for Research in Music Education, 91*, 155-159.

Sapir, E. (1951). Language. In D. Mandelbaum (Ed.), *Selected writings of Edward Sapir in language, culture and personality* (pp. 7-32). Berkeley, CA: University of California Press. (Original work published 1949)

Schleuter, L. (1994). Qualitative study of dialogue: A thought process. *Bulletin of the Council for Research in Music Education, 123*, 58-62.

Searle, J. (1976). A classification of illocutionary acts. *Language in Society, 5*(1), 1-23.

Tannen, D. (1989). *Talking voices: Repetition, dialogue, and imagery in conversational discourse*. New York: Cambridge University Press.

Tannen, D. (1993). *Framing in discourse*. New York: Oxford University Press.

Wertsch, J. (1991). *Voices of the mind: A sociocultural approach to mediated action*. Cambridge, MA: Harvard University Press.

Whorf, B. (1959). Language, mind, and reality. In J. Carroll (Ed.), *Language, thought, and reality: Selected writings of Benjamin Lee Whorf* (pp. 246-270). New York: MIT. Press & John Wiley & Sons. (Original work published 1956)

Wiggins, J. (1994). Children's strategies for solving compositional problems with peers. *Journal of Research in Music Education, 42*(3), 232-252.

Williams, D. (1997). *Listening while performing: Music listening processes as revealed through verbal reports of wind instrumentalists during rehearsal*. Unpublished doctoral dissertation, Northwestern University, Evanston.

Yarbrough, C., Price, H., & Hendel, C. (1994). The effect of sequential patterns and modes of presentation on the evaluation of music teaching. *Bulletin of the Council for Research in Music Education, 120*, 33-45.

Younker, B. A. (1997). *Thought processes and strategies of eight, eleven, and fourteen year-old students while engaged in music composition*. Unpublished doctoral dissertation, Northwestern University, Evanston.

Zerull, D. (1993). *The role of musical imagination in the musical listening experience*. Unpublished doctoral dissertation, Northwestern University, Evanston.

PART II

FOCUS ON SOCIAL AND INSTITUTIONAL CONTEXTS AND ISSUES

CHAPTER 8

CHARTER SCHOOLS

Embracing or Excluding the Arts?

James R. Austin and Joshua A. Russell

ABSTRACT

Administrators from 122 charter schools in 15 states completed a 27-item questionnaire that addressed school demographics, programmatic issues and curricular issues specific to music. Data were analyzed to determine the status of music as a curricular subject, as well as the relationship of institutional variables to music instruction. Results were interpreted in relation to national data regarding public school music education. Music is part of the regular curriculum in 70% of participating charter schools; some schools only offer music on a limited, informal basis after school. Availability of music instruction is associated with grade level configuration, school enrollment, and individuals/groups involved in establishing and designing schools. While music instruction is not as commonplace in charter schools as in traditional public schools, charter schools that do offer music provide comparable instructional time. Course offerings, however, appear narrower in scope, formal curricula are less likely to be followed by music teachers, and fewer teachers of music are highly qualified.

Diverse Methodologies in the Study of Music Teaching and Learning, pp. 163–182

Public schools are not merely schools *for* the public, but schools of publicness: institutions where we learn what it means to *be* a public and start down the road toward common national and civic identity. They are the forges of our citizenship and the bedrock of our democracy. Yet we seem as a nation to want to disown them. (Barber, 1997 as cited in Goodlad & McMannon, p. 22)

The charter school concept springs from the desire of many people for higher student achievement and greater, more positive educational results in public schools. That is in part why politicians as different as Bill Clinton and Lamar Alexander both support the charter school idea—they see it as a way to increase student achievement. (Nathan, 1999, p. 12)

INTRODUCTION

Educational reforms typically grow from seeds of discontent concerning the performance of traditional public schools. Charter schools represent one of the most significant and popular manifestations of educational reform during the past quarter century. Though charter schools commonly are linked to the recent wave of reform that began with the publication of *A Nation at Risk* in 1983, their origin actually may be traced back to earlier alternative school initiatives, such as open schools of the 1960's and magnet schools of the 1970's (Schneider, Teske, & Marshall, 2000). School choice—the prerogative for parents to open enroll their children in any public school situated anywhere—underlies alternative school creation in general and the charter school concept in particular. The Minnesota School Improvement Coalition, a partnership of state Parent Teacher Association members and business leaders formed by then Governor Rudy Perpich in the mid-1980s, was the nexus for both school choice (1988) and charter school (1991) legislation (Murphy & Shiffman, 2002).

Since the first charter schools were established in Minnesota in the early 1990s, there has been a steady increase in the number of states with charter school legislation (one state in 1991, 33 states in 1998-99, 40 states in 2006-07) and the number of charter schools in operation nationwide (one school in 1992, 1,100 in 1998-99, over 3,600 in 2006-07). Charter school enrollment also has grown. In a recent analysis of school choice trends (including but not limited to charter schools) conducted by the National Center for Education Statistics, researchers found that the proportion of students attending a public school of choice increased 4% between 1993 and 2003 (Tice, Princiotta, Chapman, & Bielick, 2006). Despite such growth, charter school enrollment still represents less than 2% of all K-12 public school students in the United States.

The charter school concept is not clearly understood. Public approval of charter schools grew from 42% in 2000 to 53% in 2006. Yet, most individuals believe they are private schools that teach religion, charge tuition, and select students based on ability (Rose & Gallup, 2006). All of these are fundamental misconceptions. Charter schools may be broadly defined as publicly funded schools of choice that operate free of district and state regulations but that are held accountable for student achievement and performance standards (Murphy & Shiffmann, 2002).

Charter school proponents view self-governance—freedom from bureaucratic policies and regulations that often stifle innovation and build frustration within traditional public schools—as key to improving student achievement and providing accountability (Nathan, 1999). Competition, a staple of free market economics, also is considered necessary to drive widespread adoption of proven innovations and systemic change within public education. A common rationale for charter schools is that they will foster greater experimentation (i.e., "break the mold" schools) and improved practice. Indeed, research shows that a broad range of curricular and instructional approaches can be found in charter schools (Manno, Finn, Bierlein, & Vanourek, 1998; McLaughlin & Henderson, 1998). Some schools reflect a very conservative philosophy while others promote progressive education ideals. In a few instances, charter schools serve unique student populations (e.g., gifted or at-risk students) and/or emphasize a particular curricular strand (e.g., information technology).

Charter schools are not universally supported. Anticharter school sentiments are evident in efforts by state policy makers, local school districts, teacher unions, and public interest groups to prevent passage of new charter legislation, limit the number of new charter schools, and cap charter school funding (Manno, 2006). Manno observes that funding misappropriations by charter school leaders, their failure to adhere to testing requirements, governance disagreements, and overreporting of enrollment has given charter school critics reasonable cause for concern.

Critics often contend that charter schools are elitist; minority students enrolled in charter schools come from higher income households than those enrolled in comparable public schools (Carnoy, Jacobsen, Mishel, & Rothstein, 2005). Information about charter schools tends to be distributed among a network of highly interested and involved parents, enrollment is on a first-come first-served basis, and transportation services are seldom provided. As a result, many charter schools have rather homogeneous student populations that do not necessarily reflect the demographics of neighborhoods in which they are situated. In Denver, Colorado, for example, minority students constituted 74% of the student population in the late 1990's. PS 1, a charter high school, had a minority population of 41%. When compared to the Colorado average of 28% at that time, PS 1 appeared to be serving a higher minority population. When compared to other neighborhood schools, however, PS 1 served far fewer minority students (American Federation of Teachers, 1999).

While charter school proponents promise greater academic accountability than traditional public schools, as of 1999 only 32 schools nationwide had lost their charters. Moreover, the majority of these charter revocations were due to financial irregularities rather than poor academic performance (Manno, 2006). In an analysis conducted by the Center for Education Reform in 2002, only 1% of 154 charter schools that closed were shut down for academic reasons. This finding held true when the analysis included only charter schools that had been open for 3 or more years. Even when charter schools fail to meet accountability standards, they may stay in operation for an extended period of time. In a survey of charter school authorizers conducted by the U.S. Education Department, more than one half reported having difficulty closing a charter school that was failing (Carnoy et al., 2005). The American Federation of Teachers (1999) cites vague legislative language in many charter laws, insufficient state and sponsoring agency personnel to provide adequate oversight, and the lack of comparable data from charter and public schools as important reasons why increased accountability in charter schools is "problematic and difficult to substantiate" (p. 7).

Despite the breadth of curricula found in charter schools, most policy analysts view the general curricular trend as one of decreased experimentation and increased uniformity (Lubienski, 2003). Charter school names, missions, and curricula often reflect, at best, a certain degree of innovative traditionalism or localized variations on practices already common within the larger public school realm. Edison, a for-profit company that manages many charter schools, for example, uses "Success for All" as its primary reading program. This program, however, already has been implemented in over 700 public schools affiliated with more than 400 different school districts (American Federation of Teachers, 1999).

Many charter schools rely on national curriculum models that are prescriptive in nature, and charter school leaders often define success and approach accountability in terms of back-to-basics ideology (Murphy & Shiffman, 2002). This emphasis on basic knowledge, coupled with assessment practices that consistently target reading, writing, and math outcomes, has had the net effect of narrowing the curriculum in many charter schools. Data recently reported by the Center for Education Reform (2006) confirm that the majority of charter school curricula might be viewed as more representative of traditional or conservative thinking (e.g., college prep and international baccalaureate programs, direct instruction, core knowledge sequence, school-to-work initiatives, outcome-based education) than innovative or progressive ideals (e.g., thematic instruction, Montessori/Waldorf philosophy, arts focused learning, cyber instruction, constructivist learning, bilingual education).

Other common criticisms of charter schools pertain to the quality of teaching and learning. There is no compelling evidence of superior learning and achievement among students who attend charter schools (U.S. Department of Education, 2003), and charter schools achievements often are viewed as coming at the expense of traditional public schools (i.e., the best students and basic resources are siphoned away). A greater proportion of charter school teachers do not meet federal "highly qualified" standards—72% of charter school teachers are certified compared to 93% of regular public school teachers (Strizek, Pittsonberger, Riordan, Lyter, & Orlofsky, 2006). Finally, many charter schools have difficulty finding adequate facilities and start-up funding, which may place de facto limits on expensive and specialized curricular programs such as music and the other arts.

STUDY IMPETUS: COLORADO CHARTER SCHOOLS

Colorado's Charter School Act, the second in the country, was passed in 1993 with the explicit goal that charter schools develop and experiment with learning approaches not already available in public schools. Individuals who wish to start a charter school in Colorado must seek approval from the local school board. If the local board rejects the proposal, it can be appealed to the state board of education, which can turn down the appeal or require the school board to work out differences with the charter applicant. There is no limit regarding the number of charter schools that may exist at one time. There were two charter schools in 1994-95, 67 in 1999-2000, and 107 in 2004-05. Colorado has consistently had one of the highest per capita enrollment rates for charter schools, currently trailing only Arizona in that regard. In contrast to national trends, Colorado charter schools enroll a smaller percentage of minority students and fewer students qualifying for free or reduced-rate lunch than traditional public schools, and charter schools predominantly exist in White, wealthy suburban areas. The core knowledge curriculum (Hirsch, 1987) has been adopted by the largest proportion of charter schools in Colorado (Fitzgerald, 2000; Fitzgerald, Green & Peebles, 2003).

A recent review of the League of Charter Schools Web site (www.coloradoleague.org) revealed that as of 2007, there were 129 charter schools in operation within Colorado. The grade level configuration evident in these schools varies greatly (see Table 8.1), which raises questions about the logic underlying student grouping decisions, complicates the process of comparing charter schools to traditional public schools, and makes music class scheduling potentially problematic (see Table 8.1).

Anecdotal data obtained from Colorado music educators suggest that school choice and charter school legislation has had many unintended consequences. Open enrollment decisions made by parents on the basis of convenience (i.e., school proximity to their workplace) or a desire to have their children attend charter schools with strong precollegiate programs, for example, have resulted in completely unpredictable patterns of enrollment in music classes. Idiosyncratic enrollments, in turn, have threatened the quality and existence of school music programs (i.e., music instructors struggle to meet minimum class size requirements or maintain adequate instrumentation) while undermining feeder program and curricular articulation processes once considered vital to music program success.

With this backdrop, we posed the question: Are charter schools embracing or excluding the arts? Our investigation arose in response to a need for more definitive information about the impact of educational reforms, such as charter schools, on arts education. We sought to determine whether charter schools provide access to the arts instruction, as reflected in music education course offerings and student participation/enrollment rates, comparable to that of traditional public schools.

Arts Education and Charter Schools

Published vignettes depicting individual cases of successful music instruction in charter schools are available (Riddell, 1997; Rudatis, 1997), and some authors contend that charter schools should embrace "talent

Table 8.1.   **Frequency of Grade Level Configurations for Colorado Charter Schools**

Grade Level Configuration	Frequency
K-3, K-5, K-6, K-7, K-8, and 1-8	72
K-9, K-10, K-11 and K-12	19
5-8, 6-7, 6-8, and 7-8	8
5-12, 6-12, 7-9, 7-10, and 7-12	9
9-12, 10-12	17
By student age	2
Information missing	2

development" as a measure of success (Opp, Hamer, & Beltyukova, 2002). Riddell (1997) observes:

> Both school choice and charter schools offer new opportunities for creativity and innovation.... Rather than see these new opportunities in a negative light because they unsettle the current system, arts educators might see in these opportunities a chance to become involved in an invigorating school. Moreover, a wide range of school options allows for the creation of more models of excellence in arts curricula. These examples do not detract from, but reinforce, the mission of improved education in all schools. (p. 7)

Our search of major educational research databases revealed no published studies of arts education in charter schools. A decade ago, Austin (1997) conducted an exploratory study of music instruction in Colorado charter schools. He found that 70% of elementary charter schools included music in the curriculum, while 35% of secondary schools offered music instruction (traditional ensemble classes, specialty instrument classes, or nonperformance classes). A majority of charter schools (60%) did not employ highly qualified music educators, relying instead on professional artists, avocational educators, or parent volunteers. He concluded, at that time, that Colorado charter schools were not providing arts education on par with other public schools.

More recently, two dissertations have focused on the status of arts disciplines in charter schools. Ferguson (2006) conducted a program evaluation of three schools (two charter and one district partnership) managed by the Edison Schools, Inc. General music instruction typically occurred twice a week for 45 minutes per class, but instrumental music instruction was not offered in any of the schools. By design, music was frequently used as a tool for improving student achievement in other disciplines. The quality of music instruction was further hampered by classroom management concerns, lack of access to school computer-based technologies, budget uncertainties, and staffing turnover/shortages. Two of the five music teachers were not state certified; the three certified teachers were seen as implementing the most age appropriate and effective teaching methods.

Henderson (2006) compared advanced placement art instruction in two public 4-year high schools: one traditional school and one charter school. While art instruction in the traditional school was characterized by sequential learning, assessment benchmarks, and explicit directions for completing major projects, the charter school's art instruction was more individualized and flexible in approach. Students attending the traditional high school were oriented toward high academic achievement and good grades, while charter school students expressed greater interest in the artistic process. Students at both schools valued the emotional and creative benefits derived from art education, but few individuals expressed interest in art as a viable career choice.

Clearly, the charter school phenomenon has gained traction among politicians, parents, and some school decision makers. While there are differing points of view concerning how effective charter schools have been in providing access to students of diverse backgrounds, promoting curricular innovation, or meeting accountability standards, most researchers and policy analysts agree that support for charter schools and the principles they represent is unlikely to wane in the near term. Given the dearth of research related to the impact of charter school policies on the availability and quality of arts/music education, a survey study of music instruction in charter schools was undertaken.

Study Purpose

The purpose of this study was to explore the status of music - the most pervasive and prominent arts education discipline (Carey, Kleiner, Porch, & Farris, 2002)—in public charter schools. More specifically, we considered course offerings, instructional time, student participation, teaching facilities, teacher qualifications, and institutional support related to music instruction. We also examined relationships between charter school characteristics and the status of music instruction. Finally, we compared results for charter schools represented in this study against national data for music instruction in U.S. public schools.

METHODOLOGY

A survey instrument was designed to collect data from charter school principals, headmasters, or directors. Questionnaire items were patterned after measures employed in recent state or national level school surveys (Fitzgerald, 2000; Education Commission of States, 1995; U.S. Department of Education, 2003, 2004). A draft version of the questionnaire was piloted and reviewed by three university faculty members with expertise in music education and/or school policy issues. The final version of the questionnaire consisted of 27 items that address five general topics: charter school demographics; philosophical basis of the school curriculum and partnerships that were involved in the school's inception; course offerings, student participation, and amount of instructional time devoted to music; music teacher qualifications and experience, and the teacher's role in school decision making; and perceived importance and support for music education by stakeholders.

Sample and Procedures

Web sites affiliated with various state education departments, the National Center for Educational Statistics, and the Charter School Clearinghouse were used to identify charter schools in operation during the 2005-06 school year. The questionnaire was mailed to a stratified random sample of 400 charter school administrators representing the 15 states with the largest proportion of charter schools in the United States (Arizona, California, Colorado, Florida, Georgia, Massachusetts, Michigan, Minnesota, New Jersey, New York, North Carolina, Ohio, Pennsylvania, Texas, and Wisconsin).

Fifteen questionnaires were returned unopened due to a change in the school's mailing address; new addresses for these schools were found and duplicate questionnaires were mailed. Twenty-two questionnaires were returned due to the recent closing of schools; a replacement strategy was used to randomly select additional schools in each affected state. An e-mail reminder was sent to administrators who had not responded after three weeks. A total of 122 completed questionnaires representing 25 elementary schools, 36 secondary schools, and 61 elementary/secondary schools in all 15 states sampled were returned (response rate = 31%).[1]

Despite the low response rate, schools in our sample were reasonably representative of the larger population of charter schools in the United States (Center for Education Reform, 2006; U.S. Department of Education, 2004). Our sample, for example, included 43% urban schools as compared to 50% for all U.S. charter schools, 50% K-8 or K-12 schools as compared to 35% for the United States, and a median school enrollment of 341 as compared to 297 for the United States. Our sample also was representative of national charter schools with respect to music teacher qualifications (87% of music teachers in our sample were licensed/certified as compared to 79% for the nation), and curricular orientation (11% arts-focused schools in our sample, as compared to 7% for the nation).

RESULTS

Because of the wide range of grade level configurations represented in our sample, descriptive results are presented in the aggregate for all charter schools. Music instruction is part of the regular curriculum in 70% of participating charter schools. Several schools do not offer music instruction during the school day, but instead sponsor after-school or extended-day sessions through which private lessons are taught by artists-in-residence or more informal exploratory activities occur. Among schools that do not offer any music, three serve specialized populations (deaf children, court-supervised juveniles, pregnant and parenting teens) and five are rural schools where funding does not allow for a music teacher to be hired.

Factors Associated With Availability of Music Instruction

Availability of music instruction is significantly associated with grade level configuration (χ^2 = 10.98, p = .004); music is offered in 84% of schools with a combination of elementary and secondary grade levels, but only in 64% of elementary schools and 53% of secondary schools. School enrollment also is connected to music instruction (χ^2 = 6.45, p = .040); music is offered in 83% of large schools and 74% of moderate size schools, but in only 58% of small schools. While music is more commonplace in suburban schools (82%) than rural (65%) or urban (63%), this association is not statistically significant (χ^2 = 4.28, p = .118). The association between school characteristics and music instruction is depicted in Figure 8.1.

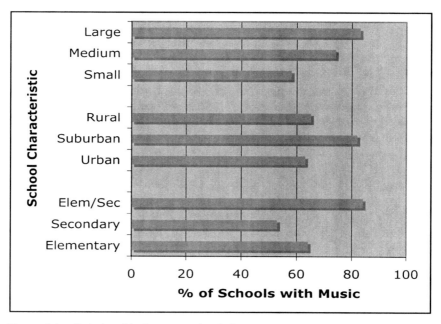

Figure 8.1.   Relationship between school characteristics and availability of music instruction.

The availability of music instruction also hinge on the individuals or groups responsible for designing a charter school. When parents are involved in charter school design, for example, music instruction is more likely to be offered ($\chi^2 = 4.82$, $p = .028$) than if parental involvement is absent. Alternatively, when state-level service agencies ($\chi^2 = 9.64$, $p = .002$), students ($\chi^2 = 6.89$, $p = .009$), teachers ($\chi^2 = 5.73$, $p = .017$) or consultants ($\chi^2 = 4.40$, $p = .036$) play an important role in designing the charter school, music instruction is less likely to be offered (see Figure 8.2). The philosophical/curricular orientation of a charter school has a negligible impact on music instruction. Not surprisingly, music is more likely to be offered in schools that adopted the arts as an academic focus ($\chi^2 = 4.15$, $p = .040$) and less likely to be offered in schools that have a vocational focus ($\chi^2 = 4.48$, $p = .034$).

Descriptive Results for Charter Schools With Music

General music, found in 56% of schools with music instruction, is the most common curricular offering. Electives in chorus are available in 43%

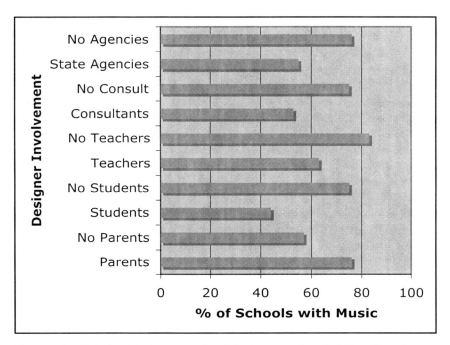

Figure 8.2. Relationship between school designers and availability of music instruction.

of the schools, band is available in 34% of schools, and orchestra or strings classes are offered in 18% of schools. For charter schools that offer music instruction, an average of 64% of students are enrolled in general music, 14% are enrolled in choir, 10% are enrolled in band, and 3% are enrolled in orchestra. We were not able to determine the proportion of students enrolled in more than one type of music class, so simply adding these percentages likely will provide a distorted picture of overall enrollment. Other required classes include music exploratory and music appreciation at the secondary level, and other electives include recorder, guitar, and African drumming ensembles at the elementary level. Trustworthy enrollment figures for these classes were not available.

In schools that offer music, instruction typically occurs twice a week in 50-minute periods for the entire school year. Instructional formats vary widely, however, with a few schools offering an hour of music daily for the entire school year, other schools providing students with music three times a week for only one quarter, and some schools scheduling music as part of a 5-week block that rotates with art and physical education. Music classes are commonly taught in a dedicated classroom with specialized equipment, though in over 40% of the schools music instruction takes place in regular classrooms (21%) or nonclassroom (20%) settings.

Approximately 85% of the schools that offer music employ fully-qualified music specialists who have degrees in music and are licensed to teach music, with the majority of those instructors teaching in a full-time capacity. Partially qualified music instructors, with a teaching license but no music degree, are found in just less than 10% of schools. Regular classroom teachers are responsible for teaching music in 8% of the charter schools. Artists-in-residence, with extensive music training and/or degrees but no teaching license, occupy positions in 12% of schools. Slightly over one-half (54%) of schools reported that the highest level of education attained by any music teacher was a bachelors degree and, on average, charter school music teachers had 11 years of teaching experience.

A majority of charter school administrators at schools with music programs reported that music teachers are expected to follow a written curriculum guide (57% indicating "yes"), do have input in determining the music curriculum that is taught (93% indicating "yes"), and do participate on school decision-making teams or leadership councils (72% indicating "yes"). Music specialists, however, do not always have the opportunity to provide input on funding allocations for music instruction (52% of school administrators indicating "no"), and music is not typically included in school mission statements or goals (62% indicating "no"). On average, administrators reported extensive support for "the arts as part of a high quality education" and believed that other charter school teachers/ staff and parents also were moderately-to-greatly supportive of the arts.

Factors Associated with Curricular Importance of Music

We assessed the degree to which curricular importance—as reflected by average amount of weekly instructional time and availability of a dedicated music room—was impacted by other variables in charter schools that offer music. Grade level configuration had a significant effect on amount of instructional time for music ($F = 29.003$, $p < .001$), with secondary schools averaging 198 minutes of instruction per week, elementary schools averaging 73 minutes, and combined elementary/secondary schools averaging 90 minutes. No other variables were significantly linked to our measures of curricular importance.

Comparing Charter Schools and Public Schools

National-level data on the status of arts education in public elementary and secondary schools were compiled by the National Center for Educational Statistics during the 1999-2000 school year (Carey et al., 2002). Because of the limited size of our sample and the 6-year difference in data collection, a direct statistical comparison of our findings for charter schools with the most recent national data on music/arts instruction in public schools was not advisable or even possible. A comparison of general data patterns, however, does provide a preliminary basis for interpreting the status of music instruction in charter schools.

Data comparisons suggest that music instruction is less likely to be offered in charter schools than in traditional elementary and secondary public schools. Charter schools that offer music typically configure instruction into larger blocks of time than public schools, but the duration of classes is generally longer in public schools (i.e., a greater proportion of public schools offer music classes for the entire academic year). Charter schools are less apt to employ full-time licensed specialists to teach music, which is not surprising given the autonomous nature of these institutions. A smaller proportion of charter schools provide a dedicated space for music instruction and written music curriculum guides are less available in charter schools. Table 8.2 summarizes the comparisons between charter schools and traditional elementary and secondary public schools.

DISCUSSION

Most researchers investigating charter schools have focused on student achievement, as reflected in scores on state or national-level assessments (U.S. Department of Education, 2003). Often lost in the contradictory

Table 8.2.   Comparison of Charter and Traditional Schools

	Charter Schools (All Grade Level Configurations)	Traditional Elementary Schools	Traditional Secondary Schools
Music instruction	70%	94%	90%
Length of class (per day)	50 minutes	38 minutes	Data not available
Average annual hours of music instruction	52 hours	46 hours	Data not available
Average days of instruction per week	2 days	2 days	Data not available
Number of weeks of class	36 weeks in 64% of schools	36 weeks in 93% of schools	Data not available
Employ full-time licensed specialist	64%	72%	91%
Provide a dedicated space	59%	67%	91%
Have a written music curriculum	57%	81%	80%

Note: Data for traditional elementary and secondary schools from Carey et al., 2002

interpretations and heated debate over test results is the question of learning (Carnoy et al., 2005). Specifically, what kind of evidence is required to make judgments about the impact of charter schools on student learning? Programmatic and curricular issues, which may serve as one barometer of student learning, have been underinvestigated, particularly in disciplines not currently targeted by statewide and national assessments (social studies, vocational studies, physical education, and the arts). No published research has examined music education within charter schools, let alone compared music offerings and instruction in charter schools to that found in other public schools. This study is an initial step in determining whether students have an opportunity to study, experience, and make music in charter school contexts.

We launched this investigation by posing the question—Are charter schools embracing or excluding the arts? Our answer is a qualified *neither.* Administrator responses imply that music, as a representative arts discipline, is offered in a majority of charter schools and that a majority of charter school students likely receive instruction in music. Moreover, one out of ten schools claims the arts as a curricular emphasis, if not a curricular focus per se. As such, one can hardly conclude that charter schools are neglecting the arts.

The music instruction provided in charter schools, however, does not appear to be at a level completely commensurate with that of traditional public schools. The utilization of longer instructional periods—a common feature of charter schools - may be viewed as an asset at the secondary level, but a developmentally inappropriate practice at the elementary level (Music Educators National Conference, 1994). Moreover, the fact that year-long music study is found in only two thirds of charter schools may limit the extent to which students are able to maximize skill development, establish continuity of learning, and come to value music as an important area of study. So, from this vantage, we cannot conclude that charter schools, as a group, necessarily embrace the arts. Given the findings related to the availability of written curricula and teacher qualifications, it seems plausible that charter school music instruction may function more as a supplemental activity, as a means of integrating instruction, or as a tool for reinforcing learning in so-called core subjects, rather than as a distinct/important curricular area.

Clearly, additional research is needed to assess the impact of the charter school movement on music/arts education and determine whether any charter-public school discrepancies reflect differing values, funding deficiencies, or other institutional barriers (Sarason, 1998). Large-scale surveys that equate charter and traditional public schools on the basis of student demographics and other important variables would provide for more direct and meaningful comparisons of curricular content, student enrollment, and achievement outcomes. Case studies would better allow researchers to explore the *quality* of music instruction and learning. Policy analyses are needed to further explore relationships among charter school legislation, school creation, teacher hiring and retention trends, curricular ideology, and school accountability practices.

Several important policy issues emerge from our analysis. First, more consideration should be given to the authorization and organization phases of charter school creation. We found some evidence to suggest that parents may advocate for music instruction in charter schools, whereas other constituencies (teachers, students, consultants) may be less inclined to do so. We do not know, however, whether parents advocate on the basis of dissatisfaction with music instruction in traditional public schools, or aspirations for their own children to experience music in unique ways. It also is unclear why students and teachers, individuals who can and should play a more prominent role in advocating for quality music education in charter schools, are seemingly ambivalent in their support of music instruction. A greater understanding of the political dynamics that unfold during charter school creation, and how such dynamics impact decisions about music instruction (availability and implementation, teacher qualifications), might be obtained by surveying and/or interviewing individuals actually responsible for writing and revising charter documents.

We speculate that the public perception of arts programs as both expensive and elitist may work at cross-purposes when charter school committees decide whether to include arts education in the curriculum. The notion that the arts are "special" and cultivate unique talents, for example, would seem to resonate within the larger charter school community. The costs associated with providing and maintaining adequate facilities (classrooms, rehearsal rooms, practice rooms, art studios, storage space, auditoriums and other performance venues) and equipment or materials (music, instruments, art supplies, sets, uniforms, costumes), however, may be seen as insurmountable to those charged with bringing charter schools to life. Yet, one might argue that singing and listening are among the most egalitarian of all educational activities (everyone has a voice and seemingly everyone owns an iPod) and that, when annual expenditures for textbooks and instructional technology are factored in, arts instruction is no more expensive to deliver than any other subject.

A second emerging policy issue involves equity and access. If charter schools primarily exist in White, wealthy suburban areas, then it is critically important to consider the reality that these schools may represent a segregation or re-segregation of students by socioeconomic class, if not by ethnicity. Moreover, if finances are one of the thorny problems that charter schools confront, then neighborhood affluence may have much to do with whether or not the arts are part of a charter school curriculum. Even when arts programs are offered to students in charter schools, it is important to consider whether they are *required*. If so, then some secondary charter schools may do a better job of providing access to arts instruction than traditional public middle and high school music programs that characteristically reach less than 25% of the school population (National Center for Educational Statistics, 1984; Persky, Sandene, & Askew, 1999; Steinel, 1990). If not, then intraschool segregation may layer on top of inter-school segregation. Past MENC (National Association for Music Education) President Mel Clayton (2002), in a direct critique of school choice and charter schools, stated:

> We have a responsibility to do whatever we can to ensure that music programs will be available, equitably, to future generations, including children from all ethnic and economic backgrounds. We must disagree with and fight back those who would segregate our education system under the guise of programs such as charter schools or school vouchers. (pp. 6-7)

Teacher quality is a third policy issue requiring further study. There is ample evidence that teacher quality impacts student learning (Darling-

Hammond, Berry, & Thoreson, 2001). Charter schools employ fewer highly qualified music teachers than traditional public schools. This is not surprising, given that one aim of charter school legislation is to provide more flexible hiring criteria and procedures. What are the long-term implications, however, for music teaching and learning? Alternative certification aficionados and charter school advocates are not strange bedfellows. If charter schools, for example, move toward hiring performers or artists who possess a high level of content area expertise, but who lack pedagogical content knowledge, then student learning in music may be negatively impacted. Conversely, if the highly qualified teacher provision of the No Child Left Behind law actually motivates charter schools to hire individuals with music degrees and teaching licenses (presuming that someone monitors charter school hiring practices), the highly qualified teacher gap between charter schools and other public schools may narrow rather than widen.

Lastly, the ideology behind curricular frameworks found in charter schools is a policy issue that may present the most insurmountable barrier to quality music instruction. In our view, back-to-basics dogma, core knowledge, and college prep programs, direct instruction, school-to-work initiatives, and home school/cyber delivery systems—curricular approaches emphasized in over 65% of charter schools (Center for Education Reform, 2006)—may either limit access to music instruction, marginalize music learning, or confound music teacher efforts to provide students with meaningful learning experiences. It is important to recognize, however, that similar forces are impacting music programs in traditional public schools. School choice legislation, as noted earlier, is leading students away from neighborhood school music programs, and high stakes testing mandates are causing many school administrators to shift instructional time and resources toward tested subject areas and away from the arts. In this sense, music teachers in charter schools and traditional public schools are facing similar challenges.

We conclude that irrespective of policy and practical differences that characterize traditional public schools and charter schools, all students attending either type of school are entitled to engage with and learn about the arts as part of a comprehensive education. This perspective is perhaps best articulated in a position statement adopted by the executive board of the National Association for Music Education in March 1997. In an online document titled *Where We Stand: The Role of Music in American Education*, professional educators are reminded of music's fundamental importance to children:

> Because of the role of the arts in civilization, and because of their unique ability to communicate the ideas and emotions of the human spirit, every

American student, pre-K through Grade 12, should receive a balanced, comprehensive, sequential and rigorous program of instruction in music and the other arts. This includes students in public schools, private schools *and charter schools* [italics added]. (http://www.menc.org/information/prek12/stand.html)

AUTHOR NOTE

A copy of the questionnaire used in this study may be obtained by contacting the first author via e-mail (James.Austin@colorado.edu)

NOTE

1. Response rates for statewide or multi-state surveys of elementary and secondary school principals vary widely. A search of the ERIC database, for example, yielded 50 published studies of this type since 1980. Response rates ranged from 15% to 91%, with a median response rate of 60%. Obtaining high response rates in charter school research is, arguably, more challenging. Charter schools typically open/close and change locations more frequently than public schools, which makes representative sampling very challenging (U.S. Dept. of Education, 2003).

REFERENCES

American Federation of Teachers. (1999). Charter schools update. *Educational Issues Policy Brief, 9*. Washington, DC: AFT Education Issues Department.

Austin, J. R. (1997). *The status of music in Colorado charter schools: An exploratory study.* Unpublished manuscript, University of Colorado at Boulder.

Barber, B. R. (1997). Public schooling: Educating for democracy. In J. I. Goodlad & T. J. McMannon (Eds.), *The public purpose of education and schooling* (pp. 21-32). San Francisco, CA: Jossey-Bass.

Carey, N., Kleiner, B., Porch, R., & Farris, E. (2002). *Arts education in public elementary and secondary schools:1999-2000*. Washington, DC: National Center for Educational Statistics.

Carnoy, M., Jacobsen, R., Mishel, L., & Rothstein, R. (2005). *The charter school dustup: Examining the evidence on enrollment and achievement*. New York: Teachers College Press.

Center for Education Reform. (2006). *Annual survey of America's charter schools: 2005 data*. Washington, DC: Author.

Clayton, M. (2002). Educating the whole child. *Teaching Music, 9*(4), 6-7.

Darling-Hammond, L., Berry, B., & Thoreson, A. (2001). Does teacher certification matter? Evaluating the evidence. *Educational Evaluation and Policy Analysis, 23*(1), 57-78.

Education Commission of the States. (1995). *Charter schools: What are they up to?* Denver, CO: Author.

Ferguson, D. A. (2006). Music education in Edison schools: An evaluation of K-5 music education in three schools managed by Edison Schools, Inc. *Dissertation Abstracts International, 66*(7), 2524. (UMI No. 3182261)

Fitzgerald, J. (2000). *1998-99 Colorado charter school evaluation study: The characteristics, status, and performance record of Colorado charter schools.* Denver: Colorado Department of Education.

Fitzgerald, J., Green, K., & Peebles, L. (2003). *The state of charter schools in Colorado 2001-02: The characteristics, status, and performance record of Colorado charter schools.* Denver: Colorado Department of Education.

Henderson, L. K. (2006). Looking for "good practice": Advanced art education in a traditional public high school and a public charter school for the arts. *Dissertation Abstracts International, 67*(3), 816. (UMI No. 3210147)

Hirsch, E. D. (1987). *Cultural literacy: What every American needs to know.* Boston: Houghton Mifflin.

Lubienski, C. (2003). Innovation in education markets: Theory and evidence on the impact of competition and choice in charter schools. *American Educational Research Journal, 40*(2), 395-443.

Manno, B. V. (2006). Charter school politics. In P. E. Peterson (Ed.), *Choice and competition in American education* (pp. 161-171). Lanham, MD: Rowman & Littlefield.

Manno, B. V., Finn, C. E., Bierlein, L. A., & Vanourek, G. (1998, March). How charter schools are different: Lessons and implications from a national study. *Phi Delta Kappan, 79*(7), 489-498.

McLaughlin, M. J., & Henderson, K. (1998). Charter schools in Colorado and their response to the education of students with disabilities. *The Journal of Special Education, 32*(2), 99-107.

Murphy, J., & Shiffman, C. D. (2002). *Understanding and assessing the charter school movement.* New York: Teachers College Press.

Music Educators National Conference. (1994). *Opportunity-to-learn standards for music instruction: Grades pre-K-12.* Reston, VA: Author.

Nathan, J. (1999). *Charter schools: Creating hope and opportunity for American education.* San Francisco: Jossey-Bass.

National Center for Educational Statistics. (1984). *A trend study of high school offerings and enrollments: 1972-73 and 1981-82.* Washington, DC: Author.

Opp, R. D., Hamer, L. M., & Beltyukova, S. (2002). The utility of an involvement and talent development framework in defining charter school success: A pilot study. *Education and Urban Society, 34*(3), 384-406.

Persky, H. R., Sandene, B. A., & Askew, J. M. (1999). *The NAEP 1997 Arts Report Card: Eight-grade findings from the national assessment of educational progress.* Washington, DC: U.S. Department of Education.

Riddell, J. B. (1997). The political climate and arts education. *Arts Education Policy Review, 98*(5), 2-8.

Rose, L. C., & Gallup, A. M. (2006). The 38th annual Phi Delta Kappa/Gallup poll of the public's attitudes toward the public schools. *Phi Delta Kappan, 88*(1), 41.

Rudatis, C. (1997, August). Charter schools and music programs. *Teaching Music*, 5(1), 27-29.

Sarason, S. B. (1998). *Charter schools: Another flawed educational reform?* New York: Teachers College Press.

Schneider, M., Teske, P., & Marshall, M. (2000). *Choosing schools: Consumer choice and the quality of American schools.* Princeton, NJ: Princeton University Press.

Steinel, D. V. (Ed.). (1990). *Data on music education: A national review of statistics describing education in music and the other arts.* Reston, VA: Music Educators National Conference.

Strizek, G. A., Pittsonberger, J. L., Riordan, K. E., Lyter, D. M., & Orlofsky, G. F. (2006). *Characteristics of schools, districts, teachers, principals, and school libraries in the United States: 2003-2004 Schools and staffing survey* (NCES 2006-313). Washington, DC: U.S. Government Printing Office, U.S. Department of Education, National Center for Education Statistics.

Tice, P., Princiotta, D., Chapman, C., & Bielick, S. (2006). *Trends in the use of school choice: 1993 to 2003* (NCES 2007-045). Washington DC: U.S. Department of Education, National Center for Education Statistics.

U.S. Department of Education. (2004). *Evaluation of the public charter schools program: Final report.* Washington, DC. Author.

U.S. Department of Education. (2003). *America's charter schools: Results from the NAEP 2003 pilot study.* Washington, DC: Author.

CHAPTER 9

DOCTORAL STUDENTS IN MUSIC AND THEIR SOCIALIZATION INTO TEACHING

An Initial Inquiry

Susan Wharton Conkling and Warren Henry

ABSTRACT

An initial, narrative inquiry into how graduate students in music are being socialized into teaching roles included 18 students who were enrolled in a graduate-level College Music Teaching Seminar at one of two institutions. We were the instructors of those seminars, and we wanted to uncover participants' stories of socialization into teaching. The intersections of our students' stories led us to suggest that doctoral students' socialization into teaching may be complicated by the presence of International Teaching Assistants (ITAs) and the multiple cultural values they bring to schools of music, lack of understanding about adult learning theories, accompanied by lack of opportunity to observe their applications in teaching, and the

Diverse Methodologies in the Study of Music Teaching and Learning, pp. 183–200
Copyright © 2008 by Information Age Publishing
All rights of reproduction in any form reserved.

presence of computer and Web-based technologies along with perceived pressure to incorporate technology into teaching.

INTRODUCTION

We are music education professors at two different institutions, each responsible for directing a seminar, College Music Teaching, which is intended to serve doctoral students enrolled in degree programs across our respective schools of music. As the instructors, we are interested in the question of how music students become music teachers. That question has been addressed often in cases of undergraduates who are preparing for public school music teaching (e.g., Campbell, 1999; Conkling, 2003; Dolloff, 1999; Madsen & Kelly, 2002; Roberts, 1991), but it has not been taken up for graduate students in music intending to become collegiate faculty who have responsibilities in studio and classroom music teaching. How are these music students being socialized into the teacher role?

Socialization is a process through which an individual moves toward membership in a community or organization. The process is dependent upon how the individual views others and others' roles in the organization, as well as how others view him or her. Thus, socialization is dynamic and interactive. Occupational socialization describes how individuals adjust to the various power structures that exist in organizations where they make their living. VanMaanen (1976) believes that occupational socialization includes an anticipatory period, during which an individual learns about the values associated with the occupational organization. Golde's research (1998) suggests that doctoral students wrestle with questions about their abilities to act as collegiate faculty members, their desire to do the work, and most importantly, whether they feel a sense of belonging in an academic field or department. Thus, it is reasonable to view the period of doctoral education as a time of socialization into collegiate faculty roles.

Although there is scant evidence about doctoral students in music, general patterns for the socialization of doctoral students into teaching roles can be inferred from descriptions of teaching assistant training programs developed in universities throughout the United States from about 1990 onward. A 1990 policy statement by the American Association of Universities acknowledged:

> Since virtually all doctoral students, whether or not they enter the academic sector, will be engaged in not only the creation but the dissemination of knowledge, the skills acquired in learning how to teach will be fundamental to their future work. Yet in far too many programs, effective teachers are produced by happenstance rather than by design. Graduate students often

teach too much but are not sufficiently assisted in becoming effective teachers; we find this both ironic and unacceptable. (p. 3)

This statement gives some indication of the nature of the graduate experience, which has changed little since 1990. According to the *Survey of Earned Doctorates Summary Report 2005* (Hoffer et al., 2006), 71% of doctoral degree recipients relied on a teaching assistantship to fund at least part of their education. In the humanities (which includes the field of music), teaching assistantships were the primary source of funding. While institutional support pays for doctoral educations, doctoral students in turn provide universities with a consistent supply of personnel to fulfill teaching and teaching-related duties at less cost than hiring professors to perform those same tasks.

Questions remain, however, about the quality of teaching done by teaching assistants (TAs), and the extent to which graduate students conceive of themselves as teachers. Teaching assistant training has arisen in short orientation programs, disciplinary programs, and in "centers for teaching excellence" on many college campuses across the country. Descriptions of best practices in TA training programs can be found in volumes such as *Preparing Graduate Students to Teach* (Lambert & Tice, 1993) or *Preparing the Professoriate of Tomorrow to Teach: Selected Readings in TA Training* (Nyquist, Abbott, Wulff, & Sprague, 1991). A decade after these publications surfaced, however, research suggests that the implementation of best practice in preparing doctoral students to teach is far from consistent in Unites States universities. Golde and Dore's study (2000) of more than 9,000 graduate students at 28 major research universities, in many disciplines including music, concluded that aspiring collegiate faculty are interested in teaching, but their graduate educations prepare them almost exclusively for research and creative work. Davis and Fiske (2000) found in a similar survey that their graduate student respondents did not receive careful supervision in their teaching assignments. Results of Austin's (2002) study suggest that professors devote little time to helping doctoral students learning to teach, and that doctoral students recognize that there is little reward in the university for good teaching. Doctoral students in the field of music were included in Austin's 4-year study.

Of all the research literature on teacher socialization that might illuminate our understanding of the socialization of doctoral students into the college teacher role, Lortie's (2002) *Schoolteacher: A Sociological Study* stands out. In it, the author refers to five attractors to teaching, including: (1) working with people, (2) rendering service, (3) liking the school environment, (4) financial security, and (5) compatibility of the teaching schedule with other facets of life. This list provides plausible attractors to college music teaching as well. Perhaps more importantly, Lortie highlights the internalization of teaching models that occurs for individuals during their 13 or more years spent as pupils. Lortie calls this internalization "apprenticeship of observation," and he gives evidence that it is frequently more influential than any aspect of formal teacher education, including the teaching internship. The extent to which apprenticeship of observation is applicable to doctoral students in music who are preparing for their careers as collegiate faculty members remains an open question.

THE CONTEXT FOR OUR INQUIRY

We began this investigation imagining that we would examine stories of our doctoral students' socialization into the teacher role. Because we chose a narrative approach, that is, inquiry based on stories of lived experience, we recognized from the beginning that many typical considerations of research would quickly become blurry. For example, we knew that there would be no boundaries between our roles as teachers and our roles as researchers. We also knew that the stories our students told were similar to, but not synonymous with, lived experiences, and that our own experiences of becoming collegiate faculty would influence our interactions with our students. Thus, as Connelly and Clandinin (2006) indicate, "In a different time, in a different social situation … a different research text might [have been] written. There is no ultimate finality, or limiting truth, in the particular text written" (p. 485).

College teaching seminars. We each taught a seminar that met once per week for 2 hours. Believing in the importance of constructed knowledge, we formatted our seminars similarly, where reading, guest lectures, and presentation of student projects were intended to generate discussion. Our syllabi were not identical, however. As we began this research project, we compared syllabi and found that we both wanted our students to question what useful purposes technology might serve in college music teaching. Technology, then, served as a point of intersection between our seminars. We paired a student from one institution with a student from another institution and asked the pairs to exchange e-mail messages where they introduced themselves and described seminar content. We also scheduled an Internet 2 class meeting, where the pairs met each other for the first time, and they subsequently heard a lecture by the deans of the two institutions about how to search for a college teaching position.

Participants. In 2006, there were 18 students in enrolled in our two college teaching seminars: 11 were pursuing degrees in music performance, 4 in music education, 2 in music theory, and 1 in conducting. Most held teaching assistantships at our respective institutions, and a few held part-time or full-time faculty appointments at other colleges or universities. Five students had prior experience teaching at the precollegiate level.

Procedures. We were careful to develop what Clandinin and Connelly (2000) call a relational ethic with our students. We shared not only our questions, but also our notes and various drafts of research text with them. Initially, we shared three orienting questions:

1. How are doctoral students in music being socialized into the teaching role?
2. How does apprenticeship of observation reveal itself in this socialization?
3. What issues or problems are prevalent in this socialization?
   3a. Are these issues or problems unique to musicians?

Each teacher-researcher wrote field notes after his or her class session, including a description of topics covered and questions raised by students. Field notes also included a column of questions or ideas to be pursued with individual students, as shown in Table 9.1. The questions pursued with individual students became brief unstructured interviews and were transcribed. Field notes, transcribed interviews, and copies of the e-mail exchanges between pairs of students constituted the primary data for this inquiry.

ANALYSIS AND INTERPRETATION

We borrowed analysis techniques from ethnographic inquiry to separate our data from its authors and reassemble it as it directly pertained to our

Table 9.1.   Example of Field Notes

10/30: Students brought in the results of assessments that had given to their students. Most assessments were concerned with when, where, and how students practice between lessons. Ethan had an interesting design; his voice students listened to recordings of singers (Whitney Houston to Kristin Chenoweth to Renee Fleming) and described the singing, applying language of vocal production and expression they had learned in their voice lessons.	*Remember to ask Ethan about the age, gender, and ethnic mix in his studio. Review his assessment with him to see if differences in response might (plausibly) be attributed to gender or ethnicity (?).*

initial research questions. By doing so, we were able to account for patterns of socialization common among our students, and preliminarily address the idea of apprenticeship of observation.

How are Doctoral Students Being Socialized?

Most of the students enrolled in our courses held teaching assistantships at our respective institutions, they had short (5 days or less) orientations to their teaching assignments, and professors were assigned to be their supervisors. In a few cases, conversations about college level music teaching took place regularly between teaching assistant and supervisor. Although faculty mentoring of TAs is supposed to take place at both institutions, in only one case did the doctoral student's supervisor formally observe and give feedback on his teaching. Otherwise, the students reported little direct mentoring or guidance in teaching from collegiate faculty. Several of our doctoral students had also held part-time or full-time appointments at other colleges and universities, where they may also have received brief orientations to their teaching assignments, but none reported any systematic induction to or supervision of their teaching by college faculty or administrators. Compared to those doctoral students mentioned in the professional literature, our students' backgrounds and experiences appeared to be typical.

Apprenticeship of Observation

The students enrolled in our courses had spent many years as music students. Their visions of college music teaching were highly influenced by their studio teachers, exemplified in a passage from one student's philosophy of teaching:

> As a piano teacher, it is my belief that the instrument is only an incidental medium. Beyond expressing themselves through music, I want the students to become confident individuals who have the abilities to think critically and create originally. I want to help unlock their potentials, to guide and support them in the learning process, so they can eventually meet the goals they have set for themselves. This is what my piano teachers have done for me.

In schools of music, most instruction by studio teachers takes place as one-on-one tutorials, and concomitant preparation by students for lessons, juried examinations and recitals takes place in a solitary fashion in the practice room. Because so much of the work of music teaching and learning is done alone, doctoral students may have few points of comparison when they are constructing their ideas about teaching. This was borne out when several of our students were asked how studio teachers understand what and how to teach. One student responded, "They just know!" whereas another student commented, "It seems to be an advantage for a studio professor to make his work appear to be magic. If he is the only one who possesses true music teaching knowledge, then students would have to flock to him!" Still a third student observed, "Perhaps the most important part of a studio teacher's job is to recruit virtuosic students. In this way, the teacher works as a caretaker of already developed talent." These statements do not argue against apprenticeship of observation, which may take place among music students bound for a college teaching career, but they complicate such apprenticeship by suggesting that students perceive little agreement in the profession about the content or strategies of music teaching.

FURTHER NEGOTIATION OF ANALYSIS AND INTERPRETATION

Clandinin and Connelly (2000) warn against smoothing over the narrative text, writing:

> It would be tempting to view this overall process of analysis and interpretation as a series of steps. However, this is not how narrative inquiries are lived out. Negotiation occurs from beginning to end … [as further] texts are composed to develop points of importance in the revised story. (p. 132)

We found three points of importance, intersections of our students' stories, which required further inquiry and development. First, 8 of 18 students enrolled in our courses were international students, and 7 of 8 international students spoke a language other than English as their first language. The ways in which these international students obtained and navigated their teaching assistantships were intriguing. Second, throughout the semester, our doctoral students tended to identify the characteristics of good music teaching in the same way as some people identify good art: they knew what they liked. Those with prior experience teaching pre-collegiate students were sometimes able to describe applications of child and adolescent development theories to music teaching; however, we observed our students' surprise as they learned about adult learning theories and thought about how those theories might be applied in music studio and classroom teaching. Finally, although we planned for the topic of technology in music teaching to figure prominently in our seminars, we were not prepared for our students' stories of feeling pressured to incorporate technology into teaching.

To make sense of these points from our students' stories, we needed to turn to research literature for additional information and clarification. By interweaving the research literature and our students' stories, we were able to generate a fuller and more complex picture of doctoral students' socialization into teaching.

International Teaching Assistants

A survey conducted in the fall of 2005 by the American Association of Community Colleges, American Council on Education, Association of American Universities, Council of Graduate Schools, Institute of International Education, Association of International Educators, and National Association of State Universities and Land-Grant Colleges concluded that international student enrollment is at least stabilized, if not increasing, at most United States colleges and universities. Increases in numbers of students from China and Korea were especially notable (Open Doors, 2005). The demographics of our schools of music closely resemble this national survey, with Korean and Chinese students making up the largest percentage of foreign enrollment, and their numbers at least stable, if not trending upward.

When we asked the international students how they were awarded teaching assistantships, they explained to us that they took the Test of English as a Foreign Language (TOEFL). According to Yule and Hoffman (1990), a higher TOEFL score may be a better predictor of teaching success, but by itself does "not guarantee that this individual will convert general proficiency into a capability to present instructional material" (p. 240). Although the iBT/Next Generation TOEFL now requires an Academic Speaking Test, there is substantial disagreement about whether it reflects English language skills that are important in all academic disciplines (Papajohn, 2006). To teach music typically requires establishing a learning environment, questioning, and providing feedback; these discourses might be similar to those employed in other disciplines (Axelson & Madden, 1994). Yet, music teaching is distinguished by its reliance on terminology derived from Italian (*forte, diminuendo, staccato, andante, tutti, etc.*). Furthermore, teacher modeling is a central strategy for music teaching, unlike in other disciplines where it may be considered a compensatory strategy (Axelson & Madden, 1994). These discourses and skills common to music teaching are not included in the iBT/Next Generation TOEFL. Our international students consistently reported that no professor or administrator assessed these teaching skills before a teaching assistantship was awarded. They realized that little evidence existed about whether they were qualified to teach music, yet many of them were immediately assigned to teach 10-12 students per week in studio lessons. Although the ITAs continued to be pleased with their teaching assignments, through institutional structures they received a strong message that English language competency and teaching competency are one in the same.

Flowerdew and Miller (1995) define several cultures that exist in higher education and the extent to which teaching is affected by these cultures. The researchers define *disciplinary culture* as "the theories, concepts, norms, terms ... specific to a particular academic discipline" (p. 366), and they point out that the technical terminology of any academic discipline is likely to remain constant across languages, most often because technical terms cannot be translated. However, Flowerdew and Miller also make the case that *ethnic culture* strongly affects teaching and learning, especially when the teacher's ethnic culture is different from the students' culture. To underscore this point, the authors contrast Confucian and Western values related to teaching and learning. For example, teachers influenced by Western values may favor an interactive classroom style, while their Chinese students value effacement and silence. Our own students confirmed this type of cross-cultural confusion in music lessons and courses. A Chinese student, whose teaching responsibilities included keyboard class, reported her initial shock when freshman students raised their hands to ask questions. "In my culture, students never ask questions. It is disrespectful to the teacher's authority." Two Korean students related stories of lectures, master classes, and ensemble rehearsals where it was typical for them to sit near other Korean speakers in order to translate and clarify. These students expressed that Koreans typically value success for all, rather than just for the individual; yet professors have accused them of cheating or being distracted when they translate for their peers. Even a Canadian student recounted how, in her first days teaching of secondary violin, she assumed that students had well-developed aural skills, and she frequently made reference to solfege syllables to help students recognize their mistakes. "Most Canadian students who are serious about music go through a series of Royal Conservatory Examinations during their formative training, so these kinds of skills are expected." She anticipated that students from the United States would have received similar training, but found that was not necessarily the case.

Our doctoral students' stories, along with the professional literature, have led us to question the extent to which socialization into the teacher role at the collegiate level is based on assimilation of a narrowly defined set of cultural values. Could one truly argue that respect for teachers or success for all do not have a place in university-level music teaching and learning? Yet, our international students perceived that these values were ignored in the collegiate teaching environment. Additionally, because a doctoral student's ethnic culture strongly influences his or her perceptions of teaching and learning, we believe that ethnic culture somehow figures into apprenticeship of observation. The extent to which students may misapprehend the pedagogical approaches of their teachers, especially when the student's ethnic culture and the teacher's ethnic culture differ, warrants further investigation.

Adult Learning Theories and Their Application

"I appreciate how Mr. Adams encourages every student to speak during studio class, even the least experienced freshman."

"My professor incorporates vocal physiology and pedagogy into every lesson. It's not overwhelming; it's just enough to make you feel like you could help your own students solve their problems."

"Lectures were a prominent part of my undergraduate education. I thought that was normal. But did I enjoy them? Did I learn from them? No, not much."

"Of course Professor Harrison has a definite interpretation of every piece that we play. But I've seen how she's wise to allow us to try our own way first."

So went our doctoral students' descriptions of music teaching at the collegiate level. The students identified aspects of teaching that seemed beneficial and other aspects of teaching that they perceived as detrimental to music learning. None of them had previously encountered the term *andragogy,* which is associated with Malcolm Knowles and generally encompasses the study of teaching and learning behaviors in adult classroom settings. Brookfield (1986) has suggested that some use the term *andragogy* as a rallying cry "to combat what [they see] as the use with adult learners of overly didactic modes of teaching and program planning" (p. 90). Our students were very familiar with passive learner roles in the face of lecture-based teaching, and they did not favor that kind of teaching. Since most of the doctoral students saw themselves as studio teachers, however, they did not view didactic lectures as a principal mode of instruction.

Rogers' (2002) list of seven adult characteristics seemed more relevant to our students, and three of those characteristics were especially applicable to studio music teaching. First, Rogers suggested that "new students are not new people; they possess a set of values, established prejudices and attitudes in which they have invested a great deal of emotional investment" (p. 73). Second, Rogers contended that adult students arrive in the learning environment with focus and intent. Since most music students have already invested a considerable amount of time and money in instruments, lessons, and practice prior to auditions for college, it is only natural that they continue to pursue musical studies with the same intensity at the collegiate level. Third, adult students are not starting a process of growth, but rather they are in the middle of a process of growth. Rogers proposed, "Adult student participants have already invested emotional capital in acquiring ... knowledge and experience. They will expend much more in defending the integrity of this knowledge, so new learning changes will sometimes be strenuously resisted" (p. 239).

In fact, such resistance was at the core of our doctoral students' concerns about their roles as collegiate teachers. A piano class teacher explained,

> they [undergraduates] don't always understand why they have to take piano class—how mastering a Bach invention will help them with their performance on viola or trumpet—and so they don't practice enough. Sometimes I have to invent ways to keep them motivated.

Another doctoral student expressed a similar sentiment saying,

> I teach students from many different majors who have many different reasons for studying voice, and it's a lot of work to find repertoire for each student that will keep them motivated and keep them practicing. I suggest to some students that they might perform something in Italian, and they immediately turn off.

Deci and Ryan's (1985) self-determination theory is a macrotheory of motivation that helped our doctoral students not only frame their collegiate students' resistance, but also better understand the kinds of music teaching they preferred. The theory begins by acknowledging three basic human psychological needs: competence, relatedness, and autonomy. The psychologists posit that humans, regardless of gender or culture, are naturally inquisitive and display an inherent desire to learn and explore. In other words, humans are naturally motivated. However, the theory also acknowledges that motivation can be "facilitated or undermined by the interaction of the organism with the social world, resulting in either healthy development, effective functioning, and well-being, or thwarted development, diminished functioning, and ill being" (Deci & Vansteenkiste, 2004, p. 34).

Ryan and Deci (2000) have revisited the classic definitions of intrinsic and extrinsic motivation, and while they acknowledge that all humans are intrinsically motivated for particular activities, in educational settings it may be more important to consider how human beings are extrinsically motivated:

> Frankly speaking, because many of the tasks that educators want their students to perform are not inherently interesting or enjoyable, knowing how to promote more active and volitional (versus passive and controlling) forms of extrinsic motivation becomes an essential strategy for successful teaching. (p. 55)

Autonomous extrinsic motivation is characterized by willingness and choice, whereas controlled motivation is characterized by pressure and demand. Autonomy supportive teachers "hold meaningful dialogues with students, and ... suspend judgment while soliciting the opinions and concerns of students" (Williams & Deci, 1998, p. 304). In contrast, controlling teachers are critical, authoritarian and ignore students' perspectives. In studies, autonomous extrinsic motivation has been linked to greater psychological well-being, better performance, and higher quality learning (Ryan & Deci, 2000).

Technology

We were intentional about framing several seminar activities around the uses of technology for college music teaching. We expected that music and video downloading, instant messaging, blogging, and the creation of Web-based portfolios were part of our doctoral students' everyday lives. We were surprised, however, to learn that our students' beliefs about technology echoed Bowers (1998) who suggests, "[students believe that] computer mediated thought and communication represent a superior and more empowering form of learning" (p. 49). Ferdig (2006) similarly comments that

> Technology is so new and exciting to many teachers (and even researchers) that it is often put into the classroom devoid of any content-learning goals. (This refers to the straw-person argument that technology can just be dropped into a setting, and it will magically transform the practices of both the teachers and the student.) (p. 755)

Acknowledging the myths that surround technology, some of our doctoral students, particularly those who held full and part-time faculty appointments, intimated that they felt institutional pressure to incorporate computer and web-based technologies into their college music teaching.

That sense of pressure may stem from external pressures on the university such as improving time-to-graduation rates, improving access to instruction, and reducing costs associated with instruction. The recent report, *A Test of Leadership: Charting the Future of Higher Education* (United States Department of Educationm, 2006), known also as the *Spellings Report*, for example, recommends "support for the dissemination of technological advances that lower costs" (p. 20), so university administrators may believe that technology is a panacea for fiscal challenges and the increasing demands to accommodate "non-traditional" student populations.

Most university and college teachers have little formal training to use technology for teaching (Bates & Poole, 2003), and the additional workload often associated with technology is "perhaps the most serious barrier to its increased use" (p. 17). While it is true that most institutions offer technology support, faculty often do not know what questions to ask, and the technology support staff do not know what faculty need, particularly as it relates to specific fields and their subdisciplines ("Face-off" 2005).

For music faculty, in particular, there are no guidelines to help decide between mastering new video editing software and memorizing a new concerto, between creating a hybrid music theory course and polishing an article for a prestigious journal, or between having chat hours with students and meeting them face to face. While all of these activities present potential enhancements to music teaching and learning, not all of them receive equal institutional reward. Furthermore, the reward for teaching with technology can vary greatly between collegiate-level institutions.

Most importantly, measuring teaching or learning related to technology is extremely difficult (Jones & Paolucci 1998), and there is surprisingly little research evidence to demonstrate that technology improves the quality of teaching for professors or produces more efficient learning for students. Ferdig (2006) suggests that research tends to describe the outcomes of technology use

> in terms of what X media ... will do for teaching and learning writ large. The growth that we have made in looking at pedagogy and people ... is forgotten if we do not include both in the assessment and then implications of the performance of the technological innovation. (p. 757)

Socialization into college teaching cannot avoid weighing the use of various technologies. As suggested by Bates and Poole (2003), the question collegiate music faculty must ask "is not are [technologies] better or worse, but in what context and for what purposes are technologies used best?" (p. 51). We wonder about what institutional supports are in place so aspiring collegiate music teachers can explore this question in depth.

PROVISIONAL CONCLUSIONS, LINGERING QUESTIONS

This inquiry was highly situated, and because of its narrative nature, not replicable even at our own institutions. Nevertheless, because of this initial inquiry about the socialization of doctoral students into teaching, we can offer some provisional conclusions and raise more informed questions for further investigation. If it is true that most doctoral students in music are dependent upon teaching assistantships for funding, they are already being socialized into the teacher role. We in colleges and schools of music granting doctoral degrees should openly acknowledge that the ecology and the economy of the university require the work of TAs. We should be intentional in the consideration of doctoral education as a time of socialization into faculty roles, and a fundamental part of our mission should be to help address doctoral students' questions about their abilities to act as collegiate faculty members, their desire to do the work, and whether they feel a sense of belonging in the music field or department.

Due to their many years of musical studies prior to enrollment in graduate degree programs, we should assume that doctoral students in music have undergone apprenticeship of observation, particularly with their applied teachers. Our inquiry suggests, however, that observations of music teaching can be extremely different among doctoral students, leading toward their perception that college music teaching is highly idiosyncratic. One of the factors that may affect doctoral student's apprenticeship of observation is his or her ethnic culture, especially when it differs from a teacher's ethnic culture. Further research should investigate the myriad ways that ethnic culture may influence observation of music teaching.

Doctoral students' socialization into teaching may be complicated by the presence of ITAs and the multiple cultural values they bring to schools of music. Further complications include lack of understanding about adult learning theories, accompanied by lack of opportunity to observe their applications in teaching, and the presence of computer and Web-based technologies along with perceived pressure to incorporate technology into teaching. Since none of these complications appear to be unique to the field of music, further research should examine promising practices related to the socialization of doctoral students into faculty roles that might be occurring in other disciplinary areas of the university.

Stories from ITAs indicated the possibility that insufficient data is collected during the admission process about doctoral students' prior experience and abilities in music teaching, as well as their dispositions toward teaching. How could new admission strategies be generated that might address this issue? One requirement might be that prospective doctoral students submit a teaching resume alongside the performance resume. A video recording of a doctoral student's teaching might also be required for admission, but departments would need to develop clear criteria for evaluating the quality of teaching represented in the videos. The purpose of collecting evidence about prospective doctoral students' teaching experiences and abilities during the admissions process should not be to prevent doctoral students from obtaining a teaching assistantship; rather, it should be to assign each doctoral student to an assistantship where his or her skills and dispositions can be best employed, and to gain clearer understanding about the kinds of supervision and mentoring that will be necessary for the teaching assistant.

Understanding adult learning theories can help TAs assess and build on collegiate students' prior experience, and account for apparent resistance to new ideas and performance techniques. Furthermore, adult learning theories suggest that the teacher should try to take the perspective of the student in order to provide the kinds of autonomy support that encourage the student to be self-directed in learning and provide motivation for the student to continue learning long after his formal education has ended. How can the doctoral student most effectively develop understanding of adult learning theories? Where are these theories systematically applied in collegiate level music teaching, and what influence does such application have on music learning outcomes?

Evidence for how specific technologies improve music teaching and learning must be compiled if prospective collegiate teachers are to make appropriate judgments about the use of technology in teaching. Which technologies provide increased access to high quality music instruction for rural, nontraditional, and other students? How can technologies bring institutions together to share music teaching and learning resources? Which technologies can be used to provide autonomy support, and thus foster self-directed learning for college music students? Likewise, we should have evidence of the ways in which particular technologies might be harmful to music teaching and learning. For example, in what ways do online music courses discourage peer-to-peer learning? Deans, department chairs and other administrators must craft careful guidelines for faculty about how technological innovation figures into promotion and tenure decisions. As part of the socialization experience, those guidelines could be shared with doctoral students to help them make important decisions about how their time and other resources should be allocated.

So, we return to our original question: How do music students become music teachers? This inquiry, though situated, suggests that doctoral students become music teachers by observing their own teachers, but such observation may be complicated in several ways, including by doctoral students' ethnic culture, their concerns about student learning, and perceived pressure to utilize technology. As calls for accountability in higher education increase, we must recognize that preparing doctoral students for teaching is essential to the long-term survival of colleges of music, and, indeed, of the entire university. Continued inquiry regarding the socialization of doctoral students into faculty roles will not only deepen our understanding of how to best prepare teachers, it will also lead toward a future professoriate that values teaching and insists that good teaching should be rewarded in higher education.

REFERENCES

American Association of Universities. (1990). *Institutional policies to improve doctoral education: A policy statement*. Washington, DC: Author.

Austin, A. E. (2002). Preparing the next generation of faculty: Graduate school as socialization to the academic career. *The Journal of Higher Education, 73*(1), 94-122.

Axelson, E. R., & Madden, C. G. (1994). Discourse strategies for ITAs across instructional contexts. In C. G. Madden & C. L. Myers (Eds.), *Discourse and performance of international teaching assistants* (pp. 153-185). Alexandria, VA: TESOL.

Bates, A. W., & Poole, G. (2003). *Effective teaching with technology in higher education: Foundation for success*. San Francisco: Jossey-Bass.

Bowers, C. A. (1998). The paradox of technology: What's gained and lost? *Thought and Action Journal, 14*(1), 49-57.

Brookfield, S. D. (1986). *Understanding and facilitating adult learning*. San Francisco: Jossey-Bass.

Campbell, M. R. (1999). Learning to teach music: A collaborative ethnography. *Bulletin of the Council for Research in Music Education, 139*, 12-36.

Clandinin, D. J., & Connelly, F. M. (2000). *Narrative inquiry: Experience and story in qualitative research*. San Francisco: Jossey-Bass.

Conkling, S. W. (2003). Uncovering preservice music teachers' reflective thinking: Making sense of learning to teach. *Bulletin of the Council for Research in Music Education, 155*, 11-23.

Connelly, F. M., & Clandinin, D. J. (2006). Narrative inquiry. In J. L. Green, G. Camilli, & P. B. Elmore (Eds.), *Handbook of complementary methods in educational research*. Mahwah, NJ: Erlbaum.

Conole, G., & Oliver, M. (1998). A pedagogical framework for embedding C&IT into the curriculum. *Association for Learning Technology Journal, 6*(2), 4-16.

Davis, G. & Fiske, P. (2000, April). *Results of the 1999 PhDs.org graduate school survey.* Paper presented at the Re-envisioning of the PhD Conference, Seattle, WA.

Deci, E. L., & Ryan, R. M. (1985). *Intrinsic motivation and self-determination in human behavior.* New York: Plenum.

Deci, E. L., & Vansteenkiste, M. (2004). Self-determination theory and basic need satisfaction: Understanding human development in positive psychology. *Ricerche di Psicologia, 1*(27), 23-39.

Dolloff, L. A. (1999). Imagining ourselves as teachers: The development of teacher identity in music teacher education. *Music Education Research 1*(2), 197-297.

Face-off: Technology as teacher? (2005, December 9). Transcript of debate between Carol Twigg and Cliff Stoll. *Chronicle of Higher Education.* Retrieved March 1, 2007, from http://chronicle.com/weekly/v52/i16/16b01201.htm

Ferdig, R. E. (2006). Assessing technologies for teaching and learning: Understanding the importance of technological pedagogical content knowledge. *British Journal of Educational Technology, 37*(5), 749-760.

Flowerdew, J., & Miller, L. (1995). On the notion of culture in L2 lectures. *TESOL Quarterly, 29*(2), 345-373.

Golde, C. M. (1998). Beginning graduate school: Explaining first-year doctoral attrition. In M. S. Anderson (Ed.), *The experience of being in graduate school: An exploration* (Directions for Higher Education, No. 101) (pp. 55-64). San Francisco: Jossey-Bass.

Golde, C. M., & Dore, T. M. (2000, April). *Findings from the survey on doctoral education and career preparation.* Paper presented at the Re-envisioning of the PhD Conference, Seattle, WA.

Hoffer, T. B., Welch, V, Jr., Webber, K., Williams, K., Lisck, B., Hess, M., et al. (2006). *Doctorate Recipients from United States universities: Summary report 2005.* Chicago: National Opinion Research Center. Retrieved from NORC Web site http://www.norc.uchicago.edu/issues/docdata.htm

Jones, T. H., & Paolucci, R. (1998). The learning effectiveness of educational technology: a call for further research. *Educational Technology Review, 9*(2-3), 10-14.

Lambert, L. M., & Tice, S. L. (1993). *Preparing graduate students to teach.* Washington, DC: American Association for Higher Education.

Lortie, D. (2002). *Schoolteacher: A sociological study* (with new introduction). Chicago: University of Chicago Press.

Madsen, C. K., & Kelly, S. N. (2002). First remembrances of wanting to become a music teacher. *Journal of Research in Music Education, 50*(4), 323-332.

Nyquist, J. D., Abbott, R. D., Wulff, D. H., & Sprague, J. (Eds.). (1991). *Preparing the professoriate of tomorrow to teach: Selected readings in TA training.* Dubuque, IA: Kendall/Hunt.

Open Doors (2005, November). *Fall international student enrollment survey: Survey results.* Retrieved January 22, 2007 from http://opendoors.iienetwork.org/?p=Fall2005Survey

Papajohn, D. (2006). Standard setting for next generation TOEFL Academic Speaking Test: Reflections on the ETS panel of international teaching assistant developers. *Teaching English as a Second Language Electronic Journal, 10*(1). Retrieved January 22, 2007, from http://www.tesl-ej.org/ej37/toc.html

Roberts, B. A. (1991). Music teacher education as identity construction. *International Journal of Music Education, 18*, 30-39.

Rogers, A. (2002). *Teaching adults*. Philadelphia: Open University Press.

Ryan, M. R., & Deci, E. L. (2000). Intrinsic and extrinsic motivations: Classic definitions and new directions. *Contemporary Educational Psychology, 25*, 54-67.

United States Department of Education. (2006). *A test of leadership: Charting the future of U.S. higher education*. Washington, DC: Author.

VanMaanen, J. (1976). Breaking in: Socialization to work. In R. Dubin (Ed.), *Handbook of work, organization, and society* (pp. 67-130). Chicago: Rand-McNally.

Williams G. W., & Deci, E. L. (1998). The importance of supporting autonomy in medical education. *Annals of Internal Medicine 129*(4), 303-308.

Yule, G., & Hoffman, P. (1990). Predicting success for International Teaching Assistants in a U.S. university. *TESOL Quarterly, 24*(2), 227-243.

CHAPTER 10

THE ROLE OF IRBs IN MUSIC EDUCATION RESEARCH

Linda C. Thornton

ABSTRACT

The Institutional Review Board serves to ensure researchers exercise respect for persons, justice, and beneficence in their research interactions. However, social science and education researchers often find the biomedical-based regulations overly restrictive. Researchers in these fields voice concerns regarding informed consent, the definition of research, and discipline-specific ethical issues. Also, local Institutional Review Boards interpret the federal regulations in highly disparate ways. The purpose of this paper is threefold, to (a) present a scenario from my own experience that highlights researchers' frustrations with Institutional Review Boards, (b) summarize the discussion of Institutional Review Board issues within educational and social science fields, and (c) present suggestions for improving interactions with Institutional Review Boards, ranging from individual to national-level changes.

Diverse Methodologies in the Study of Music Teaching and Learning, pp. 201–214
Copyright © 2008 by Information Age Publishing
All rights of reproduction in any form reserved.

THE ROLE OF IRBS IN MUSIC EDUCATION RESEARCH

A considerable portion of music education research involves the participation of human subjects. By engaging in this research, music educators are ethically responsible for protecting the welfare of participants both physically and emotionally. Also interested in the welfare of research participants, Institutional Review Board (IRBs) at colleges and universities exist to ensure that research participants are treated with respect, justice, and beneficence. Researchers associated with institutions of higher learning must clear their research procedures through the local IRB prior to collecting data for a project. Therefore, the IRB can directly influence how music education researchers address the questions in their field.

Many disciplines similar to music education, such as the social sciences, history and education, have been engaging in conversations regarding the influence of the IRB in research. As highly public cases of human subject mistreatment have resulted in ever-closer scrutiny of research projects (Brainard, 2001; Cohen, 2007), higher education faculty members have become increasing frustrated with the nature of IRB regulations and procedures. At this time, music education as a field has not actively participated in the discussion as has other fields; yet the concerns are likely shared. The purpose of this paper is to share the nature of the conversation with the music education community by describing a discipline-specific case of my own interactions with multiple IRBs, summarizing cross-discipline issues in existing literature, and presenting some suggestions for addressing the concerns raised in the paper.

OVERVIEW

The protection of biomedical research subjects was the original intent of human subjects review. Over time, the purview of IRBs expanded to include all research conducted using federal funds. Eventually, most universities voluntarily extended their reviews to all research conducted in association with the university, whether or not the project receives federal funding. As the scope of the IRB expands, university researchers, especially those outside biomedical fields, are questioning the value and role of the IRB. For example, the American Association of University Professors (AAUP) contends the very act of IRB committee members determining if research is "worth the risk" is a violation of academic freedom (AAUP, 2006).

Of additional concern to researchers is that IRB review can interfere with the development of the ethics of one's own discipline, creating a situation in which the discipline's ethics are directed by biomedical ethics that may or may not apply (Church, Shopes, & Blanchard, 2002). Greater unease is caused by the very real potential for the questions being asked in a profession to be guided by what can be done (or allowed), rather than what needs to be examined. Research by students who need to graduate and faculty who are working under the tenure clock has surely been impacted by the need to "get through" the IRB, rather than asking questions most pertinent to them and the profession (Church et al., 2002; Hamilton, 2005).

Further, the lack of correspondence between the regulations necessary for biomedical research and research methodologies, procedures, and risk found in the social sciences is the source of many discussions among social science and education researchers (AAUP, 2001, 2006; Brainard, 2001; Bosk & DeVries, 2004; The Center for Advanced Study, 2005; Church, Shopes, & Blanchard, 2002; DeTardo-Bora, 2004: Dougherty & Kramer, 2005; Hamilton, 2005; Hemmings, 2006; Marshall, 2003). Hamilton summarizes the position of many researchers by stating:

> From the apodictic to the assertoric, there is a persistent temptation to apply procedures, methods, claims, and, more recently, regulation developed for the medical sciences to social sciences. The IRB system is often nonsensical when applied to social research; the rules are not right or wrong, but irrelevant. (p. 193)

THIS RESEARCHER'S STORY

The present paper resulted from the process of conducting another research project. Music education majors at 26 schools of music throughout the United States were the potential participants for completing a questionnaire indicating their influences for choosing music education as a profession (Thornton & Bergee, 2008). In this questionnaire, no personal information regarding race, habits, or preferences was being collected—only descriptive data such as each student's major instrument (saxophone, voice, etc.), age, and anticipated year of graduation.

The 26 universities were chosen based on meeting the criteria for "major" schools of music. These universities all had Carnegie I classification (now known as Research Extensive), were members of Association of American Universities, and had accreditation from the National Association of Schools of Music. The discussion in this paper refers to those universities that met the criteria stated above.

Since the human participants involved were college students, my institution considers the population to be protected, and therefore not exempt (although survey research is to be exempt except when confidentiality is a concern). My IRB identified four requirements that needed to be met before data were collected. First, my institution was to be excluded from the data collection, as was the institution of the coauthor (this reduced the universities available for the study to 24). Second, the researchers were to receive permission from the IRB at each university from which students were recruited to be included in the study. Third, the participants were not to complete the survey during class time but rather on their own time. Lastly, the students were to return the survey to a place that was public enough that the students might be accessing the location for other reasons, yet private enough that their professors would not see who had or had not completed the survey. The potential number of subjects for this study was a few thousand. The final population sample was 250.

The second requirement, receiving permission from each IRB of the universities involved in the study, was the impetus for the present paper. Consistent with literature in other fields, some problems with IRBs are due to the local implementation of federal regulations, which is highly disparate (Hamilton, 2005). It is not the purpose of this paper to criticize individual campus IRBs, but rather highlight the array of differences among somewhat similar institutions.

When I found myself in a position of having to collect permission from 24 universities, I met with the reviewer from my IRB to ask if there was a more reasonable way of meeting their criteria for review than having to complete forms at 24 different universities. The IRB reviewer suggested I submit my approved, home IRB application to each university upon contact, and they could then choose to review that application against their own standards. Given the nature of the regulations, and similarity of the institutions, I believed this suggestion would be very helpful. However, I quickly found this not to be true.

The first observation in attempting to receive permission from 24 universities was the inconsistency in name and systematic location of the office. A search for "human subjects" or "institutional review board" on the main web site of the university occasionally led to the IRB, but often did not. Some universities have their offices under the auspices of a research dean, some in the schools of medicine, and some in a separate area that does not seem to have any reporting structure related to the rest of the university. While this information may seem irrelevant, certainly the guiding organization of an office could exert influence, oversight, and philosophy in a variety of ways.

Of the 24 institutions contacted, only nine institutions (37.5%) accepted the application that had been approved by my own IRB. Of special note, one institution informed me that my IRB and that institution have a reciprocal agreement, in writing, for IRB approvals. Therefore, with the agreement already in place, no further action was necessary.

The remaining approximately two-thirds of the universities responded in a variety of ways. The range of responses is represented by the following extremes. One institution responded with what amounted to confusion as to why the office was being involved if permission to conduct the research had already been given by an IRB. My explanation that my IRB required this information seemed to further baffle the IRB member at the contacted institution. It took considerable prompting to receive the required written consent from this institution.

At the opposite extreme, another institution contacted me three times for further information after I had completed their application. One request asked me to adjust some of the language in the informed consent letter, which then needed to be approved by my own IRB as a change in methodology. The next request was for the exact number of students in the school of music and the exact number of music education majors in order to determine the possible size of the subject pool (they would not accept an estimate). The final contact informed me that the faculty member identified as the principle investigator (PI) for the local campus had not been certified through their human subjects training. Therefore, the PI would need to complete this training before further consideration of the project. Since the PI had already served as the point person for the other requests for additional information, it was becoming apparent that the simple request to serve as PI and distribute and collect questionnaires was becoming more than a small favor. Pursuit of approval at this institution was abandoned.

Ten universities (41.67%) required me to complete the human subjects application from their own office, despite the completed and approved application received from my IRB. For some universities, this procedure was a daunting and overwhelming task, while for others it was relatively simple. I could only imagine the range of freedoms researchers at the various institutions must enjoy, or suffer, based on the information requested and the procedures in place at their universities. The 10 forms I completed varied from two-page documents asking for general information about the project and addressing each of the IRB criteria (e.g., recruitment) to forms eight pages in length, with up to four additional attachments of information.

Based on my experiences with these IRBs around the country, a number of issues can, and do, impact the nature and quality of research in our field. While my story does not highlight all of these issues, it raised many questions for me. These questions and others are summarized well by Dougherty and Kramer (2005): (a) are IRBs protecting human subjects or the institution, (b) do IRBs end up supporting research or shaping the nature and outcome of research, (c) is it appropriate that an oversight committee such as an IRB has no oversight itself, and d) in some cases, does the involvement of the IRB create more risk to human subjects than not?

CONCERNS

As mentioned at the beginning of this paper, concerns with IRBs are being discussed by many researchers in the social science and education fields. Stories of frustrating and unreasonable requirements such as that above, have been published along with calls for reform. The following describes three general areas of concern among researchers related to IRB review.

Informed Consent

Many researchers note that the notion of informed consent and qualitative research are not compatible (Bosk & DeVries, 2004; Church et al., 2002; Detardo-Bora, 2004; Hemmings, 2006; Malone, 2003). Of primary concern is that informed consent is technically impossible in a qualitative methodology. Because the methods emerge from events that will occur in the future, a researcher is not able to identify all potential risks to subjects, nor inform them of everything that could occur as a result of their agreement to participate. In addition, the relationships developed in qualitative inquiry can be intimate. As in any other human interaction, a letter cannot guarantee that a participant will not feel hurt, abandoned or used (Bosk & De Vries, 2004; Hemmings, 2006). Finally, social science and educational researchers may find it difficult to identify risks for the participants because they do not view their participants' involvement as risky (Bosk & DeVries, 2004).

The assurance of confidentiality is important to the informed consent procedure. The IRB requires the researcher to design procedures to protect the identity of the human subjects, write a letter that explains how the confidentiality will be guaranteed, and ensure each participant signs, and therefore understands, the letter. However, in historical research, confidentiality or anonymity actually jeopardizes the credibility of the research (Brainard, 2001; Church et al., 2002). Further, in many case studies and other qualitative research, Malone (2003) considers the assurance of confidentiality to be a false promise. The reality is that among research circles, someone who is interested enough to read the research could likely determine the identity of the participants just by knowing the field and the author and by using a modest amount of investigation. "It came down to this: anybody who mattered would know" (p. 805). Therefore, the promise of confidentiality made to participants in some situations is at best misleading and at worst a lie.

As alluded to in the previous paragraph, the notion of informed consent also assumes that by reading a well-crafted letter, participants truly understand the methodologies and practices in which they are about to engage. In Malone's (2003) experience, participants who were university professors and doctoral students well-trained in qualitative methodologies were not fully able to anticipate the consequences and implications of participating in her research. Therefore, it seems questionable if any participant in any research study can give consent that is truly informed.

Another issue for many researchers is the invasive nature of informed consent. A positive rapport with participants is imperative for collecting the thickest descriptive data. In ethnographic research, "Informed consent is an ongoing interaction between the researcher and the members of the communities being studied" (Church et al., 2002, p. 3) However, using the informed consent procedures designed for biomedical research in a qualitative setting can compromise this relationship (Marshall, 2003). Hamilton (2005) describes the informed consent process as "contamination of the natural world" (p. 195). Further, Hamilton contends that informed consent procedures can be frightening to subjects, especially marginalized populations. The process, therefore, seems to encourage the study of comfortable, main-stream populations and discourages examination of others.

In qualitative or quantitative education research, acquiring parent or guardian, as well as participant, permission can significantly delay or limit research participants, even when the research procedures are very similar to normal instructional procedures. Normal instructional procedures are to be exempt from review, according to the federal regulations, but the need to protect children usually overrides this stipulation. One outcome of this informed consent procedure can be that only nonmarginalized students, whose parents or guardians will sign and return a form, are the majority of participants in many research projects.

The Nature of Research

The Common Rule, as it is known, is part of Title 45, part 46 of the Code of Federal Regulations governing the IRBs. The Common Rule defines what research is subject to review, "this policy applies to all research involving human subjects conducted, supported or otherwise subject to regulation by any federal department or agency which takes appropriate administrative action to make the policy applicable to such research" (United States Department of Health and Human Services, 2005, para. 46.101). As mentioned earlier, most universities have opted to review all research regardless of funding.

However, based on the wording of the regulations, the question becomes what is research and what is not? The practice of teaching is very closely aligned to the practice of research. So where is the line drawn between research and practice? When does normal experimenting with procedures, reflecting, tweaking, and experimenting again leave the realm of practice and become research? If a faculty member approaches a teacher with a research question and procedure, and the teacher is intrigued and agrees that she, too, would like to find out this information about her students, if she delivers the procedures is it practice, but if the faculty member does, then is it research? The very nature of research such as action research and practitioner research purposefully straddles the line of research and practice and therefore seems to be very confusing to the IRBs (Detardo-Bora, 2004; Pritchard, 2002).

It has long been argued that IRBs have not considered non-quantitative methods viable. Therefore researchers contend that IRBs dictate research procedures more quantitative in nature to suit their own review protocols. While this disinterest and misunderstanding about qualitative methodologies may be waning, a number of researchers contend a highly variable stance among IRBs exists on this issue (Detardo-Bora, 2004; Hemmings, 2006; Malone, 2003; Pritchard, 2002). Education as a profession, and educational research, is served well by acknowledging multiple ways of knowing, as represented through a wide variety of methodologies such as action, practitioner, case study and ethnographic research (Hamilton, 2005). As nonquantitative methods have gained acknowledgement and respect within their fields, it seems the IRB system needs to also adapt to accommodate a broader view of research.

Ethical Issues

Treating people in the right way is at the heart of human subject protocols. However, there is perhaps no greater divide among people in this world than that of what is "right." The treatment of women under Taliban rule was seen as unjust to Westerners, but "right" to the Taliban. The capitalist principles intractable in United States society are currently in question in other parts of the world. Therefore, how is it possible for a society, agency, or office to come to consensus about what is "right?" At what point can someone be certain that benefits truly outweigh the risks?

At what point can we know that "justice" has been ensured? In a society in which the definition of "human" is in question (a fetus? a clone?) the notion of a single idea of fairness and respect seems unrealistic.

The Belmont Report, originally published in 1979, serves as the guiding document for the ethics and principles for the IRBs. However, Pritchard (2002) contends the philosophical traditions for the three guiding principles, respect for persons, justice and beneficence, are inherently contradictory and therefore makes meeting all three criteria technically impossible. In addition, Weijer (2004) argues that the creators of *The Belmont Report* ultimately stripped the report of references to its philosophical and ethical backgrounds because the authors could not agree on what those should be.

As mentioned earlier in this paper, researchers contend field-specific ethical concerns for human subjects are being marginalized by IRB reviews. The Illinois white paper discusses "mission creep" by IRBs "caused by rewarding wrong behaviors, such as focusing more on procedures and documentation than difficult ethical questions" (The Center for Advanced Study, 2005, para. 2). Hamilton (2005) concurs that focus on procedures and so-called petty crimes are actually harming the discussion of appropriate ethics and behaviors by researchers. Further, a possible repercussion of the incongruence between IRBs and social science researchers is that IRB review is actually driving the course of research within the discipline. "Lack of understanding generates misunderstandings, which can cause students ... to abandon controversial or challenging inquiries in favor of more innocuous studies to minimize the risk of brutal IRB review" (Hemmings, 2006, p. 16).

In an attempt to keep the discussion somewhat balanced, it is worthy to note that the frustrations raised by social scientists are real, but could be necessary on some level.

> There is more than a whiff of hypocrisy in imposing obligations on others—in this case, physicians and medical researchers who cannot be trusted because their self-interest makes unreliable their judgments of others' best interests—while resisting those very same obligations for oneself because our work is harmless, our intentions good, and our hearts pure. (Bosk & DeVries, 2004, p. 256)

SUGGESTIONS FOR IMPROVEMENT

The literature, my experience, and common sense indicate several suggestions that could be explored to help the IRB process work better for social science and education researchers. These suggestions range from long-term and far-reaching changes to fairly simple adjustments that can be done on an individual basis.

Research

The authors of the Illinois white paper suggest conducting research regarding IRBs as one way to determine the working relationship between IRBs and researchers. It is argued that even a basic investigation, collecting descriptive data about case loads and types of research sent to the boards, would be useful. However, at the time the report was written, such basic descriptive data were not available on a national scale. The white paper's authors note that while accounts of extreme situations with researchers and IRBs (such as the present paper) abound, without data such stories can only assumed to be exceptions (The Center for Advanced Study, 2005).

Another, although somewhat ironic, course of action would be to systematically investigate the role of the IRB in the research process. However, gaining approval for this type of research has been found to be somewhat intrusive itself (Dougherty & Kramer, 2005). The IRB must approve the study, even if the IRB is the subject. Any appeal of the process goes to the IRB. Again, as Dougherty and Kramer asked, what kind of oversight is there for the overseers?

Changes in Regulations

In a 2006 report, AAUP suggests revision to the IRB regulations so all studies involving autonomous adults in surveys, interviews, or public observation would be exempt. Technically, this is already true, but the IRB still reviews the research to determine that it does not need to be reviewed. The AAUP suggests that such research be truly exempt, following the ethical guidelines of researchers' respective professions, with no review by the IRB at all.

Another suggestion is to have a separate review process with different regulations based on subject vulnerability (biomedical compared to social science), by discipline (education and communications, for example), or by methodology (such as ethnographies or oral histories) (AAUP, 2006; Center for Advanced Study, 2005; DeTardo-Bora, 2004). My IRB, in fact, does have separate review boards for biomedical and social/behavioral sciences. However, due to the highly disparate nature of social/behavioral science research, this separation does not seem to address all the issues between researchers and IRB protocols.

Further, an exploration of other ways IRBs can work, for example in other countries, seems warranted. "In the Netherlands, for example, social science research is exempt from review unless it places a demonstrable physical or psychological burden on its subjects" (Bosk & DeVries, 2004, p. 259). It seems possible that a broader view of the nature of protection could be in order.

Changes at the Local Level

Much of *The Belmont Report* and the Federal Code of Regulations governing IRBs is interpreted by the local IRB. This was clearly shown in the above vignette, as well as discussed by Hamilton (2005). Suggestions for helping the IRB process work better for social science and education researchers have been posed. The most prominent suggestion is for greater social science presence on IRBs (Bosk & DeVries, 2004; Church et al., 2002; Fitch, 2005; Hemmings, 2006; Marshall, 2003). Hemmings further suggests that teachers could be included in reviews of education research to help constitute "normal" educational practice. Most importantly, researchers with experience in social science research need to have a significant, not token, voice in the review process (Church et al., 2002; Fitch, 2005; Marshall, 2003).

In addition, it seems minimally necessary for IRBs to have an appeals process in place (AAUP, 2006; Bosk & DeVries, 2004). Currently, if a researcher does not agree with the stipulations of the IRB reviewer, there is no recourse for the researcher, or option for third-party opinions. There does not appear to be any regulation at the federal level that would prevent local campuses from creating an appeals process.

Based on my multicampus interactions, a logical step could also be for more institutions to develop reciprocal agreements. The institution I encountered with this agreement in place is very similar to my own. Perhaps institutions within conferences (Big Ten, Big Twelve, etc.), at the very least, could enact such agreements to simplify cooperation among researchers.

By contrast, educational researchers can work to increase their own knowledge as to how IRBs work (Bosk & DeVries, 2004: Church et al., 2002; Fitch, 2005; Marshall, 2003). Further, Fitch (2005) recommends how researchers interact and approach the IRB could make the review process smoother. She suggests that researchers consider, as teachers, how we prefer to be questioned. Approaching the IRB officer politely, with specific questions, and with a due respect to the profession in which they work will often find a more open door and satisfactory answers.

Involvement of Professional Organizations

Many disciplines have developed a code of ethics and position papers designed to help IRBs understand the needs of the discipline and guide their reviews of research. The American Anthropological Association (AAA), for example, has published a code of ethics (AAA, 1998), confidentiality and field notes (AAA, 2003), and a statement on ethnography and institutional review boards (AAA, 2004) on their Web site.

Similar documents are also in place in the field of education. The American Educational Research Association (AERA) houses a social and behavioral sciences working group on human research protections, "an interdisciplinary group of scientists established to examine and suggest ways to enhance the protection of human subjects in the social and behavioral sciences" (AERA, 2005, para. 1). This working group was established in 2001 by the National Human Research Protections Advisory committee, and later found a home within the office of AERA. The working group produces reports on issues such as "Risk and Harm." In addition, the group has delivered day-long courses on human subjects topics presented at meetings of the American Sociological Association and AERA, among others.

The working group appears to have instigated many positive discussions and positions regarding the role of human subjects in research. However, Bosk and DeVries (2004) raised objections to what they perceived as an overbalance in favor of hard-science positions in the make-up of the working group. For example no ethnographers were members of the committee. In addition Bosk and DeVries object to the working group having sponsored a conference regarding IRB "best practices." They argue the title of the conference alone "reinforces the link between the rules that regulate biomedical research and rules that regulate social and behavioral science research. For many social scientists, this linkage is precisely the problem" (Bosk & DeVries, 2004, p. 252).

AERA also has developed ethical standards for educational researchers, published on their Web site (AERA, 2004). Included are guiding standards for research populations, educational institutions, and the public. These standards are clearly aligned with the principles followed by IRBs, including information regarding rights to informed consent, confidentiality, and respect for persons. Also included are more specific items related to honesty, integrity, and sensitivity.

Music education researchers clearly support and abide by research ethics similar to those stated by AERA. It could be extremely helpful for music education researchers to develop a best practice model that could help communications with IRBs regarding the unique aspects of music education research, as per the Church et al. (2002) suggestion. Music education research can include the medium of sound which sometimes requires psychometric testing of hearing and/or perception, the need for video and/or audio recording of participants, and one-on-one meetings with children, as in a lesson setting. Further, experiences with music can be quite intense and personal, and qualitative perspectives on these experiences are invaluable to the field. Many other aspects make music education research unique, and a document produced by researchers in the field could greatly enable music education researchers to have more positive outcomes in their interactions with IRBs.

There appears to be an active dialogue in regard to social scientists and the IRBs. It seems the conversation is becoming louder and louder, in fact (AAUP, 2006; Cohen, 2007). Music education researchers would be wise to be present at the conversations in order for their special needs to be considered. The data presented in this paper are used for the purpose of illustrating that the standards, criteria, procedures, and priorities of IRBs around the country are highly variable. Demands for more consistency, cooperation, and sensitivity toward nonmedical research procedures are clearly in order. I believe IRB offices are committed to protecting human subjects, and have deep respect for the responsibility they are assigned. However, in the 30 years since the inception of these procedures, not enough has been done, especially in the social sciences, to make sure that human subjects are being protected and the research process is not extraordinarily inhibited.

REFERENCES

American Anthropological Association. (1998). *AAA code of ethics.* Retrieved April 1, 2007, from http://www.aaanet.org/ar/irb/index.htm

American Anthropological Association. (2003). *AAA statement on confidentiality of field notes.* Retrieved April 1, 2007, from http://www.aaanet.org/ar/irb/index.htm

American Anthropological Association. (2004). *AAA statement on ethnography and Institutional Review Boards.* Retrieved April 1, 2007, from http://www.aaanet.org/ar/irb/index.htm

American Association of University Professors. (2001). *Protecting human beings: Institutional review boards and social science research.* Retrieved July 30, 2006, from http://www.aaup.org/statements/redbook/repirb.htm

American Association of University Professors. (2006). *Research on human subjects: Academic freedom and the Institutional Review Board (2006).* Retrieved March 30, 2007, from http://www.aaup.org/AAUP/About/committees/committee+repts/

American Educational Research Association. (2004, November). *Ethical standards: II. Guiding Standards: Research populations, educational institutions, and the public.* Retrieved March 15, 2007, from http://www.aera.net/aboutaera/?id

American Educational Research Association. (2005, December). *Social and behavioral sciences working group on human research protections.* Retrieved March 15, 2007, from http://www.aera.net/AboutAERA/Default.aspx?menu_id=90&id=669

Bosk, C., & De Vries, R. (2004). Bureaucracies of mass deception: Institutional review boards and the ethics of ethnographic research [Electronic version]. *Annals, AAPSS, 595,* 249-263.

Brainard, J. (2001, March 9). The wrong rules for social science? [Electronic version]. *Chronicle of Higher Education, 47,* A21.

The Center for Advanced Study. (2005). *The Illinois white paper: Improving the system for protecting human subjects: Counteracting IRB "mission creep."* Retrieved March 31, 2007 from University of Illinois Web site: http://www.law.uiuc.edu/conferences/whitepaper/summary.html

Church, J., Shopes, L., & Blanchard, M. (2002). Should all disciplines be subject to the common rule? [Electronic version]. *Academe, 88*(3), 62-70.

Cohen, P. (2007, February 28). As ethics panels expand grip, no field is off limits. *New York Times.* Retrieved March 23, 2007, from http://www.nytimes.com

Detardo-Bora, K. A. (2004). Action research in a world of positivist-oriented review boards [Electronic version]. *Action Research, 2,* 237-253.

Dougherty, D. S., & Kramer, M. W. (2005). A rationale for scholarly examination of Institutional Review Boards: A case study [Electronic version]. *Journal of Applied Communication Research, 33*(3), 183-188.

Fitch, K. (2005). Difficult interactions between IRBs and investigators: Applications and solutions [Electronic version]. *Journal of Applied Communication Research, 33*(3), 269-276.

Hamilton, A. (2005). The development and operation of IRBs: Medical regulations and social sciences [Electronic version]. *Journal of Applied Communication Research, 33*(3), 189-203.

Hemmings, A. (2006). Great ethical divides: Bridging the gap between institutional review boards and researchers [Electronic version]. *Educational Researcher, 35*(4), 12-18.

Marshall, P. A. (2003). Human subjects protections, Institutional Review Boards, and cultural anthropological research. *Anthropological Quarterly, 76*(2), 269-285.

Malone, S. (2003). Ethics at home: Informed consent in your own backyard [Electronic version]. *Qualitative Studies in Education, 16*(6) 797-815.

Pritchard, I. A. (2002). Travelers and trolls: Practitioner research and institutional review boards [Electronic version]. *Educational Researcher, 31*(3), 3-14.

Thornton, L., & Bergee, M. (2007). *Career choice influences of music education students at major schools of music.* Manuscript submitted for publication.

United States Department of Health and Human Services. (2005, June). *Code of federal regulations Title 45 public welfare: Health and Human Services Part 46 protection of human subjects.* Retrieved March 31, 2007 from http://www.hhs.gov/ohrp/humansubjects/guidance/45crf46.htm#46.101

Weijer, C. (2004, November). *Ethical and policy issues in research involving human participants.* Retrieved March 15, 2007, from http://www.onlineethics.org/reseth/nbac/hweijer.html

ABOUT THE AUTHORS

Melissa Natale Abramo is a doctoral candidate at Teachers College, Columbia University, as well as music instructor and department chairperson in a middle/high school in Westchester County, NY. Her research interests include narrative inquiry, poststructural and feminist theory, instrumental music, and music technology. Her dissertation work utilizes narrative and poststructural analysis to explore the construction of instrumental music teacher identity.

James R. Austin is associate professor of music education and associate dean for undergraduate studies in the College of Music at the University of Colorado in Boulder, where he teaches graduate courses in research methodology and assessment, and directs master's theses and doctoral dissertations. His research interests include student motivation and self-concept development, teacher education, classroom-level assessment, and school/arts policy implications of educational reform. He has authored numerous articles and book chapters, and serves on the editorial boards of three major music research journals.

Margaret H. Berg is associate professor and chair of music education at the University of Colorado, where she teaches undergraduate instrumental methods and graduate courses in foundations of music education, string pedagogy, and qualitative research. Her research interests include the social psychology of music education, string/orchestra pedagogy and curriculum development, and teacher education. She is on the editorial board of the *Journal of String Research* and *American String Teacher* and has authored articles and book chapters on various topics in music education.

Deborah Bradley is assistant professor of music education in the Department of Curriculum and Instruction and the School of Music at the University of Wisconsin-Madison, where she teaches undergraduate courses in general and multicultural music and graduate courses in sociology of music education. Her research focuses on issues of race, racism, and social justice in music education. She is the author of several articles published in international journals including *Action, Criticism, and Theory for Music Education, Music Education Research,* and *Philosophy of Music Education Review* (forthcoming).

Liora Bresler is a professor at the College of Education at the University of Illinois at Urbana Champaign and at the School of Art and Design, a fellow at the Academy of Entrepreneurial Leadership, and affiliate professor in the School of Music. Recent publications include a coedited book on context and culture in elementary and early childhood arts education (Bresler & Thompson, 2002 by Kluwer), a book on International Research in Education (Bresler & Ardichvili, 2002 by Peter Lang), a book on embodied curriculum (Bresler, 2004, by Kluwer), and the *International Handbook of Research in Arts Education* (Springer, 2007). Bresler serves as an editor for a book series: *Landscapes: Aesthetics, Arts and Education,* for Springer and is the cofounder and coeditor of the electronic journal *International Journal for Arts and Education* (2000-). Most recently she won the Distinguished Teaching Life-Long Career Award at the College of Education (2004), the Campus Award for Excellence in Graduate and Professional Training at the University of Illinois (2005), the Edwin Ziegfeld Award for distinguished international leadership in art education by the United States Society for Education Through Art (2007), and the The Lin Wright Special Recognition Award by the The American Alliance for Theatre and Education (2007).

Mark Robin Campbell is associate professor of music education at The Crane School of Music, SUNY at Potsdam, where he teaches undergraduate and graduate courses in music teaching, learning, philosophy, and curriculum. His research focuses on the thinking and socialization processes of preservice music teachers. He is editor of several collections of works and is author of numerous published articles and studies.

Susan Wharton Conkling is associate professor, chair of the Music Education Department, and affiliate faculty in conducting and ensembles at the Eastman School of Music, University of Rochester. Her teaching includes choral conducting and methods, curriculum, and college teaching seminar, and her research focuses on the socialization processes of music performers and teachers.

Teryl L. Dobbs is assistant professor of music education at the School of Music and in the Department of Curriculum and Instruction, University of Wisconsin-Madison. She teaches undergraduate courses in instrumental music education and graduate courses in current issues and ability-dis/ability issues in music teaching and learning. Her research interests include discursive practices within the music classroom and dis/ability issues in music education.

Warren Henry is associate professor of music education at the University of North Texas, where he serves as associate dean for academic affairs. His primary research areas include university teacher preparation and professional development partnerships. He is the author of numerous published articles and maintains an active schedule as a clinician throughout the country.

Joshua A. Russell is assistant professor of music education at the University of Arkansas at Fayetteville where he teaches undergraduate and graduate courses in music teaching, assessment, psychology, and string pedagogy. His research interests include educational policy, teacher education, string education, and psycho-social/cognitive development in musical learning and teaching. He has contributed to several music education practitioner and research journals.

Margaret Schmidt is associate professor of music education at Arizona State University, where she teaches undergraduate and graduate courses in string and instrumental music education, psychology, and teacher education. Her research focuses on the development of preservice and novice music teachers' thinking and choice of teaching practices. She has published articles in music education and teacher education journals, and is director of the ASU String Project.

Linda Thompson is assistant professor of music education at Lee University, Cleveland, TN, where she teaches undergraduate and graduate courses including music methods, curriculum, and research. Additionally she is the coordinator for the Master of Music-Music Education program at Lee. Her research interests include teacher education and the preservice teacher socialization. She has published in both music education and music therapy journals.

Linda Thornton is assistant professor of music education at The Pennsylvania State University, where she teaches undergraduate and graduate courses in instrumental pedagogy and methods, music psychology, and music education history and research. Her research involves the development of instrumental musicians and teacher identity formation. She is the author of several publications and maintains an active schedule as a clinician, conductor, and performer.

Peter Whiteman is the director of the Center for Education, Research and Children at the Central Coast Campus of the University of Newcastle, Australia, where he teaches in the early childhood teacher education programs. His research interests include early childhood musical development and education, children's symbol systems, and reconstructed childhoods. Currently, he is involved in an Australian/US collaborative project with young children as music researchers and is also undertaking commissioned research for a government agency.

Printed in the United States
126339LV00002B/43/P